PRAISE FOR IMMIGF

"Patrick has made me realise that even the most mundane and ubiquitous words can have an endlessly fascinating story."

—**Betty Chen**, founder of ARTiculations

"Patrick has always had the unique ability to get you caring about things you didn't realize you cared about. This book will make you care about why you talk the way you talk."

—**Mr. Beat**, educational YouTuber and author of *The Power of Our Supreme Court*

IMMIGRANT TONGUES

BOOKS BY THE AUTHOR

The Origin of Names, Words and Everything in Between (2018)

The Origin of Names, Words and Everything in Between: Volume II (2021)

IMMIGRANT TONGUES

Exploring How Languages Moved, Evolved, and Defined Us

PATRICK FOOTE

MIAMI

Cover Design: Elina Diaz
Cover Photo/illustration: stock.adobe.com/alehnia, stock.adobe.com/Aleksander Nordaas, stock.adobe.com/peacefy
Interior Illustrations: Patrick Foote
Layout & Design: Elina Diaz

For permission requests, please contact the publisher at:
Mango Publishing Group
5966 South Dixie Highway, Suite 300
Miami, FL 33143
info@mango.bz

For special orders, quantity sales, course adoptions and corporate sales, please email the publisher at sales@mango.bz. For trade and wholesale sales, please contact Ingram Publisher Services at customer.service@ingramcontent.com or +1.800.509.4887.

Immigrant Tongues: Exploring How Languages Moved, Evolved, and Defined Us

Library of Congress Cataloging-in-Publication number: 2025938537
ISBN: (print) 978-1-68481-815-0, (ebook) 978-1-68481-804-4
BISAC category code: LAN009010 LANGUAGE ARTS & DISCIPLINES / Linguistics / Historical & Comparative

"English? Who needs that?
I'm never going to England."

—Homer Simpson

TABLE OF CONTENTS

WHERE ARE YOU FROM?

Whenever someone asks me the incredibly innocent question "Where are you from?" I am always left feeling a tad uncertain about my answer. I was born in London, moved to the small coastal town of Bognor Regis with my family when I was five, and in my mid-twenties decided to pack up my life and move four hours away from most of my friends and family to Plymouth, a city I had spent no more than a couple weeks collectively exploring. So, my answer to where I am from is kind of up for debate. I was born in one place, lived most of my life in another, and now live somewhere else entirely. The true answer to the question of where I call home I guess is "all of the above." In the grand scheme of humanity, my three answers to this question are relatively tame. Others have called completely different parts of the world home across their life. These are places where they made friends, planted their roots, and formed a life they love. Languages, in many ways, are resoundingly similar.

If you were to look at a map of our modern world and see the most widely spoken language in each nation, you would quickly notice that not every nation gets its own unique tongue. While France might speak French, and Japan Japanese, French can also be found across various parts of Africa. Meanwhile, a language like Spanish (which unsurprisingly derives from Spain) is spoken by the majority of nations south of the US border. Then we have English, the language of my home nation, which has become a widely spoken language in every continent on the planet, even that big cold one in the south. These languages, like myself and many others, have found homes in places where they were once foreigners.

Since the inception of language, the tongues we speak have migrated with us far and wide. The journeys these languages have undertaken can in many cases be both wonderful and heartbreaking. Words that originated on a tiny island have gone on to be spoken by masses of people. In many cases, these languages are spoken by more people in different lands as opposed to where they originated from. In some rarer cases, these languages are no longer even spoken in their place of origin. It's easy to take for granted the spread of languages across the globe. For example, whenever I have had to prepare for a trip across the Atlantic to spend some time in the Land of the Free, remembering to pack a phrase book is never on my to-do list. I simply get off my however-many-hours long flight and carry on talking the way I do back in Blighty.

English, of course, didn't just magically appear all of a sudden in the USA and become their primary tongue. Neither did Portuguese in Brazil, French in Cameroon, or Arabic in Egypt. These languages and many others journeyed away from their birthplaces, across land, sea, and sky to cement themselves in their new homes. It is these journeys that we will be covering in this book. No two languages' journeys are identical, but there are undoubtedly many similarities in these journeys. Many languages migrated slowly over time, finding themselves at home in new places so subtly, we barely think of them as immigrant tongues. Others, however, rocked up more or less overnight and quickly asserted their dominance, thanks to foreign powers wanting to claim land in parts of the world formerly unknown to them. Their languages finding new homes was often a byproduct of these exploitations. Due to this, foreign tongues have had varying success at finding new homes. In some cases, they are spoken across a huge portion of a continent, in many cases they become the go-to language for a country, and on occasion they are spoken by a small community of people in a land. While we all know that English and French are spoken in Canada, the fact that Welsh is spoken by a pocket of people in Argentina flies much further under the radar. We'll get to it, don't worry.

It's worth remembering that, in most cases, languages didn't find new homes in empty lands. When the Spanish arrived in South America, the continent already had ample tongues. A sad reality of many of these language journeys is the fact that, in making themselves at home in new places, they simultaneously displaced other languages, either greatly reducing the number of native speakers or killing them off entirely. This book is just as much about covering the languages that were already being spoken in these corners of the globe as it is about the foreign languages that found new homes.

If you hadn't already noticed, some languages have immigrated far more than others. I have already mentioned English, Spanish, and French and this will definitely not be the last you hear of them. The reasons why languages like these Western European ones became so globally spoken will become clear as you progress through this book. Though, I imagine many of you will already have a pretty good understanding as to why this is the case.

Something else I really wish to highlight in this book is just how much many of these immigrant tongues have evolved in their new homes. The English spoken in the USA and the English spoken in the UK are resoundingly different. As is the English spoken in Australia or New Zealand. A language can feature different words and phrases in its new home, ones that were never introduced or never really accepted back in their place of birth. In some cases, languages have changed so much, they are actually classified as whole new languages. The technical term for these is daughter languages, and we delve into a few of them in this book too.

The final thing I should address before we begin looking at these journeys is who I am. Prior to the writing of this book, I have spent many years making content on my YouTube channel, *Name Explain*. While the channel started out just looking into the origins of names, it has since expanded into looking at other elements of language too. I have also previously written two other language-centred books, *The Origin of Names, Words & Everything in Between: Volume I* and *The Origin of Names, Words & Everything in Between: Volume II*. A large amount of the videos I make for internet consumption focus on history, language, and geography. As this book is more or less about the history of the geography of language, you should, hopefully, feel in pretty safe hands.

A QUICK NOTE ON LANGUAGE FAMILIES

The concept of language families is used throughout this book. The idea amounts to grouping languages together based on similarities. Language families often contain many branches, with each of those branches containing multiple languages. The closer two languages are in their family, the more alike they will be. While French and Hindi are both part of the Indo-European family, they are on completely different branches: the Romance and Indo-Iranian branches, respectively. French has more in common with its fellow Romance language, Spanish, while Hindi has more in common with the Indo-Iranian Bengali. Some families contain thousands of languages, others just a handful. Here are some of the most notable language families along with some branches and languages, focusing mainly on the tongues covered in this book. This has been heavily condensed for ease's sake. In reality, there's a lot more minutia between them, e.g. the Germanic branch of the Indo-European family actually splits into smaller branches like Low Franconian or Anglo-Frisian. But who doesn't love a book that starts with a list of key players?

THE INDO-EUROPEAN LANGUAGE FAMILY

The Germanic Branch: English, German, Dutch, Swedish, Icelandic, Afrikaans

The Romance Branch: French, Italian, Spanish, Portuguese, Romanian

The Balto-Slavic Branch: Russian, Polish, Ukrainian, Latvian, Lithuanian

The Celtic Branch: Welsh, Irish, Scottish Gaelic, Manx, Bretton

The Indo-Iranian Branch: Hindi, Persian, Sanskrit, Bengali

THE URALIC LANGUAGE FAMILY

The Ugric Branch: Hungarian

The Baltic-Finnic Branch: Finnish, Estonian

The Sami Branch: Northern Sami, Southern Sami, Ter Sami

THE TURKIC LANGUAGE FAMILY

The Oghuz Branch: Turkish, Turkmen, Azerbaijani

The Karluk Branch: Uzbek

The Kipchak Branch: Kazakh

THE ATLANTIC-CONGO LANGUAGE FAMILY

The Bantu Branch: Swahili, Zulu, Kirundi

The Volta-Niger Branch: Yoruba, Igbo

The Savannas Branch: Miyobe, Gur, Kulango

THE AFRO-ASIATIC LANGUAGE FAMILY

The Semitic Branch: Arabic, Hebrew, Maltese

The Berber Branch: Tuareg, Tashlhiyt, Shawiya, Kabyle

The Cushitic Branch: Somali, Oromo, Beja

The Egyptian Branch: Old Egyptian, Middle Egyptian, Coptic

THE SINO-TIBETAN LANGUAGE FAMILY

The Sinitic Branch: Mandarin, Jin/Cantonese, Wu, Yue

The Tibetic Branch: Standard Tibetan, Khams Tibetan, Amdolese

The Burmish Branch: Burmese, Achang, Zaiwa

THE JAPONIC LANGUAGE FAMILY

The Japanese Branch: Japanese

The Ryukyuan Branch: Okinawan, Miyako, Kikai

THE KOREANIC LANGUAGE FAMILY

The Korean Branch: Korean

The Jeju Branch: Jeju

THE ALGIC LANGUAGE FAMILY

The Algonquian Branch: Cree, Ojibwa, Arapaho, Cheyenne

The Yurok Branch: Yurok

The Wiyot Branch: Wiyot

THE IROQUOIAN LANGUAGE FAMILY

The Northern Iroquoian Branch: Mohawk, Seneca, Huronian

The Southern Iroquoian Branch: Cherokee

THE UTO-AZTECAN LANGUAGE FAMILY

The Nahuan Branch: Nahuatl, Pipil

The Numic Branch: Comanche, Timbisha, Shoshoni

The Piman Branch: O'odham, Tepecano

THE ARAWAK LANGUAGE FAMILY

The Northern Branch: Taíno, Garifuna, Arawak, Piapoco

The Southern Branch: Asháninca, Machiguenga, Iñapari

THE QUECHUAN LANGUAGE FAMILY

The Quechuan I Branch: Ancash, Huánuco, Yaru

The Quechuan II Branch: Cuzco, Cajamarca-Cañaris, Kichwa

THE AUSTROASIATIC LANGUAGE FAMILY

The Vietic Branch: Vietnamese, Arem, Phong

The Khmer Branch: Khmer

The Munda Branch: Santali, Mundari, Ho

THE AUSTRONESIAN LANGUAGE FAMILY

The Malayo-Polynesian Branch: Māori, Tongan, Hawaiian, Fijian, Malagasy

The Philippine Branch: Tagalog/Filipino

The Malayic Branch: Malay, Indonesian

THE PAMA-NYUNGAN LANGUAGE FAMILY

The Paman Branch: Umpila, Koko-Bera

The Nyungan Branch: Noongar, Galaagu

PART I

EARLY MIGRATIONS

ANTIQUITY TO THE ELEVENTH CENTURY

WHAT HAVE THE ROMANS EVER DONE FOR US?

LATIN ACROSS EUROPE

Languages have been migrating for pretty much as long as there has been language. Antiquity is full to the brim with language migration, many of which went on to shape the languages of our modern world. Latin is quite possibly the best example of that. The tongue of Rome is quite famously a dead language, meaning it is not spoken in a meaningful way by a large society of people. Even Vatican City, famously known as the smallest country on the planet which once prided itself on having Latin as an official language, has greatly downplayed the use of it. The importance of this dead tongue starts to make more sense when you realise just how pivotal it has been in shaping many other languages which originated in Europe, before spanning out across the globe. Latin is seen by many as a means of allowing you to understand many other languages; it can be seen as a foundation language of sorts.

Latin's influence on other languages varies between tongues. Its strongest influence lies with the Romance languages. These are a family of languages which all have Latin as a direct ancestor. Think of Latin as a great great great grandparent, and the modern Romance languages as their descendants. The Romance languages include the likes of Italian, Spanish, French, and Portuguese, found across Western Europe. Yet, the offspring tongues of Rome didn't just travel west. Romanian, the official language of Romania, can be found to Rome's east, nestled primarily around Slavic-speaking nations. Even languages that are not direct descendants of Latin have been influenced by the ancient language to varying degrees. The distinctly Germanic language of English has been inspired heavily by the words of Rome; it is believed around 60 percent of all English words have their roots in Latin. German, too, has been inspired by Latin, though nowhere near to the extent English has been. Even the Slavic tongue of Polish borrowed from Rome in its early development. The influence of Latin can even extend to a language like Japanese. Many Japanese words are adaptations of English words, like their word for accessory, *akusesarii*. This was borrowed and adapted from English, and English borrowed and adapted it from Latin's word *accessorius*. Make no mistake about it, it could be argued that Latin is one of the most influential languages on the global stage, and the language that has travelled and evolved further than any other. Latin's millennium-spanning migration came into being thanks, of course, to the Roman Empire, which originated on the boot-shaped peninsula found in the south of Europe which now houses the nation we call Italy.

Despite being the language so deeply linked with Rome and its empire, it might seem odd at first to know that this language's name has no relation to Rome. This is because when Latin first emerged in the middle of the eighth century BC, the city and the Empire were not a thing yet. In fact, their mythological founder was only just born around this time. What did exist, however, was the region of Latium, a very old term for the region in the centre of modern Italy that the city would eventually be founded in. One of the key things that the people of Latium had in common was the language they spoke, which was named after the region as Latin. Though, at this time Latin was still emerging and far from its final form, the earliest form of Latin is now retrospectively referred to as Old Latin.

Latium claimed just a small area of this peninsula, the rest of which was split between other groups of people who all spoke their own languages. While on our modern maps Italy is a single entity, that certainly wasn't the case in this pre-Roman world. People who spoke a language dubbed Faliscan lived just north of Latium, Umbrian and Oscan to the south of it, and farther north Etruscan was spoken. While Latin, Umbrian, and Oscan were all related to one another, Etruscan was part of its own isolated language family. Yet, despite this, it was probably the one that had the biggest influence over Latin, as the Latin alphabet (the one you are most likely reading this in right now) was derived directly from the Etruscan alphabet. Most of these other languages spoken across the Italian Peninsula would eventually die out. Their deaths came as Latin grew in significance, once the Kingdom of Rome was founded, which would go on to become the Roman Republic, and eventually the Roman Empire.

Rome's legendary founding took place on the twenty-first of April, 753 BC, which ties in neatly to our earliest known records of Latin. Undoubtedly, the brothers of Romulus and Remus would have been speaking an early form of the tongue. It was these two brothers who were thrown into the river Tiber, where they were expected to die, only to be found and nursed on the milk of the she-wolf. The two lads would grow up to found cities of their own. Romulus eventually killed his brother Remus in a fit of rage, and founded his city of Roma, which we call Rome in English. There really isn't too much evidence as to how true this tale is, but it's this story which most go to when looking into the founding of the city.

In its early days, Rome was just one of the many city states that could be found on the Italian Peninsula. Through an urge for more resources, land, and simply clashing with their neighbours, the humble city state expanded. By 264 BC, Rome had claimed the entirety of the peninsula, a few centuries after it had shifted from being a kingdom to becoming a republic. The expansion of Rome across the entire boot of Italy led to the end of many of those previously mentioned languages that were once spoken there. We can only imagine a world where the might of Rome didn't squash all these other ancient tongues; maybe the nation would be brimming with linguistic diversity to this day. Faliscan is thought to have ceased around 150 BC, and Oscan around 79 AD. While it's thought that these languages simply went extinct, as they were so similar to Latin, the idea that they merged isn't entirely out of the question. It was by 100

BC that the language is considered to have stopped being Old Latin and instead formed into Classical Latin; this evolution of Latin is dubbed classical for a good reason. It's the kind of Latin synonymous with Rome. Rome had now claimed all of the boot, greatly expanding their land and people, yet more land and more people required even more resources to thrive. Rome also found itself with some new neighbours, ones who were far less similar to them in their languages and customs. The Roman Republic was now introduced to wider Europe, which they saw as their answer to that resources problem.

As the centuries waned, Rome easily claimed more land across the continent and, as a result, spread their influence and language. Interestingly enough, Rome never forced their customs onto their claimed land too heavily, allowing their new subjects to carry on living life as they saw fit and carry on speaking their languages. Rome never demanded that everyone learn Latin. It was due to these relaxed rules that the Republic, and eventually Empire, thrived for so long and was able to grow to such a huge size. Many places were seemingly under Roman rule in name only, with the lives of ordinary subjects not changing all that much. Latin was still able to thrive in these conditions. It was the official language of the empire, so even if you didn't speak it in day-to-day life, it was hard to avoid. As it was the language used by the most influential people in the empire, it's easy to understand why it would go on to influence languages across the territories they claimed. Rome would claim the Iberian Peninsula (which they dubbed Hispania at the time and is now home to the nations of Spain and Portugal) in 218 BC. Gaul, which made up the majority of modern France, would go to them in 50 BC. And Dacia would come under Roman rule in 106 AD, Dacia being the older name for what now makes up modern Romania. It would be in 117 AD that Rome would reach its maximum size, claiming a majority of Europe, the westernmost points of Asia, and most of the northern coast of Africa. This sets the scene as to how Latin came to shape so many modern languages in Europe, especially the major ones that are direct descendants of it: Italian, Spanish, Portuguese, French, and Romanian.

Before the arrival of Rome, the Iberian Peninsula was home to a completely different set of languages—none of them of Romance origin like the ones that now dominate the land. One of the most prominent of these was a language we now refer to as simply Iberian. The oldest evidence we have of this language dates to the sixth century BC and featured its own unique script. While we know what it looks like, something we aren't as sure about is what family it originates from. It could have been an isolated language, meaning it has no relation to any other, or it could possibly have been part of the Vasconic family, a very small family of tongues which today now only has one living member, Basque, a tiny language still spoken in a northern nook of modern Spain. It's considered to be one of the oldest and most complex languages in Europe and could honestly have a whole book about it unto itself. The peninsula was also home to other languages, a couple of which are a tad more identifiable. Celtiberian and Gallaecian were two languages of the Celtic language family which were once spoken there. While they no longer exist, the Celtic languages are still spoken to varying degrees, most prominently on the islands just north of Iberia.

In the time before Rome, in the land we now call France, there was another Celtic language. We mentioned that, during the time of the Empire, the land that made up the majority of modern France went by the name of Gaul, and the people who lived there were also known as the Gauls, and their Celtic language was dubbed Gaulish. Gaulish actually had a fairly good run, all things considered. Over to the east, however, the Dacian language was spoken in Dacia. This is another language of fairly isolated origins but was, too, dropped when Romans came along and dubbed the land after themselves when it became Romania.

These languages managed to survive to varying degrees once Rome claimed their homelands. The pre-Roman Iberian languages died around the first century AD while Gaulish and Dacian held out for a few hundred more years. We can only imagine what life was like for these pre-Roman settlers of Europe when the Empire came knocking on their door. For centuries, the land they called home was unique to them—a Gaulish farmer would have lived a simple, relatively small life alongside their fellow Gaulish speakers. This would have been completely upheaved with the arrival of Rome. Suddenly, they were dealing with higher powers who spoke a language incredibly different to their own. Day by day, the Gaulish they all spoke would have been slowly usurped by Latin, thanks to the power and influence Rome held in Europe at this time. Until we arrived at the point we are at today, when Gaulish is just another tongue lost to the past. Thankfully, Rome didn't enforce their language quite as strictly as they enforced their taxes. While Latin would have been seen as the tongue of prestige and upward mobility in Ancient Rome, many in the wider empire carried on speaking their native tongues in everyday life, while picking up bits of Latin to communicate with their new Roman overlords. This allowed for something quite remarkable to happen.

Latin and all these other languages started to intermix with one another, and new languages evolved. The Latin spoken in Iberia became intertwined with those Celtic and Iberian languages, while the Latin spoken in Dacia got mashed together with the Dacian tongue. It got to a point over the centuries that there really wasn't just one Latin language anymore. What replaced it instead were a series of different dialects of Latin, which are collectively referred to as Vulgar Latin. In our day and age, vulgar isn't the most pleasant of terms; we use it to describe something that deeply offends us. However, it simply comes from the Latin *vulgaris* which means ordinary or common. It was in only the seventeenth century that it picked up its modern meaning. While I am sure that these vulgar versions of Latin felt vulgar (in our sense) to those who felt they spoke the language in its purest form, it's these vulgar Latin dialects that paved the way for the modern Romance languages. That would take some time, as while these places were under Roman rule, the true form of Latin could still maintain prominence and influence. Yet, in the same way that Rome wasn't built in a day, it wasn't destroyed in a day either. Rome's decline was gradual and happened for a myriad of reasons, chiefly because the empire was so damn big. In an age prior to the instant communication we all take for granted, controlling an empire of that size was quite the challenge. This led to war within the empire itself and the eventual splitting of Rome into the Western and Eastern Empire in 395 AD. While Eastern Rome would thrive for centuries under the guise of the Byzantine Empire, they dropped Latin fairly quickly in favour of Greek and other languages. Western Rome collapsed in on itself in 476 AD, and with its death also died a central influencing body for the Latin language in Europe.

Yet the people who were once subjects of Western Rome didn't just stop speaking Latin once the empire was dead. For most of them, enough time had passed that the pure forms of their old tongues had been forgotten and a vulgar form of Latin was probably all they knew, so it would be pretty hard for them to just stop speaking it all of a sudden. These Vulgar Latin dialects carried on being spoken in their respective regions, only now there was no Latin-speaking empire to influence them. This finally allowed these forms of Latin to reach their next step and slowly shift into the languages we know today.

On the Iberian Peninsula, the various Vulgar Latins are thought to have differentiated enough into the modern languages of Portuguese and Spanish around the ninth and thirteenth centuries respectively. Meanwhile, the Vulgar Latin spoken in Gaul became French in the eighth century. Romanian, however, is thought to have emerged a lot later down the line, around the sixteenth century. Of course, these languages didn't just go from being Vulgar Latin to their modern forms overnight. Each one slowly evolved from older versions of the language to the forms we know today. Many of them are still changing, especially in parts of the world they eventually migrated over to.

Latin wasn't even safe from corruption in its homeland. Of the widely spoken Romance languages, Italian is thought to be the closest to Latin, though smaller Romance languages like Sicilian and Sardinian are thought to be closer. When Western Rome fell, even the peninsula wasn't free from influence. The Latin spoken there intermingled with outside tongues, like the Germanic languages spoken by "barbarians" from the north who ransacked the land. On top of this, without the rule of Rome, the common people didn't bother all that much with speaking Latin in the prim and proper way. This all led to the emergence of Italian as its own language, starting in around the fourteenth century.

The modern Romance-speaking nations did not make up the entirety of the Roman Empire's land though. It included places like the island of Great Britain, Asia Minor (now Turkey), and Northern Africa. The reason these places no longer speak a child of Vulgar Latin is because these lands would eventually have other tongues migrate to them. A really interesting case is with Greek, however. Greece was under Roman rule, yet the Greek language existed prior to Rome and didn't get squashed by the presence of Latin, and is still spoken to this day. This is thanks to multiple reasons. First off, the land where Greek is spoken was fairly inaccessible in the ancient past, as the land is a mixture of mountains and islands, so the language could kind of just carry on doing its thing free of interference. Secondly, Greek was a highly respected language. Much of Rome was influenced by the Greek culture that came before it. It's important to remember the Eastern Empire would adopt it as their official language.

The death of this once mighty language might seem sad, but in reality, Latin served its purpose. Like many parents hope to achieve, Latin created children that have carried on its legacy. In the same way Latin migrated and evolved across Europe, many of its offspring have done the exact same thing across the wider world. Latin's descendants can be found in overseas places like Africa and, perhaps most noticeably, Latin America. While no countries currently speak Latin, it has continued to thrive in the Christian Church. Latin has been the de facto language of Catholicism ever since the Roman Empire made it their official religion in 380 AD. In the church, Latin continued to evolve way after the fall of Rome. Today, the kind of Latin spoken by the church is known as Ecclesiastical Latin, or simply Church Latin for those of us who struggle with big words. It was this kind of Latin that was once the official language of The Vatican City, before even they ditched it. Latin might not be relevant all that much as a spoken language today, yet its movement around across Europe and evolution into the Romance tongues we know today is one of the most influential migrations to ever take place on our planet. It was, however, far from the first immigrant tongue. Across the Mediterranean Sea and way farther south, a group of languages migrated across vast swaths of land hundreds of years before Romulus and Remus even suckled on the milk of the she-wolf.

HOPING TO FIND SOME OLD FORGOTTEN WORDS

BANTU LANGUAGES ACROSS AFRICA

Africa is possibly the continent most deeply linked with migration. From the migration of the great wildebeest across the Serengeti, to the multitude of birds that migrate to the continent to seek warmer weather in the winter months. Even humans started life in Africa before we, too, migrated to pretty much every corner of the earth. It should come as no major surprise to find out that languages have also migrated across the continent. Africa is home to a selection of immigrant tongues which originated from other parts of the world. Yet, before languages like English, French, and Arabic arrived in the land, native tongues took great strides across the jungles and deserts of Africa and cemented themselves in parts of the continent they did not originate from. One of the most impressive of these being the migration and expansion of the Bantu languages.

The Bantu languages are a branch of the larger Atlantic-Congo language family. Notable Bantu tongues include the likes of Zulu, Xhosa, Lingala, and the most widely spoken, Swahili, which acts as something of a lingua franca for a large chunk of Southern Africa. A lingua franca is the title a language earns when it becomes a tongue of international communication, or just communication amongst people who all speak different languages in close proximity. Today, they are seen in places like a United Nations meeting or even the Olympics Opening Ceremony. Across history, many different tongues have been considered lingua franca for different parts of the world; in this nook of Africa, it is undoubtedly Swahili. Today, these various Bantu languages can be heard across Central Africa all the way to the continent's southern tip. To many, the Bantu languages are the definitive native tongues of the continent, and all of them originated from one part of the land via one initial language.

Proto-Bantu is the name given to the hypothetical first Bantu tongue. It's believed to have come into existence in around 4500 BC, which is an outstandingly long time ago. We have not been able to pinpoint the precise location of its origins, but it's believed to have all started somewhere along the western coast of Central Africa. Possibly along the Sanaga and Nyong rivers which are now located in the modern nation of Cameroon. Funnily enough, despite being the probable homeland of the Bantu languages, the most widely spoken tongues in the nation are now French and English, two languages that migrated there from Europe far later down the line. It seems the most spoken Bantu language in the country now is Bulu, spoken by the Bulu people of the land.

The Proto-Bantu speakers stuck to this small region of Africa for around 2,000 years. Across this two-millennia nonmigratory period, these Bantus progressed in a way the rest of Africa did not. During this time, the majority of people in sub-Saharan Africa were living as hunter gatherers or foragers, still using basic stone tools. The Bantus were comparatively far more advanced. They had a better understanding of farming and agriculture, combined with not only stone tools but access to iron from ores they discovered. Iron not only gave them better tools for farming but stronger weapons for warfare. In many ways, the Bantus were living in the Iron Age while other parts of Africa were still in the Stone Age. After a stationary 2,000 or so years of living in modern Cameroon, Bantu speakers started moving, which saw the beginnings of a period of history known as The

Bantu Expansion. This migration of Bantu speakers did not happen overnight; it was quite the opposite. Roughly starting in 2000 BC and only ending in 1500 AD, that's a migration lasting 3,500 years! I don't think even the wildebeest migrate for that long of a period. As this migration started so long ago and occurred in a part of the world that left little to no written evidence for us to uncover later down the line, there is a lot up in the air in regard to what actually happened. The best evidence we have of these migrations are the many Bantu tongues that were birthed in their path. One of the key things we aren't too sure about is why these Bantu people decided to start moving across Africa in the first place. Theories range from them exhausting their local resources, sicknesses, warring with other tribes, to the romantic idea that they had an urge for adventure. What we seemingly know for sure is that the Bantu people started moving and left that trail of languages in their wake.

What that trail was exactly is (once again) up for debate, though there is a consensus over exactly how the Bantu migration took place. From their homeland in modern Cameroon, the Proto-Bantu speakers fanned off into different directions. Some trekked eastward, finding themselves amongst the continent's eastern coast and great lakes. Others travelled directly south from Cameroon and plundered Africa's deepest points. When these travels are seen on maps, they look like easy little jaunts, however, that would be far from the truth. In reality, these Proto-Bantu speakers would have walked the continent over hundreds of years. While boats would have been utilised, there were no horses to pull the carts. This was a migration primarily taken on foot. All while navigating the scorching sun, torrential rains, and vicious wildlife Africa has at its disposal.

By the middle of the second millennium AD, roughly 2,500 to 3,000 years since their migrations began, Bantu speakers now called the majority of sub-Saharan Africa home. The southeast of sub-Saharan Africa is seemingly the land which they never manage to plant roots in. Yet, these Bantu migrants didn't find homes in unoccupied lands. The rest of Africa was thriving in its own way during these migrations and peoples from parts of the continent the Bantus arrived in spoke languages unrelated to theirs. This most likely included tongues from other African language families like Nilo-Saharan, Cushitic, and the Khoisan languages, famed for the unique clicking noises that are part of their language. As Proto-Bantu speakers settled in lands where these other speakers lived, their languages would have slowly intermixed with one another, which ultimately gives us the many Bantu languages found across Africa today. This includes the likes of Kimbundu and Ovambu found along the western coast; Lunda, Tetela, and Bemba in the centre of Africa; then, across the eastern coast of Africa, we find languages like Zulu, Makhuwa, and Gogo. All these tongues across the continent derived from that single Proto-Bantu language. While some of these languages might be widely unheard of to people in places like Europe and the Americas, they are spoken by huge swaths of people. The aforementioned Makhuwa (a language I can, hand on heart, say I had never heard of prior to the writing of this book) alone has over four million speakers—that's double the number of Estonian speakers out there.

Language was not the only thing that the Bantus brought to these parts of Africa that were new to them. They introduced the new areas where they migrated to their customs, cultures, and relatively far more advanced technologies and skills like iron smelting and more efficient farming. These were some of the key reasons why Bantu languages were able to spread so successfully. How advanced Bantus were compared to other African people at this time could have been akin to Europeans introducing advanced technologies to natives of the New World, though that was still many years down the line. This not only allowed the Bantu languages to spread but their customs and ideals, too. Across modern Africa, this has created a somewhat unified Bantu identity across millions of people even if they do not speak the exact same Bantu language. However, this unified identity has also caused rifts with some non-Bantu-speaking Africans. One extreme case is with the Baka people, a non-Bantu hunter-gatherer tribe who live in the wilderness of Cameroon, the Republic of Congo, and Gabon. They have claimed in recent times that they are facing racial harassment from Bantu people for being supposedly inferior to them. It is unfortunate to know that this concept of racial superiority can be found even in the depths of Africa.

These migrations led to that original seed of Proto-Bantu evolving into over 400 Bantu languages spoken across the continent. The most prominent of them by and far is Swahili, as I mentioned. It's natively spoken by over five million people, with another eighty million able to speak it as a second tongue. It has the status of an official language in Tanzania, Rwanda, Uganda, and Kenya, as well as having recognition as a minority language in Angola, Burundi, Mozambique,

Zambia, and the Democratic Republic of Congo. Swahili began life as just one of the many Bantu languages left in the wake of their expansion. It originated on the eastern coast of Africa and, for some time, many believed that it wasn't actually a Bantu language—instead, it is believed to have originated with Arab traders who often worked down the eastern coast of the land in the far past. We now know, however, that Swahili is definitely Bantu, though it certainly does have a heavy Arab influence. This includes various words of Arabic origin finding themselves at home in Swahili, something truly unique for a Bantu language. This is seen prominently in the numbers of Swahili. Their words for the numbers of one, two, three, four, five, eight, and ten (*moja, mbili, tatu, nne, tano, nane*, and *kumi* respectively) are of Bantu origins. While their names for six, seven, and nine (*sita, saba*, and *tisa*) are all astoundingly similar to the Arabic names for these numbers (*sita, sabea,* and *tise*). We can only imagine why it was six, seven, and nine in particular which adopted Arabic names; perhaps they were more prominent numbers in the realm of ancient trading and bartering.

Trade with Arabs is one of the key reasons why Swahili spread and went on its own journey. It was this language that Arabic merchants used whilst in Africa and, while they initially bartered with just Swahili speakers on the Eastern Coast, they eventually travelled farther into the continent. As they went farther, they carried on using Swahili, as it was the only African language they knew, allowing this Bantu language to find a home deeper into Africa. This spread of Swahili ramped up with the arrival of Christian missionaries in Africa. Missionaries have one goal in mind: to spread their religion as far and wide as possible. To them, Africa must have seemed like a blank canvas of sorts to influence as they pleased. Today, Christianity is the most followed religion in Africa, so a job well done I suppose. Their key to converting the continent was being able to speak the same language as the people they were trying to bring to Team Jesus. As Swahili had already picked up a strong following, it made logical sense that it would be the language they would choose. Suddenly, countless Christian missionaries were learning Swahili to aid their religious expansion. As they brought the word of God to new corners of the continent, they brought their newly adopted tongue with them too. This cemented Swahili even more so into the land.

Swahili is even an official language of the African Union and is seen by many as the lingua franca of the continent. This Bantu tongue seems to wish to position itself as the definitive African tongue—one that is African born and bred and not a language thrown onto it through colonial powers. Today, Swahili is the second most spoken language in Africa by the number of people who have it as their native tongue. Ultimately, the prominence of Swahili (and the vast range of Bantu languages as a whole) boils down to the simple fact that, thousands of years ago, those Proto-Bantu speakers on the other side of the continent started to migrate for some unknown reason.

Though, as mentioned, Swahili is only the second most spoken first tongue of Africa. The first is Arabic, which obviously isn't Indigenous to Africa. How Arabic gained such prominence on the continent is a different story altogether.

A WHOLE NEW WORLD

ARABIC ACROSS NORTH AFRICA

In 570 AD, which is roughly midway through the aforementioned Bantu expansion, a baby was born in the city of Mecca on the Arabian Peninsula, east of Africa's northern coast. His full name would have been something along the lines of Muhammad ibn Abdullah ibn Abdul-Muttalib, but to most people he would have just been known as Muhammad. This is none other than the Muhammad who would go on to form the religion of Islam. It would be a little while longer until his Islamic Golden Age came to fruition. What was far from a baby at this time was the language being spoken in the corner of the peninsula he was born in, Arabic. The earliest evidence we have of Arabic dates back to the ninth and eighth centuries BC and we call this form of the language Proto-Arabic which, if you couldn't guess from the name alone, is resoundingly different to the Arabic many people speak today. In the realm of language families, Arabic is part of the

large Afro-Asiatic family, sitting specifically on the Semitic branch, meaning its closest relatives are languages like Aramaic and Hebrew.

The tongue first emerged in the northwest of the peninsula and at first would have intermingled with languages that are now long gone like Akkadian of Ancient Mesopotamia and Eblaite which was spoken in Ancient Syria. While these languages died out, Arabic lived and spread from its starting point in the northwest, trickling down across the entire peninsula. From its inception in the ninth century BC, the language changed dramatically. Over the centuries, new sounds, letters, and words were weaved into the language. The fourth century AD saw the introduction of the Arabic script. By the sixth century AD, the language had transitioned to a phase retroactively referred to as Classical Arabic. It was this version of Arabic that Muhammad would have been speaking in 610 AD when, at the age of forty years old, he made his first revelation.

The legend goes that, while meditating in a cave near to his home in Mecca, Muhammad was visited by none other than the angel Gabriel. The angel started to speak, reciting words Muhammad believed to be straight from God (Allah in Islam), and informed him that he was the next prophet. Before this, there was no single dominant religion in Arabia. Christianity and Judaism had taken some hold there, as well as various unique religions in the land. This was about to change as Muhammad went back to Mecca to explain what had just happened to him. He called upon the people to worship this one true god who just spoke to him. Minus a small following of people, the wider city rejected him and his new idea of Islam. This led to Muslim persecutions in Mecca and by 622 CE, Muhammad and his followers retreated to the nearby city Medina where, unlike in Mecca, Islam was accepted and grew rapidly. While Islam was freely followed in Medina, there were still struggles, including many attacks on Muhammad and his religion from various non-Islamic tribes and people. He seemingly fought back and won against many of these attacks. The idea of Muhammad as this great military general is something not often talked about, but the battlefield was yet another place he excelled in. Though, this came at the expense of those who he beat on the battleground. By 630 AD, he returned to Mecca where Islam was finally accepted in the city, yet he wouldn't live too long to see how much the religion would prosper as by 633 AD he, too, died.

If you could not guess by now, the migration of the Arabic language and the spread of Islam are incredibly intertwined with one another. As the religion was founded in an Arabic-speaking part of the world, it became the de facto language of the religion. Meaning, when the religion eventually migrated to other parts of the world, in most cases Arabic came along for the ride. While Muhammad established a foundation for Islam with Arabic as its defining language, it didn't spread all too far under his watch—it reached no farther than the cities of Medina, Mecca, and the surrounding area. It was the Islamic rulers who followed Muhammad that would spread Islam farther, into the rest of Arabia, which was already speaking Arabic, northward into the wider Middle East, and eventually westward into a land that was speaking a variety of different tongues at the time, none of them being Arabic.

While North Africa is (obviously) part of Africa, it is in many ways very different to the rest of the continent. Its proximity to Europe and having a coast along the Mediterranean means the region played a big role in the European age of antiquity, with much of the land coming under Roman rule. Even prior to the Romans, the region hosted its own native powers who would shape the world, namely the Ancient Egyptians, one of the most celebrated and important cultures to ever grace our planet. North Africa is defined by the Sahara Desert, the largest hot desert on the planet. This acted as a natural barrier of sorts and was a key reason why the Bantu-Migrations didn't spread to the north of the continent. This allowed languages in North Africa to evolve and migrate in their own ways. By the time Muhammad founded Islam, a large portion of North Africa was under Byzantine rule. The official languages of the Byzantine Empire fluctuated between Latin and Greek. Other tongues were spoken here, too. A truly fascinating one is African Romance, a Romance language which emerged from Latin speakers arriving in the region thanks to Rome. It would be incredible if Africa still had its own unique Romance language, but the language died out seemingly quickly once Islam arrived in the region.

The most noteworthy native pre-Islamic North African languages have to be the various Berber tongues. These are the languages of the native Berber people. Specific Berber tongues are ones such as Tashlhiyt, Shawiya, and Kabyle, all of which stemmed from some unknown Proto-Beber language. They are among the oldest languages in the region, believed to have originated somewhere around the Nile prior to 2000 BC. It was around this time that the Berbers, too, migrated westward across North Africa, bringing their languages with them. The Berber languages collectively make up their own branch of the Afro-Asiatic family, meaning they are something of a distant cousin to Arabic. Unlike African Romance, Berber can still be heard across North Africa today, with there being an estimated fourteen million speakers of various Berber languages. That is undoubtedly a large number, but it pales in comparison to the 150 million Arabic speakers on the continent, most of which live in the north.

What this establishes is the fact that, at the time of Muhammad's death, North Africa was speaking a mixture of languages ranging from ones brought in from Europe like Latin and Greek to ones of native roots like the Berber languages. Following Muhammad's death, a new Muslim leader had to be decided on, with the title going to a man named Abu Bakr, a close friend of Muhammad's. It was under Bakr's reign that Islam really started to expand. He became the first ruler of the Rasidun Caliphate, with a Caliphate being a kind of Islamic empire. This Caliphate had one aim which was to expand Islam as far as possible. From its beginnings in 632 until its demise just twenty-nine years later in 661 AD, it did a fairly good job of that. Under its four rulers (Abu Bakr, Umar, Uthman, and Ali), Islam was able to spread across the entire Arabian Peninsula and north of it. While by this point Arabic was already the lingua franca of sorts for Arabia, its expansion northward of it saw Arabic plant its first seeds somewhere other than the deserts of Arabia. This spread of Islam and Arabic was achieved through various ways, including war, notably the brutal Ridda Wars which pitted the Rashidun Caliphate against various tribes of Arabia, which saw Islam conquer the peninsula. The Caliphate had secured the entirety of Arabia as well as land north of it like modern-day Syria and Iraq. It was at this point, under the control of their second leader, Umar, that the Rashidun Caliphate finally turned toward the west and went to land that lacked Islam and Arabic: North Africa.

Crossing the Sinai, the Rashidun Caliphate found itself in the land of Egypt. Long gone were the pharaohs and the pyramids were crumbling remains of the empire that once stood here. At this point, the land of Egypt was instead under Byzantine rule, well, just about anyway. Prior to the arrival of the Rashidun Caliphate in Egypt, the Byzantines had spent the last decade or so fighting another empire, the Sassanids, for control over the land. The land that makes up Egypt is deeply

valuable as the Nile gives it some of the most fertile soil in the area, hence why
Ancient Egypt thrived in the area for so long. By the time Islam cropped up in
Egypt, the Byzantines were exhausted from fighting the Sassanids. This led to a
quick and decisive victory for the Rashidun Caliphate, which saw Egypt come
under their rule in 642 AD. For the first time since 30 BC, Egypt was not under
any kind of Roman rule. This was the first time that Islam, and of course Arabic,
planted its roots in African soil, and it would be far from the last time.

By the time the Rashidun Caliphate met its demise in 661, its reach across
North Africa included the majority of modern-day Egypt, the north of modern
Libya, and the southeastern cusp of present-day Tunisia. It was here that Arabic
first spread into the region. The Rashidun Caliphate ended not due to another
empire defeating it, but instead via unrest within the Caliphate itself. Their third
ruler, Uthman, was assassinated in his own home by rebel soldiers after growing
discontent. This resulted in advisor Ali becoming their fourth and unknowingly
final ruler. Tensions were high enough and one person in particular was deeply
unhappy with the death of Utham. Muawiya was a governor of Syria and the
head of another noteworthy Muslim clan, the Umayyads. He demanded justice
for the murdered Caliph, but Ali didn't give it to him. It was not only Muawiya
who was enraged, but so were many of Muslims who came to his side. Civil war
broke out in this Islamic empire, which ultimately resulted in the death of Ali by
assassination too. So came the end to the first Islamic Caliphate, but in its place
rose another: the Umayyad Caliphate led by Muawiya in 661.

This Caliphate lasted a far longer time than its predecessor—for just under
a hundred years, dissolving in 750. In just short of a century, the Umayyad
Caliphate saw the Islamic Empire reach its greatest expanse; treading farther
east into Asia and westward in North Africa, its soldiers and settlers traversing
lands once ruled by Pharaohs and Emperors of Rome. Decade by decade, they
encroached on more North African land, easily claiming it from the waning
Byzantine Empire that held it before them. By 698, the Umayyad Caliphate had
claimed the entirety of the Byzantine's North African land and supplanted Arabic
as the language of power there. The residents of former Byzantine land quickly
saw Arabic become the reigning tongue. Others deeply affected by the expansion
of the Umayyad Caliphate would have been the Berber people, who had for so
long called North Africa home. Initially, they attempted to resist the incoming

Muslims, but through destruction of their homes and lives, as well as persuasion on the pros of Islam, many Berbers allowed them in. To this day, many Berbers speak Arabic and follow Islam.

The Caliphate reached its maximum size in 720, where it covered the previously mentioned North African claims that the Rashidun Caliphate has obtained, but even more of modern-day Libya, the entirety of modern Tunisia, a large chunk of present-day Algeria, and all of present-day Morocco. The Umayyad Caliphate even crossed the Strait of Gibraltar and took over the majority of the Iberian Peninsula. Arabic and Islam hasn't had as much of an impact on modern Spain and Portugal, especially compared to the persisting impact it has had on North Africa. This Islamic Empire became so large that parts of it received new names; the western part (which covered most of North Africa) became known as the Maghreb, which simply means the western land. This is a term that has stuck with the nations of North Africa (minus Egypt) to this day. The other part of the empire which covered Egypt, and their Middle Eastern claim, was called the Mashriq, which unsurprisingly more or less means the eastern land.

Arabic was planted as the key language of North Africa and it even trickled down to more southern parts of the continent. Nations like Chad, Mauritania, and Sudan which lie just below the true north of Africa have Arabic-speaking communities. Arabic became prominent in these places not only due to the Islamic Empire extending into land north of them but also due to things like interacting with Arabic traders and nomadic Arab clans who settled here too. The farthest south Arabic found itself in Africa in a major way is seemingly across the island nations of Comoro which have Arabic as one of their three official languages. This, once again, would have been as a result of merchants traversing the Indian ocean, and while they were there, they influenced the Bantu tongues, too, which were traversing sub-Saharan Africa at the time.

Like the Rashiduns before them, the Umayyad Caliphates, too, were not destined to rule forever. They would be overthrown in 750 by the Abbasid Caliphate for a variety of reasons. Though, the Islamic Empire lived on after the Umayyads, it was under them that it reached its largest expanse, and it was they who did a huge amount of the heavy lifting bridging Islam and Arabic into land it did not originate from. The land of North Africa, over the years, would shift from power to power before it all eventually landed in its current form with the nations of Morocco, Algeria, Tunisia, Libya, and Egypt making up the continent's northern coast. All these nations have Arabic as an official language. Egypt, unto itself, is the most populous Arabic-speaking nation today. There are probably more Arabic speakers in Egypt alone than there are in the entire Arabian Peninsula today, where the language derived from. The Arabic dialects spoken in these countries are far from identical to each other, seemingly. The tongue's vast migrations led to it evolving and each nation has its own dialect of Arabic influenced by other factors and tongues in these lands.

The dialects of Arabic spoken across North Africa can be split into two categories: Maghrebi Arabic and Egyptian Arabic. Maghrebi Arabic splits down even further into smaller dialects of Arabic such as Moroccan, Algerian, Tunisian, and Libyan Arabic, spoken in their respective countries. While each of these sub-dialects have their own unique features, one of the overarching things about Maghrebi Arabic are its influences. A variety of languages have influenced Maghrebi Arabic based on geographic and historic reasons. Those native Berber languages have survived this rise of Arabic in the land and gone on to shape the tongue of Arabia in these places. The Moroccan Arabic word for key, *saaroot*, comes from Berber roots, while other forms of Arabic use the word of *miftah*. It is not only Berber that has played a role in forming the Maghrebi dialects. European languages like Spanish, French, and even Italian have dipped their toes into these forms of Arabic. We already know that the Islamic conquest led to Iberia becoming Muslim territory, so it only makes sense why some Spanish words would also travel back across the Strait of Gibraltar. Italian might seem odd at first, but it makes way more sense when you realise just how close the southern tip of Italy actually is to North Africa. Tunisian Arabic especially has a stronger Italian influence. In parts of Tunisia, it's quite likely you'll hear ice cream being referred to as *jilati* as opposed to *buaza*, which is the more commonly heard Arabic word for the creamy goodness. *Jilati* obviously comes from the quintessentially Italian gelato. As for the French influence in the Maghreb, that comes down to the fact that many years down the line, post-Muslim conquests in this part of the world would become ruled by France and their language would migrate here. Many of these nations even have French as an official co-language.

Beyond just words, however, there are other differences. Maghrebi Arabic dialects are often seen as being spoken faster than other kinds of Arabic. It's believed this is thanks to the Berber influence. Berber languages often drop vowels, so it makes many words naturally quicker to say. This surrendering of vowels has snuck its way into many Maghrebi Arabic pronunciations. The Maghrebi Arabic dialects all have their own unique names too. *Darija* for Moroccan, *Derja* for Algerian, *Tūnsi* for Tunisian, and *Lībi* for Libyan.

Egyptian Arabic, on the other hand, is mainly spoken in just Egypt. It may seem odd for Egypt to get an Arabic dialect all its own but, as mentioned, it's the largest Arabic-speaking nation on the planet. With over 100 million speakers and the land's unfathomably long history, it only makes sense the tongue would shift in its own way there. Berber seems to have influenced Egyptian Arabic less so, but the Coptic languages of Ancient Egypt have survived the millennia to be present in the Arabic now spoken in the land. The simple word of *ah*, meaning yes in Egyptian Arabic, comes from these roots. At some time between the pyramids being a modern tomb and them being a tourist trap, the Ottomans claimed Egypt—this meant Turkish shaped the Arabic here too. Ōḍa meaning "room" in Egyptian Arabic, derives from Turkish's *ooda*. It's *ghurfa* in other forms of Arabic. The language of Egyptian Arabic itself is simply known as *Masri*.

All these forms of Arabic lie on a dialect continuum, meaning that their intelligibility between one another can vary. Dialects that are geographically closer to one another will be more alike and easier to understand. Thankfully, we now have Modern Standard Arabic. This is a neutral version of the language that is taught across the Arabic-speaking world and acts as a lingua franca between all the speakers. Many Arabic speakers use Modern Standard Arabic for formal situations but will fall into their regional dialects amongst friends and family. Modern Standard Arabic allows speakers of any version of the tongues, whether they be found in the land the language was initially conceived in or the depths of the Maghreb, to understand one another.

We can only imagine if Muhammad knew when he had his first revelation what an impact his teachings would have on the world. For it not only birthed the second most followed religion on the planet but set in motion the language he spoke finding a home in another continent and evolving in that land in all kinds of ways. He sparked the beginnings of a huge change in the world, he sparked the beginnings of (as Jazmin sang out on that flying carpet) a whole new world.

FROZEN IN TIME

THE BIRTH OF ICELANDIC

Around the time of the founding of Islam, Europe had somewhat recently found itself in a period we now call the Middle Ages. It's a period seen by many to have started with the fall of Western Rome in 476 AD and it doesn't have the best of reputations. It's thought to be a period of cultural decline in some ways. The great thinking of the likes of the Greeks and Romans was instead replaced with unequivocal religious obedience. Many deem the Middle Ages as a time where human progress took a step backward; this isn't entirely true. Many things did take a step forward. One language in particular took a great leap across sea and sky to not only migrate to a new home but evolve into a whole new tongue entirely.

Old Norse, the language of the Vikings, had its origins in the second century AD, emerging in Scandinavia. It started life as a northern variant of the Proto-

Germanic language spoken to the south of it. Old Norse would become the grandparent of the North Germanic language branch which includes Swedish, Danish, and Norwegian. These tongues are similar to Old Norse, but another language was eventually formed. It's this one that has the strongest family resemblance to Old Norse—that being the tongue of Icelandic. There is minimal difference between Old Norse and modern Icelandic; in fact, many Icelandic speakers alive today can read Old Norse scriptures with relative ease, there being only a few differing words and letters in the languages. For instance, the *Landnámabók*, an Old Norse text dating from the twelfth century detailing the settlement of Iceland, can be read by an Icelandic speaker with minimal effort. A Swedish or Danish speaker would struggle with it more so. If this doesn't impress you as an English speaker, I would suggest you try and read an English text from the twelfth century. Icelandic also lacks any dialect variety. An Icelandic speaker who lives in Raufarhöfn, in the nation's far north, will use the exact same words and pronunciations as an Icelandic speaker who lives in Vík, on Iceland's south coast. This is, once again, remarkable, especially when compared to British English, where the name for a bread roll changes every few miles. It's as if the tongue of Old Norse was frozen in time on the shores of Iceland.

Icelandic stayed so close to Old Norse down to the lack of outside influences on the language. The island that makes up the bulk of the nation is over 500 miles away from mainland Europe. While now a flight to Iceland from Europe is pretty swift and simple, getting to this land in the past was quite the challenge. Only the bravest of souls and toughest of boats could make this voyage. Other Old Norse descendants connected to the rest of Europe became influenced by other languages over the years, while Icelandic stood frozen, unaffected by the changing world across the sea.

Today, Iceland is resoundingly proud of its ancient, relatively untouched tongue. This pride has manifested into something known as linguistic purism. Purism in language is the idea that a language maintains no outside influence from other tongues. While English may borrow from Latin, German, and French, Icelandic intends to not take words on loan and sticks to just the words of its ancient language. This can prove interesting when it comes to forming new words for new concepts. For example, when the language first came into being, computers weren't really a thing, at least in the sense we know them today. "Computer" ultimately comes from Latin origins. This means that Icelandic can't simply use this word or slightly adapt it into their tongue, as that would mean diluting the language with a small dab of Latin. To combat these kinds of issues, new words are coined from Icelandic's old lexicon. The actual word for computer in Icelandic is *tölva*, which is a combination of Icelandic words meaning number and prophetess, as if a computer is some kind of magical number crunching female deity. As someone who doesn't really understand how exactly computers work, comparing them to some kind of magical number god seems fitting.

Loaned words have found themselves migrating into Icelandic occasionally, however. This is chiefly seen in the form of branded names for things created outside of the island. Coca-Cola is still called Coca-Cola even in Iceland, they haven't had to adapt the name or craft a new one for it. Icelandic linguistic purism is seemingly no match for global capitalism. While foreign brand names have snuck into the language, something that has had a much more difficult time of sneaking in are foreign human names. Iceland is incredibly picky when it comes to the names of its citizens. Icelanders must have names that fit the structure of the Icelandic language. There's even a list of approved names you can choose from, with there being just over 4,000 names on this list. If you choose to give your baby a name that isn't on the list, it has to be approved by the Icelandic Naming Committee, who are very much a real thing. Names they have rejected include the likes of Damien, Theo, and Mario. This all might come off as a tad silly and restrictive, but Iceland is fiercely proud of its language and views itself as a pure tongue in a world full of mongrel languages. They even have a special day for their language—the sixteenth of November is Icelandic Language Day in the nation. Iceland's insistence on keeping their tongue pure might seem stuffy and overprotective, but it's an incredible conservation effort to keep a tongue in this form. It's an effort that many other languages have unfortunately not been able to afford and, as a result, are no longer on this planet.

This effort has allowed Iceland to pride itself on just how old and unchanged its language is, but the idea of there even being a language spoken at all on this landmass is a relatively new idea. While the first notion humans had of Iceland came in 325 BC, when Greek explorer Pytheas spotted the land on one of his epic voyages, he seemingly didn't stick around or even touch its soil or stone. He didn't name it Iceland either. The island of Thule appears on many ancient maps and was known during the time of Ancient Greece and Rome. Thule was this supposedly northernmost island in the world. Many days away, even from Britain, and surrounded by icy waters. Thule could potentially have been Iceland in reality, but we aren't entirely sure. True settlement of Iceland came around hundreds of years later. There is some evidence that Irish monks were actually the first to settle in the land in the latter half of the eighth century AD. They seemingly didn't leave all too much of an impact here. Some argue, though, that the Celtic Irish language is one of the few to have influenced Icelandic due to ties between the Land of Ice and Fire and the Emerald Isle. Prior to this, no one group of people had conclusively called Iceland home. Unlike many other cases when a foreign tongue immigrated to a new land, there was not a native language already there. Iceland was a barren, uninhabited land full of little more than volcanoes, ice, and some puffins. This also explains to us why Icelandic has remained so pure and unchanged. There was no native language to influence it like we see in other cases of immigrant tongues.

It was in the ninth century when Iceland came to the interest of the Norse; by this point, Vikings were well on their way to pillaging and exploring the world beyond their fjord-laden homeland. Iceland was a landmass known to them and, in 868, a Norseman named Flóki Vilgerðarsson set off on the first known deliberate voyage to the land. This epic journey involved the use of ravens to help him find the island, knowing they would fly toward land. Once he finally came to the land, what struck him most were the wide fjords full of drifting ice. It was due to this that he named this land Iceland, or *Ísland* as it was in Old Norse and (unsurprisingly) still is in Icelandic. While Flóki spent a good amount of time in Iceland across his life, he never made a permanent settlement there. A permanent Norse-speaking community on the island would happen a few years after his voyages in 874.

We aren't entirely sure why Ingólfur Arnarson decided to leave Norway and sail the seas to find a new home. The leading theory is that he had to flee the land because he was a wanted man! Along with his half-brother Hjörleirfur Hróðmarsson, he had killed the sons of a Norse earl. This created a bitter blood feud between his own family and the earl's. After this, Arnarson fell from being a wealthy Norwegian landowner to having next to nothing to his name. Arnarson gave up on Norway and set off to find new land to call his own. He, his stepbrother, and their wives took to the seas in search of a new home. After an extended time in the harsh North Sea, Arnarson spotted a speck of land in the distance. Iceland was in sight but, as the story goes, he didn't just sail up to it and call it home. Instead, he cast two decorative stone pillars into the ocean from his ship and vowed to farm wherever those pillars turned up again, leaving his fate to the gods. Thankfully, those pillars did find themselves on the shores of Iceland, though relocating them took a bit of time. From dropping those pillars in the sea, it took Arnarson and his crew no less than three years to find them again—like searching for two stoney needles in a barren, frozen haystack. Arnarson didn't just do laps of the island looking for them during that time, though—he instead settled on another part of the island and started farming there. This area is now called Ingólfshöfði, meaning Ingólfur's residence. It was tough, but he managed it, especially during the harsh Icelandic winters with minimal sunshine.

When he heard news that the pillars had been found, he reunited with them. It was here on a small coast in the southwest of Iceland he founded a proper settlement. He named it Reykjavík, meaning steaming bay in relation to the steaming hot springs found there, and this settlement is still the capital of the nation. The founding of Reykjavík cemented Old Norse on the island, which wasn't the toughest of competitions as there weren't any other languages there to compete with. Arnarson and his crew flourished in the new village, and they wouldn't be alone for that long. Word caught on quickly about this new Nordic safe haven back in Scandinavia. The idea of empty land free to farm appealed to many Norse people of the time. Especially once King Harald of Norway came to power and ruled with an iron fist.

Iceland became a refuge for Norse speakers wishing for a fresh start free from the rule of this tyrannical king. People came en masse to Iceland and by just 930, around sixty years after Reykjavík was founded, it is believed that all habitable land in Iceland was settled by speakers of Old Norse. It takes a lot for masses of people to pack up shop and leave. Especially if it's leaving one relatively cold and harsh environment like Scandinavia for an even colder and harsher one like Iceland. Yet, the desire for a new life drove these Norsemen and Vikings to the shores of Iceland, their longboats traversing the tough waters for the promise of a new home. Norse had arrived in Iceland, and from here it kind of just stewed. Its evolution was not as pronounced as, say, Arabic in North Africa or Latin across

Europe. It shifted from Old Norse to Old Icelandic around the eleventh century and eventually became modern Icelandic in the sixteenth century. During this time, the language didn't really change all that much. There was the odd new word or pronunciation here and there but, on the whole, this language remained frozen. It hasn't remained frozen just linguistically, but frozen geographically too.

Beyond its initial migration from Scandinavia to Iceland, the Icelandic language hasn't travelled all that much in any meaningful way. It isn't the grandparent of some newer language, nor has it become the official language of any other nation due to global colonisation. Modern Iceland doesn't even have its own army— military really isn't in their blood. It hasn't stayed completely stationary, however. The language has travelled from one frozen north to another. A small Icelandic-speaking community can be found in the nation of Canada and is simply dubbed New Iceland. This small slice of a Nordic nation arrived in Canada in the nineteenth century when Icelandic migrants grew tired of the living conditions back home, especially due to the then recent eruption of Askja which blanketed swaths of the country in ash. After groups of Icelandic people attempted to make parts of the USA and even Brazil their home, a small section of Manitoba was settled on due to its fertile land, geographic similarities to Iceland, and lack of other people already living there. The area also lacked a volcano, which many Icelanders were happy with too. Today, New Iceland is home to the largest group of Icelandic people outside of Iceland and, while the language can still be heard, it's far less prevalent than it was in the past. However, the region still celebrates its Icelandic roots with a yearly festival to commemorate their Viking ancestors. My personal favourite thing about New Iceland has to be the name of their largest settlement, Gimli. Though, it's not directly named after everyone's favourite dwarf, unfortunately.

ARABIC & LATIN'S LOVECHILD

THE BIRTH OF MALTESE

The Semitic languages are notable for their uniquely written scripts. From the delicate curves of Arabic to the archaic letters of Hebrew. One Semitic language bucks this trend entirely, however. Not only does it lack its own unique script, it uses another far more popular one entirely. On a tiny island nestled within the Mediterranean, something truly unique happened. Across history, via multiple different human/language migrations, a new tongue was born which is nothing but Semitic and Arabic in its parentage. Yet, in its written form, it looks far more akin to a language like Italian or English. This is the only Semitic language that natively uses the letters of Rome, the Latin script which is now seen in languages across the globe. This Arabic-Latin hybrid is the language of Maltese, the national tongue of the island nation Malta.

Looking at the geography of Malta starts to give you an idea as to why Maltese is this unique hybrid. The islands that make up this tiny nation are tucked neatly between the Italian island of Sicily and the North African coast, their nearest African neighbour being the Arabic-speaking Tunisia. Yet, despite its small stature, Malta has had a long history of outsiders coming to the island and calling it home. Human habitation in Malta is believed to go a long way back, with the earliest evidence of human life on the islands coming from 5900 BC. These neolithic people are believed to have come over from Sicily and seemed to have lived simple hunter-gather and farmer lives. We don't know what language they spoke and all we have left of them are the temples they constructed and the caves they called home. This would not be the last of Sicilian migration to Malta, as the much larger island (compared to Malta, anyway) is the key in finding out how Maltese ended up as an Arabic language written in Latin. That's a long way down the line, however. Human life on these islands dates back centuries and it took a long line of linguistic influence for Maltese to become the language that it is today.

The first group of people to make a definitive home in Malta were the Phoenicians, who claimed it as their own during the eighth and ninth centuries BC. This ancient group of people originated from an area of the eastern Mediterranean known as the Levant, which now houses nations like Israel, Jordan, and the island of Cyprus off its western coast. A key reason why Malta has had so many different powers claim it over the course of history boils down to its prime location. It makes for a terrific launching point from Asia into Europe and this is exactly what the Phoenicians used it for. To them, it was a great stopping point on long sea voyages to resupply and rest up before heading back toward the open sea. The language of the Phoenicians, dubbed Phoenician, is related to modern Arabic and Maltese. This shows us that the first language spoken widely across the island was of Semitic origins, helping lay the groundwork of the modern Maltese language. Though, Phoenician is not a direct ancestor of Arabic and Maltese but more a cousin from the past.

The islands remained under Phoenicians' rule for some time, but eventually fell to the also Phoenician-speaking Carthaginians from modern Tunisia, then to the Romans and their Latin. It would stay Roman in some form all the way until 870 AD. This means that from the ninth century BC until the ninth century AD, Malta was ruled by a mixture of Semitic speakers and Latin speakers. It's no surprise that, after around 1,000 years of this intermixing, the language itself started to borrow aspects from both tongues. It was in 870, around the same time the Norse were making Iceland their new home, that Malta was first claimed by true Arabic speakers. The Aghlabid Dynasty, who were at the time ruling the Maghreb long after the Umayyad Caliphate claimed it initially. They took the islands from the Byzantine Empire claiming them in a particularly fierce siege and battle which saw countless Maltese lives lost and cities sacked. Their conquering of the islands had a devastating effect on them. It was supposedly so vicious that it left Malta with no major human population in its direct aftermath. While this could have spelt out the end of human life in Malta, thankfully, down the line, its importance on the global stage was realised yet again—allowing humans and language to thrive there once more.

Life started to spring up again in Malta in the eleventh century. It's from here that our old friend Sicily once again came onto the scene—they, too, had had their own Arab conquest. Across the ninth and tenth centuries, those same Maghrebi Arabs, the Aghlabids, chipped Sicily away from Byzantine rule. Prior to this, the island had a language unique to it: Sicilian, a Romance tongue which is still spoken to some degree today but in much smaller numbers compared to the other great Romance languages like Italian and French. A key reason why the Sicilian language's numbers dwindled was due to this Arabic rule. The Romance language of Sicily got replaced by a new Arabic language that formed on the islands, known as Siculo-Arabic or just Sicilian Arabic. The Aghlabid-ruled Emirate of Sicily also included the islands that make up modern Malta. This was probably because, by this point, the islands were once again pretty much a barren wasteland after the siege back in 870, so it might as well have been administered along with Sicily instead of being its own thing.

Thankfully, from here, the Aghlabid started to realise the true potential of Malta, like the Phoenicians and Romans had before them. Slowly, they started to immigrate from Sicily to Malta and settle there once again. Malta sprang to life like it had done in the past and blossomed with lemon trees, orange trees, and the many wonderful cities and towns we still see there today. These Arabs from Sicily also brought along the language of Sicilian Arabic with them to Malta. The language flourished there, much like the architecture and flora. It even started to evolve further on these islands. Sicilian Arabic gave birth to the earliest form of Maltese. This means Maltese is a daughter language of Sicilian Arabic, which in turn is a daughter language of Maghrebi Arabic. At this time, Maltese was primarily an oral language, meaning it didn't have much of a written form. Its adoption of the Latin script was still some time off. Though, the Latin alphabet would have undoubtedly had a presence in the land, chiefly because of its proximity to other Latin alphabet-using places and its history under Roman rule.

Our earliest evidence of Maltese using the Latin script comes to us from the fifteenth century in the form of a poem named *Il-Kantilena* by Maltese poet Pietru Caxaro. By now, Sicilian Arabic had well and truly morphed into the distinct language of Maltese. Yet, at this point, Maltese was still primarily Arabic in its lexicon. Loan words from other tongues hadn't been cemented all too much in the language yet. Despite being very much Arabic at this time, the poem is still written in the Latin script. This means we have no evidence of this Arabic tongue ever being written in the Arabic script. By the time this poem was put to paper, Malta was no longer under any form of Arabic rule. In the early days of the eleventh century, the Normans went on a bit of a conquest around Europe; perhaps most famous was their conquest of Britain in 1066. A few decades later, in 1091, they claimed Malta from the Arabs too. This brought a degree of French/Norman influence to the islands. The Latin script would have been the alphabet of choice for those in power, but due to Malta's remoteness from the rest of Europe, French didn't intervene too much. Most people would have carried on talking their Arabic-originated Maltese tongue.

A stronger French influence on the language came in the century after that poem was written. In 1530, The Knights of Malta came to rule the land. This is a religious order whose aims were primarily to defend Christianity as well as heal the wounded and sick. They originated in Jerusalem back in the eleventh century but called many places their home before landing in Malta. Their key language was French, though they may have spoken other tongues. This wasn't the last of French-speaking rule for Malta, however, as after the Knights came a certain Mr. Bonaparte in 1798. After quickly claiming the islands from the Knights, Malta became part of his empire. Just as quickly as he claimed Malta, he lost it as the British pinched Malta off of the French in 1800. The British took a great amount of care in Malta, using it once again for its strategic location as it had been used in the past. Their language of English, unlike French that came before it, did take hold on the islands. Today, English is a joint official language of Malta. Maltese has amazingly managed to remain the language of the masses on the islands in the face of outside powers.

It was while under British rule that the Maltese alphabet was actually finalised. Somehow, despite the Maltese language being in existence for hundreds of years up to this point and even being written down, its alphabet had never been formalised. In 1924, a group of Maltese writers came together and formalised the language's script, finally giving the Latin alphabet official capacity for the language. Malta would gain independence from the British forty years later in 1964. Suffice to say it took *quite* a long time for Latin to become the official script of Maltese but, by this point, it should come as no surprise that this Arabic language uses the Latin alphabet. It's the only script the language has ever known thanks to centuries of Latin language influence on these islands, as well as the huge mixture of migrations that had Malta as their final destination. Maltese doesn't just use the Latin script verbatim. In the same way its spoken form is an evolution of Arabic, its written form is an evolution of the Latin script. The Maltese alphabet features letters unique to it such as Ċ which sounds something akin to the English CH sound; Ġ, which has a J sound; Ħ, which sounds a lot like an English H; and Ż, which makes a sound similar to S at the end of words.

This makes Maltese the only Semitic language that uses the Latin script. Maltese, on the whole, also has the unique claim of being the only dominant Semitic language of a European nation. The European influence on Maltese isn't just seen in its alphabet, however. Many loan words of European origin have taken root in the tongue too. The long history of British rule in Malta means that there are words of English origin in the language. None are more interesting to myself than their word of *kitla*, meaning kettle. The British are very much associated with kettles and their cups of tea, so it only makes sense why Maltese would adopt this word from the British. Various French-speaking rulers of the islands meant that the language has also had some influence there too. The Maltese term for "good evening," *bonswa*, is pretty much just a phonetic spelling of the French *bonsoir*. Even Italian, the land of the Latin alphabet, has shaped Maltese due to how close the nations are. The Maltese word for "sock," *kalzetta*, comes directly from the Italian *calzino*.

Maltese is first and foremost a Semitic language, in spite of the European influence on its script and much of its lexicon. Maltese has a degree of mutual intelligibility with Arabic. Apparently, many Maltese speakers can understand Arabic to some degree, and the languages share around a third of their words. Of all the different dialects of Arabic out there, Maltese is often considered to be closest to the Arabic spoken in Tunisia, which is fitting given how close the countries are to one another. Of all the words of Maltese that derive from Arabic, the one that strikes me the most is their term for God. Malta is an incredibly Catholic country—it was *literally* ruled by Catholic knights for some time, yet the language's word for the supreme deity of the religion is none other than *alla*, similar to Islam's *allah*. A gentle reminder of Maltese's Arabic origins.

Maltese's birth is a truly fascinating example of a language migration. It's the final product of not one but two languages moving in together and producing offspring. A child that has elements from both its parents. It's also a reminder that, like Arabic's first movement from the Arabian Peninsula into North Africa, these migrations can be transcontinental too. It was around the same time when Maltese came into being that another Asian tongue found itself at home in European land, only this time in a much bigger way.

LOST & HUNGARY

HUNGARIAN IN EUROPE

Maltese shows us that non-Indo-European languages are present across Europe. However, they tend to lie on the outskirts of the continent, in parts of the land where other language families start to creep in. Thanks to a language migration in the ninth century, a non-Indo-European tongue found itself not only in Europe, but more or less slap bang in the middle of the continent. This was none other than the tongue of Hungarian, found in the nation of Hungary. A simple glance of the lexicon of Hungarian makes it abundantly clear that this tongue has little relation to its neighbours. An example I find incredible is their name for the nation of Italy. In the surrounding languages of Romanian, Slovenian, and German, the boot-shaped nation is called *Italien, Italija,* and *Italien,* respectively. All three of these languages are from different branches of the Indo-European family. If Hungarian was also part of this happy little family, then its name for

Italy would sound similar too. Languages of geographic closeness also tend
to sound alike regardless of familial ties. Of course, this isn't the case. The
Hungarian name is instead the mouthful *Olaszország*, which sounds nothing like
any of the other names for Italy. Even the Hungarian name for Hungary sounds
nothing like the name Hungary. Its native name is instead *Magyarország*. With
its natives being known as the *Magyars/Magyarok* and the language being called
Magyar Nyelv, Hungarian really sticks out like a sore thumb. It is, however, not a
language isolate, but rather a black sheep that's been separated from the rest of
its flock.

The rest of its flock are fellow members of the Uralic language family. This is a
language family that has its initial origins far away from the lands that now use
these tongues. The Uralic family of languages is thought to have been conceived
somewhere in the Ural Mountains—a range now housed in Russia. They are
often used as a natural border of sorts between European Russia and Asian
Russia, as well as Europe and Asia as a whole. Around the Ural Mountains today,
Uralic languages are still spoken, but in no large numbers. They are minority
languages in Russia. This includes the Samoyedic and Permic languages. These
are distant cousins of Hungarian. The Uralic languages of Mansi and Khanty can
also be found in the Urals. What makes Mansi and Khanty of so much interest to
us is the fact they are the closest relatives to Hungarian. As these three languages
all lie on the Ugric branch of the Uralic language family.

Uralic languages have thrived best away from their homelands, like a student
leaving the nest to find their real self at university. Hungarian is the most widely
spoken of the Uralic languages with seventeen million speakers. However, it is
not the only Uralic language to find a land of its own in Europe. Two branches
of Uralic languages have found themselves at home in some of the northernmost
points of Europe. The Sami branch contains the many Sami dialects which
populate the sparse wilderness in the northern tips of the Nordic countries. And
then there's also the Baltic-Finnic branch. This is the branch that houses the other
two most widely spoken Uralic languages, the ones that have come to represent
entire nations as opposed to just small pockets of people. It is in this branch we
find the languages of Estonian and Finnish, spoken in the nations of Estonia
and Finland, respectively. This paints a picture of the Uralic family all nestled
somewhat close to one another in Northern Europe and nearby Asian Russia. It's

here that the rest of Hungarian's flock grazes, and we can start to understand just how far Hungarian has wandered from its paddock.

Hungarian is not just distant from its relatives geographically; these languages have been split for a huge amount of time too. The initial split of Proto-Uralic is thought to have occurred over 4,000 years ago. For context, the split in, say, the Romance branch of Indo-European is thought to have happened around 2,000 years ago, if that. This has created varying degrees of mutual intelligibility between these languages, especially in regard to the three most prominent ones, Hungarian, Finnish, and Estonian. Take the word for "dog" in each of these languages: *kutya, koira*, and *koer* in Hungarian, Estonian, and Finnish, respectively. All three versions of this word for our best friends are similar to one another in their spelling and pronunciation. Granted, they aren't identical, but you can clearly see a relationship between them. On the other hand, we have their words for "cat." Finnish and Estonian go with *kissa* and *kass*, which are alike, while Hungarian goes with *macska*, which isn't particularly in line with its Uralic siblings.

On the whole, Finnish and Estonian are a lot more alike. They are similar, however, in ways beyond just their words. For example, Hungarian, Finnish, and Estonian all share the trait of having just one pronoun to refer to people in the third person in. There's no "he" or "she" in their language. Just ő in Hungarian, *hän* in Finnish, and *ta* in Estonian.

Though, in spite of these similarities, by and large the languages are pretty different, with Hungarian very much evolving in its own way. A Finn in Budapest would still need to pack a phrasebook. The difference in these languages would not have been as prominent in the past, in fact they would have been the exact same language. Proto-Uralic is believed to have originated around 8,000 years ago in the Ural Mountains; after 4,000 years of living together, these speakers decided to go their separate ways. One group would go on to become the Finnish and the Estonians, with some of those migrating even further and becoming Sami speakers. Those who would become the Hungarians, or *Magyars*, went in a completely different direction. Oddly enough, at first they travelled eastward, finding themselves on the western edges of Siberia, a cold and inhospitable part of the world. They relocated here around the start of the AD era and here they struggled, noticeably against the vicious and brutal Huns—one of history's most infamous tribes and people you wouldn't want to be on the bad side of. Despite the similarities in their names, the Hungarians and the Huns are not the same people, it's just a coincidence. The Huns drove these migrants out of Siberia. By the time of this exile, the language they spoke had already changed. It was around 1000 BC that it's thought the Proto-Uralic these people spoke started to shift into the first stage of Hungarian. These people needed a new home, and the quest to find one would take centuries. The early Hungarian speakers, who left their home in the Ural Mountains and found themselves banished from Siberia, realised that travelling eastward was no longer a viable option. With barren wasteland to their north and south, they were only left with one option. Step by step, they travelled westward. What aided these travels was the mighty Eurasian Steppe, a huge spread of flat, easily traversable land which spans from modern China to Hungary. This navigable land has, throughout history, helped many peoples come and go between Europe and Asia with ease. They went farther westward than any Uralic speakers had gone before and, finally, after generations of migration in the late ninth century AD, they stumbled upon somewhere that could make an exquisite home.

The Carpathian Basin is a huge area of land in the southeast of Central Europe. It's a relatively flat part of the continent, bordered by various mountain ranges, including the Carpathian Mountains where its name is derived from. It's full of great farmable land, a manageable climate, and ample rivers. It would be a suitable home for any band of wanderers. Today, the majority of Hungary lies within the Carpathian Basin, so a slight spoiler I suppose. Before the land belonged to the Hungarians, many others and their languages called this land home. While under the rule of Rome, it went by the name of Pannonia. In the sixth century after the fall of Western Rome, a group named the Avars claimed it as their home, they were a Turkic people with their own migration story and would have spoken a language somewhat similar to that of modern Turkish. Just prior to the land coming under the claim of the Hungarians/*Magyars* it did not belong to one single power. It was instead being fought over by three powers—the First Bulgarian Empire emanating from Bulgaria, the Kingdom of East Francia which had a majority of their land in what is now eastern Germany, and Great Moravia which was based in modern Czechia. It was these three empires that fought for the Basin and its geographic importance during the late ninth century.

Also around this time, the Hungarians had emigrated far enough west to find themselves on the cusp of this land.

They did not plunge straight into this fray, turning things into a "fatal four way," in wrestling parlance. Their conquering of this land came in stages. At first, Hungarian mercenaries were hired by the Bulgarians, East Franks, and Moravians to fight on their behalf. Little did these empires know that, in doing so, they were just giving the Hungarians a good idea of the lay of the land, and it was land they wanted. On the outside looking in, the Hungarians got to work on planning their conquest, and that conquest went into motion properly in 894. This was in the midst of those three other kingdoms duking it out. Beyond these three raging for the land, it was relatively sparsely populated, which made things easy for the Hungarians to claim the land fairly swiftly with their military might. The Bulgarians, East Franks, and Moravians were usurped by the Hungarians who had travelled far from their home in the Ural Mountains. By 900, the Basin was firmly under Hungarian control, the people whose ancestors were ousted by the Huns some millennia ago were now the ones doing the ousting. This, of course, occurred to the chagrin of the empires who spent decades fighting over it before the Hungarians rocked up.

From here, the Basin has stayed under Hungarian control, evolving into the Kingdom of Hungary in around 1000, and eventually merging into the famous dual monarchy of the Austro-Hungarian Empire. Before becoming the nation it is today, during all that time, their language of Hungarian shifted too. Their tongue continued to evolve in its own unique way, cut off from its relatives up in the Baltic. Modern Hungarian finally emerged in the eighteenth century. This shows us just how far away geographically and timewise Hungarian had been away from the rest of its Uralic family. This distance alone can explain to us why the language is so different from its cousins, like Finnish and Estonian. Yet, the Uralic language of Hungarian hasn't turned its nose up at its Indo-European neighbours completely. Its lexicon now contains words from the languages it shares borders with. The Hungarian word for mushroom, *gomba*, was acquired via their Slavic-speaking friends of Slovenia to their southwest, who use *goba* as their name for Mario's favourite power-up. Finnish, meanwhile, goes with the wholly Uralic *sieni* as their word for the fungus. Even Romania and their Romance language has inspired the language of Hungary. The Romanian term for bag, *pungă*, is more or less identical to the Hungarian term *punga*. The Uralic Estonian favoured the simple word *kott* as their name for a bag.

The most interesting influence of Hungarian, however, is probably the Turkish language; these two nations have a very closely shared history with one another, having been allies and enemies various times over history. This means that many Hungarian words have come from Turkish roots too. For example, they both share the same word for the humble "tray"—*tepsi*. Turkish and Hungarian are more similar than just sharing a lexicon, it seems; both languages have similar grammar and other features. In fact, they are so alike that, for some time, many linguists believed that Turkish was actually another language in the Uralic family. While we know now that isn't the case, the two languages did both undertake somewhat similar journeys to get to where they are today.

NOBODY'S BUSINESS BUT THE TURKS

TURKISH IN TURKEY

Turkish takes the crown as the most widely spoken non-Indo-European language in Europe. Instead of Uralic, Turkish sits on the Oghuz branch of the completely separate Turkic language family. It is by and far the most widely spoken Turkic language, with around ninety million people able to speak it either as their native tongue or as a second language. The language is now firmly planted in the transcontinental nation of Turkey. The fact the nation straddles the line between Europe and Asia has, throughout history, given Turkey a mystique in the eyes of many. In the past, before the age of easy travel, it was seen as Europe's last outpost and a gateway to a continent so different from the one many adventurers were leaving behind for their own migrations and journeys. In the same way

European explorers would migrate to Asia via Turkey, the tongue of the Turks migrated in the opposite direction to get to its current home.

The origin of the Turkic language family is believed to have been somewhere in northeast Asia. We can't conclusively pinpoint an exact location, but one of the most prominent theories has the language family originating from land which is now part of Mongolia. That's roughly 3,400 miles away from the country we now call Turkey. It's a staggering migration, that's for sure, but it's not the only idea we have of their homeland. Others place the origin of the Turkic family somewhere in the Altai-Sayan region, a vast expanse of land which lies within the borders of Mongolia, as well as Russia, China, and Kazakhstan. Others place their home in the Tuva region, which is now in the south of Asian Russia. While evidence can't seem to agree on where exactly the language came from, what we can agree on is that it's a darn long way away from Turkey today.

Proto-Turkic (and its speakers) is believed to have emerged somewhere around there in around 2000 BC. Meaning there's around 4,000 years between Proto-Turkic's humble origins in far flung Asia to the language being spoken in Eurasia today. Yet, we don't seemingly know all that much about the original Turkic speakers. They left no major impact in this part of the world at this time, but we seem to understand that they were fairly nomadic people. They set up shop in one area for some time before moving on to start fresh somewhere else. The first really noteworthy Turkic speakers that we know of from this part of the world are the Göktürks. The earliest evidence we have of them comes from the fifth century AD. Their language was something called Orkhon Turkic, which can also simply be called Old Turkic. While we know of them from the fifth century, they really made their mark the century after, as in the sixth century they seized power in an area known as the Rouran Khaganate. This was a region that now resides in modern Mongolia. The Rouran Khaganate is generally regarded as the first major Turkic-speaking power on the globe. This gave Turkic people not only more land, but the understanding that they, too, could expand beyond their homelands. With migration in their bones thanks to their nomadic lifestyle, Turkic people spread beyond this empire and all across Asia. Their migrations were helped, once again, by the Eurasian Steppe, following a similar route which led the Hungarians to Hungary.

By the time the Turkic-ruled Rouran Khaganate met its demise in the eighth
century, Turkic speakers had migrated a great amount, planting new Turkic
languages across the globe in their travels. We can somewhat trace these Turkic
migrations across Eurasia thanks to the spread of Turkic languages across our
globe. The major Turkic-speaking nations today can act as a bridge from their
home in the region of Mongolia to the nation of Turkey itself. Kazakhstan and
their tongue of Kazakh is Turkic and lies just east of Mongolia, the land where
these migrations most likely began. This would have been the first stop in the
migrations of Turkic-speaking travellers; many would have stopped here long
enough to form this tongue. Many would have gone farther south and had their
languages evolve into the Turkic tongue of Uzbek and Kyrgyz, now spoken in
the nations of Uzbekistan and Kyrgyzstan, respectively. Their next step toward
Europe would have seen them traverse the Caspian Sea and settle on its western
shores. Today we can also find the nation of Azerbaijan, who speaks another
Turkic language: Azerbaijani. Though, from a nomenclature perspective, the
strongest link we find between Turkish and the other Turkic languages has to be
with Turkmen, spoken in the nation of Turkmenistan, found east of the Caspian
Sea. This explains to us why Turkey and Turkmenistan have such similar names,
as they are both lands settled by Turkic speakers. These Turkic languages all have
varying degrees of mutual intelligibility with one another.

The Turkic languages' spread as a whole across western Asia into Eastern Europe
gives us a good guide as to how those initial speakers migrated across the world.
Turkey itself is the westernmost point of the Turkic sphere. Turkic speakers were
on the boundary of their final homeland by 1037. It was in this year that the
Seljuk Empire was founded. This was a Turkic-speaking empire initially set up in
modern Iran. Because of their location, they spoke a mixture of Persian as well as
a language known as Oghuz Turkic, the forebearer to the modern branch which
shares its name. This empire expanded westward over the years. By the middle
of the eleventh century, their westernmost border was shared with a certain
peninsula. This peninsula has gone chiefly by two names in the past, Asia Minor
and Anatolia. Today, it houses the bulk of Turkey. This land has, throughout
history, been highly coveted for its transcontinental location, bridging Europe and
Asia together. This has resulted in many different peoples calling the land home
prior to its establishment as Turkey.

The earliest residences we know of in Anatolia are the Hittites. They lived here as far back as the seventeenth century BC and their key language of Hittite belonged to the long extinct Anatolian Branch of Indo-European. After them came a long line of other residents, including the Trojans who's famed city of Troy could be found in one of the westernmost points of the land. Their language of Trojan is incredibly unknown to us, and we don't know what exactly it relates to either. The Phrygians came after them with their language of Phrygian. Then the Lycians and their language of the same name. All these languages, however, are long gone on our globe. The oldest language to have a presence here that is still spoken today is Persian, as the Persian Empire claimed the land in the sixth century BC. Though, by 129 BC our old friends the Romans secured it as part of their empire and their Latin grew influential there. Anatolia stayed Roman in some form for a while. The peninsula gained a huge amount of prominence when Eastern Rome made the settlement of Byzantium their capital, changing its name to Constantinople and, down the line, it would be renamed once again Istanbul.

Anatolia was still under Greek-speaking Byzantine rule by the mid-eleventh century when the Seljuk Turkic Empire were their neighbours to the east. By this point, the Byzantine Empire was not in good shape. While it wouldn't be completely wiped out for a few more centuries, this was undoubtedly an empire in decay. An empire in decay is one that grows paranoid and suspicious. The Byzantines focused their paranoia on the Seljuks to their east. Funnily enough, at this point, the Seljuks were just doing their own thing and not getting themselves involved with the Byzantines. This Byzantine paranoia reached a fever pitch in 1046 when the Byzantine-Seljuk war broke out. This war was instigated by the Byzantines who had grown fearful that the Seljuks were going to attack them first. Yet, despite starting this war, they did not end it. In the battle of Manzikert in 1071, the Byzantines were trounced by the Seljuks and lost control of the majority of Anatolia to the Turkic speakers. Finally, the peninsula was under Turkic rule.

The Seljuks set up Anatolia as its own independent power which was dubbed the Sultanate of Rûm in 1077. A sultanate is a land area ruled by a sultan. Rûm is an older word of mixed Turkic and Persian roots and was a term for Rome/ the Byzantine Empire, so the name kind of means the Sultanate of Rome, as the land it sat on had been Roman in some form for so long. In the Sultanate of Rûm, Oghuz Turkic morphed into Old Anatolian Turkish, the oldest form of the language we now call Turkish. The reason it changed was due to the wide array of influences that had come over the language. These influences are still seen in the modern language today. Many words of Turkish are Persian in origin, which makes a lot of sense as the Seljuk Empire started in Persian land. This can be seen in a word as simple as "vegetable," which is *sebze* and *sabzi* in Turkish and Persian, respectively. The word for "vegetable" is resoundingly different in Turkmen, being *gök önümler*. This comes down to the fact that this kind of Persian influence never happened in Turkmenistan. Another language that has had a great influence on Turkish is Kurdish. This Indo-European language's native homeland is just west of the Anatolian peninsula. To this day, Kurdish is still a minority language in Turkey.

From its inception in 1077, the Sultanate of Rûm lasted all the way until 1308. During this just over two-century period, Old Anatolian Turkish became a mainstay in the land. This was a huge chunk of time for a people who had historically been nomadic to stay put, so it's understandable why the language thrived here so much. The thriving of Old Anatolian Turkish, however, came at the expense of many of the previous languages spoken here in the past falling to the wayside. Two key things led to the fall of the Sultanate of Rûm and, fittingly enough for the transcontinental land, each of those events came from either side. From Europe came the Chrisitan Crusades—wars and battles fought across Europe with the intention to bring Christianity to as many people as possible. These military campaigns are often romanticized but make no mistake, despite being done in the name of religion, they were a bloody and brutal affair. The Sultanate of Rûm practised Islam which, unfortunately, made them a huge target for these Crusades.

This attack from the west was only made worse by another threat arriving from the east. From Asia, a power swept into the land that derived from the Turkic speakers' homeland: the Mongols. The Mongols would go on to form the largest contiguous Empire the planet has ever seen, which included the western edges of Anatolia. You may expect that this would have put an end to Turkic talk on the peninsula and instead everyone would be speaking a Mongolic language, yet, as we see from the current state of the world, that is far from the case. This is for a variety of reasons. The language of the Mongol Empire, Middle Mongol, never really spread like Latin did across the Roman Empire for a variety of reasons. On top of this, the Empire also spoke a variety of other languages, too, including various Turkic tongues. It's probably also worth mentioning here that the modern Mongolian language is not a part of the Turkic family despite originating in close proximity to them. It is, instead, a part of its own Mongolic language family which houses some other much less prominent tongues.

This left Anatolia Turkic-speaking but not under full Turkic control. The Turkic speakers instead split into smaller principalities on the land now known as the Beyliks of Anatolia. Each one was a small principality unto itself with its own rulers and laws. Each of these Beyliks would have also, most likely, their own dialect of the aforementioned Old Anatolian Turkish. One of these Beyliks, situated in the northwest of Anatolia, was set up by a man named Osman Ghazi and would be named after him. We don't hear too much of the Osman Beylik these days, and that's because it's better known under the Latinized version of its name: Ottoman Beylik. In this Beylik, the version of Turkish spoken became known as Ottoman Turkish.

If you couldn't guess, this humble Beylik was the earliest seed of what would become the Ottoman Empire. A quest for power, land, and wealth sent Osman and his troops to claim the entirety of the peninsula, and even beyond. By the fifteenth century, the Ottomans had claimed Constantinople from the lingering Byzantines, ending that empire, and in turn ending the last remnant of the Roman Empire which flickered into being in 753 BC. At its peak in the sixteenth century, the Ottoman Empire had claimed the entirety of the Anatolian Peninsula, a large chunk of southeast Europe, a majority of Northern Africa, and even the west coast of Arabia. Their language of Ottoman Turkish came along for this journey too. While it was the official language most normal people of the empire used, a less ornate version of it is known as Common or Vulgar Turkish.

Ottoman Turkish is a lot like the modern Turkish it would evolve into. Though, a key difference was the script it used. It used an adaptation of the Arabic script. The Ottoman Empire ebbed and flowed before its dissolution in the aftermath of the First World War. The Ottomans found themselves on the losing side of this war and what little land they had left at this point (primarily the land that makes up modern Turkey) was split between the Allied Powers. It stayed under foreign rule like this until 1922, when the Turkish War for Independence broke out. Victorious in this affair, the Republic of Turkey was founded, and this is the form that nation has to this day. By this point, the language had reached its next and final form, shifting from Ottoman Turkish into modern Turkish, at least in its spoken form, anyway. In its written form, it was still using that adapted Arabic scripture. This came to an end in 1928, when the language adopted the Latin script. This was for better integration with the rest of Europe and to help boost literacy.

This 4,000-year odyssey, which started somewhere around Mongolia with the Proto-Turkic speakers, ends here. Along their migrations, many other languages were born, like Uzbek, Kazakh, and Azerbaijani. Yet, today the most populous Turkic language can be found at the end of their travels in this transcontinental nation whose name is still an ode to those original speakers.

These early migrations show us that languages have been on the move for more or less as long as there have been languages. Yet, in the latter days of the Middle Ages and in the next phase of human history, the tongues we speak would go on to migrate and evolve in places farther than the feet of humans or even the hooves of horses could take us. Languages would find themselves at home in places where their native speakers didn't even know such tongues could exist just decades prior.

PART II

THE AGE OF COLONISATION

TWELFTH CENTURY TO
THE EIGHTEENTH CENTURY

THE TROUBLES WITH LANGUAGE

ENGLISH IN IRELAND

The true Age of Colonisation that saw many languages migrating to parts of the world which were unknown to those tongues is seen to have really kicked off in the early fifteenth century. Yet, the origins of this time period and the idea of European powers claiming land overseas can be traced back further. Many historians point to an event in the twelfth century which saw one small island claiming another nearby small island as the foundation of European colonisation. It was here that the world started to evolve even more into the one we know today, and it wasn't just the planet and its borders which were changing.

By the twelfth century, English had come a long way. Roman rule was all but a faint memory in English's homeland, with Rome leaving Britain to fend for itself in 409 AD. Yet, the memory of 1066, the Norman invasion, and subsequent rule of England, was still sharp in their collective mind as the land was still under a strong French/Norman rule and influence. All this had led to a very unique language being spoken in the land. Between the Roman's exit and the Normans entrance, a variety of Germanic settlers decided to call Britain home, especially the part of Britain we now equate to England. The other parts of the island, present Scotland and Wales, remained a tad more isolated, which allowed their own Celtic identities to flourish. These Germanic settlers ranged from tribes known as the Jutes, Angles, and Saxons. All derived from different parts of Central to Northern Europe which now make up areas of Germany and Denmark. Each tribe brought with them a Germanic language which, in England, intermixed with one another as well as received a heavy dose of Latin influence from the Romans who had previously called the land home for a few centuries. By the fifth century, these languages had birthed Anglo-Saxon, more commonly known as Old English. It was really just around 1,500 years ago that English came into being in any form, yet, in the short millennium and a half, it has gone from freshly born to spoken around the world.

Though, we are a long way from that happening in the twelfth century. By this time, the various kingdoms set up by the Anglo-Saxons, like Wessex, Mercia, and all the others you hear about in Middle Ages dramas, had merged together and, in turn, been claimed by the Normans in 1066, as every British school child knows. At this point, English acquired a large dollop of Norman influence which is still present in the myriad of words of French origin in English today. Here, English left its old age and became what we now know as Middle English. By the middle of the twelfth century, English would start its conquest around the globe, leaving its homeland and making a permanent settlement in new lands. Its initial steps were not into the Southern Hemisphere or even transatlantic. It instead found its way to a nearby island that was a little closer to home. An island that still has a somewhat troubled history with the language.

Prior to the twelfth century, Ireland had remained relatively unbothered by outside powers. Rome never laid their mites on it and, minus the occasional Viking pillage or Christian saint supposedly removing all the snakes from the land, it had more or less been left free to do as it liked. This means the language of the land, Irish, had too been unfazed. Irish belongs to the Celtic branch of Indo-European. While the Celtic identity is now heavily linked with Ireland as well as the other nearby Celtic nations like Scotland, Wales, The Isle of Man, and Cornwall, the Celtic languages actually had their origins in continental Europe. Europe used to be home to all manner of Celtic languages like Celtiberian and Gaulish. Though, as we highlighted in a previous chapter, these mainland Celtic languages were wiped out by the Romans in their conquests. Today, the Celtic languages that preside across Ireland, Britain, The Isle of Man, and in northwest France are just remnants of the once huge language family which dominated pre-Roman Europe. The earliest form of the Irish language we know of is referred to as Primitive Irish of Proto-Goidelic. That latter name derives from the fact that this is the nucleus language of not just Irish but the other Goidelic languages, a sub-branch of the Celtic branch, which also includes Scottish Gaelic and Manx. Primitive Irish morphed into Old Irish in around the sixth century and then, a few hundred years later, changed more so to Middle Irish. A unique feature of Primitive Irish and Old Irish was the writing system it used. The Ogham script was a native construct, written top to bottom and formed of simple lines and dashes to represent the sounds of the language, much like the modern Latin alphabet. It's a truly unique script that has more or less been lost to time.

What this means is that, by the twelfth century, both Irish and English were in their awkward middle phases. Yet, the lands they called home were somewhat different—England was governed by a central power, while Ireland was still split into various smaller kingdoms. These two tween languages would butt heads toward the latter half of this century. It was a mixture of events within England and Ireland which led to the Anglo-Norman invasion of the Emerald Isles. In 1126, a man named Dermot Mac Murchada became King of Leinster, one of the kingdoms of Ireland at the time making up most of the island's southeast. He was a wildly vicious leader, being more than happy to kill anyone who got on his bad side. Anyone having to live under him would not have been in a happy place. As his reign went on, he got involved in a deeply bitter rivalry with many of the other kings in Ireland, going so far as to kidnap another king's wife! By 1166, the Kings of Ireland had had more than enough of the man, forcing him into exile and packing him off to Blighty. In England, Mac Murchada had one goal in mind: getting back to his kingdom and reclaiming his throne. To achieve this, he went directly to the highest power in England.

By this time, England was on its second Henry. This Henry was the great grandson of William the Conqueror, meaning that Norman rule was still in full swing and had not been fully diluted yet into England as a whole. Henry II was not only the most powerful man in England but was, at the time, the most powerful monarch across Europe. His Angevin Empire not only included England but a large chunk of Western France. For some time, he had grown interested in placing Ireland under his watch too. This emanated from a 1155 meeting with Adrian IV, the only English pope in history thus far. As pope, Adrian's job was to make sure Catholicism was worshipped and practised in the appropriate way. The Great Schism which split Christianity into Catholicism in the west and Orthodoxy in the east had at this point only happened a hundred years before. So, the Catholic church was still trying to establish what made them more unique in comparison to the Christianity being worshipped east of them. The path Christianity had taken in Ireland was deemed by him to be the incorrect one. At this point, Ireland had always done Christianity in its own way; this stems back all the way to Saint Patrick introducing the religion in the land in 433 AD. To make it more palatable to the natives at the time, he incorporated elements of their native religion. This gave Ireland a unique flavour of Catholicism which is even seen today with the Celtic Cross that is deeply linked with the land. This spin on the religion had disgruntled Pope Adrian IV and he wanted Henry II to do something about it. It was in 1055 that the pope gave the king permission to invade Ireland to restore the faith to its rightful manner in his eyes. Just after ten years from receiving the pope's blessing/demand to invade Ireland, he was sitting in his court with an Irish king inviting him to the land.

Mac Murchada wanted the king's power and soldiers on his side when he returned to Ireland in exchange for influence and land. Henry II didn't directly agree, he instead allowed Mac Murchada to court the knights of his land to see if they would help him in return for land and power in Ireland. This allowed Henry II to indirectly invade Ireland and, if it happened to go badly, he wouldn't be the one to take the blame. Mac Murchada got to work on wooing knights, and one that came to his side was the Earl of Pembroke in Wales, Richard de Clare. De Clare joined forces with Mac Murchada in exchange for the hand of Mac Murchada's daughter Aoife. With the promise of a wife and promise of land, de Clare joined Mac Murchada in his reclaiming of Ireland. Mac Murchada ventured back to Ireland in 1167 with a handful of mercenaries, and de Clare rallied archers which were pivotal in their attack—so much so that de Clare earned the nickname of Strongbow. That's the popular retelling but there's debate over its authenticity. These 1167 skirmishes proved successful and led to the full-scale Anglo-Norman conquest of Ireland, actually ordered by Henry II, kicking off in 1169.

The rulers, warriors, and ordinary people of Ireland were nowhere near prepared for an invasion like this. They were outnumbered and outpowered by the English in every possible way. The poor Irish kingdoms either showed little resistance to the English or simply bowed to their whims. This is perhaps the first time we see English place itself in a landmass through brute strength and murder and, unfortunately, it will be far from the last. By 1171, Henry himself arrived in Ireland to view the spoils of his conquest. Mac Murchada was also put back on his throne but died the same year of some horrible illness. Post-death Mac Murchada has been portrayed as one of Ireland's most treacherous residents, the man who invited the English to their home. As Strongbow was married to his daughter, it meant that he became the next King of Leinster and, in turn, became the first Irish king of Anglo-Norman origins. In 1177, the invasion was over with the Anglo-Normans as the decisive victors. As Henry II promised the pope all those years back, he took Ireland under his control and set up the Lordship of Ireland. This was the title given to Ireland at this time under English rule. The Lordship expanded over the years to cover the majority of Ireland. It's here that the English language started to take hold of the nation. It would have been the language of power and authority. Though, the ordinary people of the land still seemingly held on to their Celtic Irish language. Roughly 400 years and six Henrys later, English really rose to prominence in Ireland and the native tongue started to dwindle.

In 1542, Henry VIII elevated the Lordship of Ireland into the Kingdom of Ireland, albeit still a kingdom under British rule. While this may sound like it gave Ireland a higher degree of autonomy, in reality this was done so Henry VIII and England could wield more influence and power over the land. As well as make sure no other foreign powers could claim Ireland. Ironically enough, it was also to make sure the pope could not try and claim Ireland back off the English. By this point, Henry VIII had ditched the Catholic church and established his own protestant Church of England, primarily for his own gain. The very same establishment which demanded Henry II claim Ireland was now trying to claim the land back from his eponymous successor. As we know now, Ireland didn't become a vessel power of another nation, including the Vatican. It stayed under English/British rule for some time, with a part of the land still a part of the UK. One of the main aims the English had for Ireland while it was its own kingdom was to bring the land more in line with England, that included language.

A key aim was to eradicate the Irish language as much as possible and instil English as the tongue of the land. Beyond just having English as the language of power in Ireland, the English took other steps to try and stamp out Irish over the years. This included exiling Irish speakers of influence from the land. Notably, many former kings and rulers during Ireland's pre-English times were removed in the aftermath of the battle of Kinsale in 1601. This was the final battle which cemented English rule in the land, and the Irish were even aided by Spain in it. With no key Irish-speaking people in the country, it proved difficult for the language to have any kind of influential voice. The late seventeenth century saw the introduction of penal laws in Ireland, too, by Oliver Cromwell, who even beyond the penal laws brought so much devastation to Ireland—killing many and sending countless to other parts of the Empire more or less as slaves. These laws heavily restricted the rights of Catholics in the land. Of course, there was a strong correlation between Catholics and Irish speakers at the time. They directly attacked the language in the fact that they made it illegal for Catholics to speak or read Irish. These exiles, murders, and laws against the old Irish way of life were excessively cruel to the people in the land. People whose ancestors had lived peaceful lives in isolation now found themselves under the thumb of the British and their tongues looked down upon. All these penal laws were only removed in 1829, but it was too little too late for Ireland, as by this point the entirety of the island had outright joined the United Kingdom along with Scotland and Wales. This cemented English even more so, with the Irish language becoming linked with the rural lower classes of the nation. Even once part of the UK, English speakers made more attempts to oust Irish through English being taught in schools. It was after all this the Great Potato Famine struck Ireland in the mid-nineteenth century, leaving countless in the country starved or dead. Many even fled the country to find more prosperous homes in countries like the USA. While the famine was a natural disaster, to this day many argue that England and the rest of the UK could have done more to support Ireland in this time of need.

This all resulted in Irish being seen as a second-class language. The tongue of the poor and uneducated living in the nation's vast countryside. English, on the other hand, had come to be seen as the language of the educated and civilised. The narrative was, if you wanted any kind of upward mobility or success in Ireland, you had to speak English. I have to state the obvious now, there is no such thing as a second-class language. Nothing in nature dictates that one language is superior to another, that's human made nonsense. But it was damning nonsense that persisted in the land and, over the years, English won out as the go-to tongue of Ireland. Even in 1920, when the majority of the nation left the UK to become an independent nation, English was still the lingo of choice. From here, the relationship between Ireland and the UK, especially in Northern Ireland, which is still part of the UK, has been tumultuous. This rocky relationship all stems from the long interconnected and exploitative relationship that Ireland has had with the UK. This manifested itself in the twentieth century as a period of Irish history known as The Troubles. The Troubles saw conflict on either side of the border, fighting for what they believed Ireland should be, and attacks ranged from assassination attempts on Prime Ministers, a massacre on the streets of Derry in 1972, and even bombings of shops and other establishments. This period of Irish history saw even more leave their homeland behind to find safe haven in places like the USA. The Good Friday agreement of 1998 is seen as putting The Troubles to an end but, beyond this, conversations still take place over Ireland, Northern Ireland, and the UK's relationship. With most of those conversations taking place in English.

English is the clear winner in regard to language in Ireland today, with well over 90 percent of the people on the island speaking it as their native language. English in Ireland has evolved in its own unique way—it is simply known as Irish English. Irish English is very similar to British English, with there sometimes being changes in word order and grammar when spoken more colloquially. Irish English is at its most unique when words from the Irish language itself are spliced within it. One of the most popular Irish words used in Irish English has to be *craic*, which ultimately means "a good time" of some description. Many words used across English varieties come from Irish too. Like "gob" being a slang word for "mouth," deriving from the Irish "*gob*," meaning "beak."

Thankfully, the Irish language exists as more than just some loan words in English. Thanks to a revival in the language in the nineteenth century, Irish is still widely spoken. There are around two million people across Northern Ireland and Ireland who can speak the language to some degree. There are thought to be a few thousand who speak it as their native tongue. The parts of the island which are seen as having Irish as their primary tongue are known as the *Gaeltacht* regions and they are found mainly across the west of the island in both Ireland and Northern Ireland. The language is even present in road signs across the land too. What this tells us is that, while Ireland may have been English's first big claim in the wider world, we can have faith that the native tongue of the Emerald Isle will shine on for years to come.

English's arrival in Ireland set a blueprint of sorts. The blueprint was the idea that a power could rock up in a new land and claim it through any means necessary, displacing and destroying the lives of those who had lived there for centuries prior. It was an awful and barbaric way to find footing in a new part of the world but, heartbreakingly, it was one that got results for those attempting it. This blueprint set by England in Ireland is one that many other European powers would follow in the centuries to come, as their world expanded in ways they never thought possible.

DEFINITELY NOT INDIA

SPANISH ACROSS THE AMERICAS

You could travel the entirety of South America and get by with the understanding of just one language—with the exception of one huge nation in particular, which has a related yet different tongue. Spanish in South America, as well as in parts of North America, is one of the most remarkable cases of a language finding a home in a new land. For context, there are around forty million Spanish speakers in the language's birthplace of Spain. In just Mexico alone, meanwhile, there are 113 million Spanish speakers. Collectively, the Americas are home to well over 400 million native Spanish speakers. The prevalence of the language in the New World is (somehow?) ultimately attributed to a person who wasn't even Spanish and was insistent that he had found India.

Christopher Columbus' legacy is a real mixed bag. For so long he was celebrated as a hero across the Americas as the man who kicked started what now call the continents of North and South America. There are many cities named after him and even the entire nation of Colombia is an ode to his legacy. Yet, a larger conversation is going on about what he actually did during his time in what was dubbed the New World. He is seen as responsible for the deaths, enslavement, and pillaging of the many native people he found in the lands. This has darkened his legacy greatly in recent years, with there even being demands to change the names of places named after him. On top of this, more recent historical analysis of the man sees him as something of a chancer, a man who grifted his way into his legacy. As the story goes, he was insistent that he had not found new land but instead found a westward passage to India. There's debate over how true this actually is. Some sources claim that Columbus lived out the rest of his days adamant that he found India. Something worth noting is that, in his day, India was a much broader term. It didn't apply to just the nation we know today but instead the larger area to its east too. It's why Indonesia's name means the islands of India.

While he wasn't Spanish (he was most probably Italian, but some believe he was Portuguese) he definitely could speak the lingo. By the time he set sail to see what lay west of Europe in 1493, the language of Spanish had morphed from its origins as a Vulgar form of Latin. The language was entering its middle era, fresh off the back of being Old Spanish for a few centuries. It was this form of Spanish that sailed across the Atlantic with Columbus and his crew, who had been sponsored by Spain to seek out new wealth and land for the nation to form an empire from. The intention was to find a westward travel route to India, so Spain didn't need to traverse all across Asia to reach what we now dub the Far East. While Columbus never made it to India, what he stumbled upon instead came to be of high value for the Spanish.

From leaving Spain on the third of August 1492, it took his ships over two months to find any land. It was on the twelfth of October that they finally made landfall. Where exactly he landed is another thing up for debate about this man. It was definitely on one of the islands which is now part of the Bahamas. Most likely San Salvador but, once again, we are not entirely sure. From here, the narrative tends to go that, with this voyage, Columbus discovered the Americas, or was at least the first European to land in the New World. Neither of these are the case. We know for sure that Norsemen landed in North America as far back as 1000 AD, though they didn't make all that much of an impact on the land. Non-Europeans, meanwhile, have called this land home for around 30,000 years. The many Indigenous people in the Americas are believed to have arrived in the land from Asia, specially via the Beringia. This is a now-sunken land mass which once connected what is now Alaska and Siberia together. It lives on as the Bering Strait, which at its narrowest is just fifty miles. From here, people dispersed all across the continent, from its Arctic north all the way down to its close-to-Antarctica south. They split into different groups and, from here, their languages developed.

In the Bahamas, Columbus' crew came across the Lucayan people, a native group who spoke a language referred to as Taíno which is part of the larger Arawakan language family which houses many of the native tongues of the Caribbean. The story goes that these people welcomed the explorers on to their island and, while Columbus and co were somewhat cordial, things turned sour when the Europeans started to ransack the island for anything of worth, like gold or pearls. They even kidnapped some Lucayans to take back to Europe with them, treating their fellow humans like wild animals. Even kidnapping wild animals to take them on a transatlantic cruise is barbaric. It's these kinds of actions that are destroying the legacy Columbus had built up for centuries.

While Columbus first landed in the Bahamas, the islands didn't offer much of worth in his eyes, so they set sail to find somewhere a tad more prosperous. To the south of the Bahamas, they came to a much larger prosperous island. Here, the land and resources were deemed much more agreeable. The native Taíno speakers who resided here also had an unpleasant experience with the Europeans, a disheartening pattern of events that repeats throughout the settlement of the Americas. Columbus, meanwhile, was so taken with the island, he dubbed it Hispaniola, meaning Little Spain. Today, the island houses the nations of the Dominican Republic and Haiti. It was here that Spanish settlement of the Americas truly began and is seen by most as the true starting point of the Age of Colonisation, which saw languages migrate to this new world and beyond. Columbus came back to Hispaniola during his second voyage in 1493. This time, he left some of his crew behind to craft a makeshift settlement dubbed La Isabela.

This was the first permanent European settlement in the Americas and, after two more voyages from Columbus in 1498 and 1502, the floodgates were open to Spanish, and eventually wider European, colonisation of this new land.

The Spanish Empire spread far and wide across the Americas. Even reaching parts of the land which are no longer predominantly Spanish-speaking, like Jamaica, Haiti, and a lot of the USA. We are here to look into the diaspora of languages on our modern globe, so lands that were once Spanish, but the language has now fallen to the wayside won't be particularly focused on. Besides Hispaniola, Cuba came under Spanish rule in 1511. Followed by Panama in 1519. The 1520s, meanwhile, were highly prosperous in the eyes of Spain. It was this decade which brought Venezuela, Mexico, Guatemala, Nicaragua, and Columbia into their sphere of influence. It was also this decade they started their conquest of Honduras, but that wasn't complete until 1939! The 1530s weren't just focused on claiming Honduras, as during this decade Peru, Ecuador, Paraguay, and Bolivia came to be ruled by Spain as well. The year of 1540 saw El Salvador fall to Spain too, another long conquest which actually started all the way back in 1524. The following year, in 1541, Chile was theirs too. Argentina, meanwhile, doesn't seemingly have one specific year in which it was conquered by the Spanish, instead taking place in parts across the sixteenth century. The final piece of land claimed by the Spanish in South America was Uruguay. This came much later in 1726. Earlier attempts were made in the early sixteenth century, but the death of a Spanish navigator via the natives of the land discouraged the Spanish from claiming it. The Portuguese, meanwhile, were not put off by this and made it part of their empire in the late seventeenth century. It was the Portuguese the Spanish took the land from as opposed to the Indigenous people directly. Don't feel too sorry for the Portuguese here, as we shall see they still had ample holdings in South America.

While the sixteenth century proved bountiful of Spain in the New World, it would have been nothing short for a catastrophe for the native people who had lived here for millennia. It would have begun with sighting ships in the distance, craft unlike anything they had seen before. When those ships arrived on their shores, the people who disembarked would have seemed alien. Adorned in clothes unlike anything they had seen before with weapons and diseases that would prove devastating.

It was these actions that shaped the modern Americas and, in order to trace
the Spanish language in the modern Americas with ease, I charted the Spanish
conquering of South America in relation to the modern States. In reality, the
borders of these countries came around a lot later. During the time of the Spanish
Empire, their claim in the New World was instead split into two major areas
known as Viceroyalties. The Viceroyalty of New Spain covered their land in
North and Central America, as well as their Caribbean islands, and land that
equates roughly to Venezuela, as that nation has for some time been linked with
the Caribbean. The Viceroyalty of Peru, meanwhile, was the collective title for
their land in the rest of South America, focused on the nation which also has this
name today. New Spain and this iteration of Peru were founded in 1521 and
1542, respectively. This set the foundation of the Spanish language to find a home
in land that only a few decades previously they had no idea existed. In around
500 years, Spanish went from being non-existent in this continent, to today being
the most widely spoken language across North and South America, with there
being over 400 million speakers. Spanish, however, was nowhere near the first
language spoken on this land. We have already mentioned the Taíno language
that Columbus encountered in the Bahamas and Hispaniola—it was also the
language of choice in other Greater Antilles islands like Jamaica and Cuba. In
reality, Taíno is just the tip of the linguistic iceberg for native languages of the
Americas. These two continents were full to the brim with native tongues prior to
the arrival of Europeans. Modern South America, unto itself, is home to around
600 Indigenous tongues, with there being an awful lot more in the past.

Native languages asides from Taíno that were being spoken in modern Hispanic
American nations around the time Columbus arrived in the land include:

- Lencan languages, spoken by the Lenca people in Honduras
- Nawat, spoken by the Pipil and Nicarao people in El Salvador and
  Nicaragua respectively
- Kalinago, spoken by the Kalinago (formerly Carib) people in Costa Rica,
  Venezuela, and many of the small Caribbean islands now collectively
  known as the Lesser Antilles
- Boruca, spoken by the Boruca and Diquis people in Costa Rica

- Chibcha, spoken by the Chibcha people in Costa Rica and Venezuela, as well as being something of a lingua franca for the Musica Confederation in Colombia
- Cueva, spoken by the Cueva people of Panama
- Aymara, spoken by the Aymara people in Bolivia
- Cacán, spoken by the Diaguita people of Argentina
- Guaraní, spoken by the Guaraní people of Argentina and Paraguay
- Charruan languages, spoken by the Charrúa people of Uruguay

Once again, these languages have been geographically pinned to their modern nations to help us more easily understand where they were spoken. The Nawat-speaking Pipils, for example, definitely did not refer to their homeland as El Salvador, the concept of a nation by this name would have been completely alien to them prior to the arrival of Europeans. Probably, the most well-known of pre-Columbian languages are the various Nahuatl, Mayan, and Quechuan languages spoken by the Aztec, Maya, and Inca civilisations, respectively. These are not three singular languages, but instead collections of smaller languages belonging to different families. Nahuatl is a branch of the larger Uto-Aztecan family with languages like Huastec, Guerrero, and Ometepec. The Mayan languages form a family unto themselves which houses a language simply called Maya, as well as ones like Q'eqchi', and Mam. Quechuan, too, is a family with languages like Kichwa and Cuzco amongst its branches.

The civilisations that spoke these languages were more than just simple hunter gatherers or farmers, as history so often unfaithfully depicts when it comes to the Americas of the past. They had incredible societies, large ornate cities, and empires unto themselves. The Aztec capital of Tenochtitlan was the largest in all of pre-Columbian America at its peak having a population of over 200,000. For comparison, London in the fourteenth century (when Tenochtitlan was founded) is thought to have had a population of just 80,000. As incredible as these empires and civilisations were, they all met a similar fate. The stories of how the Spanish Empire claimed land from these peoples are similar to one another. Imagine conquistadors barging in with weaponry, like steel swords and even huge horses, that the Indigenous people could not match. The Spanish would happily murder any native who stood in their way. Many of those they didn't kill directly would fall ill to diseases the foreigners brought with them that the natives had

no immunity to. Their homes were not safe from the Empire either as they were
more than happy to ransack and destroy the mighty settlements the likes of the
Aztecs, Maya, and Inca had crafted. The Mayan civilisation was located around
modern Mexico, Belize, Guatemala, and Honduras. The Spanish came for it in
1517, yet the conquest was only completed over a hundred years later in 1697.
Shortly after the start of their Mayan conquest, the Spanish came for the Aztecs
in 1519. The Aztecs, sadly, fell much quicker than the Inca. With their land in
central Mexico being fully absorbed into the Spanish Empire by 1521 when their
beloved city of Tenochtitlan was decimated. Today, Tenochtitlan forms the basis
of modern Mexico City. The last of these great powers, the Inca Empire, was
located in South America. On its western coast, across land we now call Peru,
Ecuador, Bolivia, and Chile. Conquest of this land started in 1532 and came to
an end in 1572 when the land was secured by the Spanish. This would have had a
huge effect on the tongues of the land too. Year by year, the Indigenous peoples of
the land, who spoke this wonderful plethora of languages, would have heard their
own languages fall to the wayside as Spanish quickly became the tongue of trade
and politics in their home. It was nothing short of devastating.

This was a similar story for the many smaller groups of people who first called
this land home too. It was a systematic sacking of an entire continent in the name
of power. While this could have been a tragic end to these ways of life, many of
these native languages are thankfully still with us today and spoken to varying
degrees. In the face of destruction, many native people went into hiding in more
remote parts of the land. Free from Spanish invasion, they set up their own
smaller communities of speakers, many of which have flourished into the present.
The tongue of the Aztecs, the Nahuatl languages, are still spoken by around two
million people in smaller pockets of Mexico. Mayan languages have around six
million speakers. And the Quechuan tongues have over seven million speakers
across their homeland. The single native language with the largest population,
however, goes to Guaraní spoken in Argentina and Paraguay with well over six
million speakers. Others, however, have not been so lucky; the entire Chibchan
family of languages, which includes tongues we already mentioned like the
Lencan languages, Boruca, and Chibchan itself, is partially extinct. Though,
what's most notable is the fact that Taíno, the first native language Columbus
heard in the New World, is now nothing but a distant memory.

Yet, in the same way the natives lost their land to the Spanish, the new descendants of those who initially migrated here eventually found their own freedom. One by one, across the nineteenth century, parts of the Spanish Empire in the Americas found their independence. Yet, by this point, Spanish had supplanted all of the Indigenous languages here and still reigns supreme. Though, in the short, roughly 500 years Spanish has been at home in this part of the world, it has evolved in so many ways. Most areas of Hispanic America have their own dialect of Spanish. There's Mexican Spanish, Ecuadorian Spanish, even Amazonic Spanish. Collectively, these versions of Spanish can be referred to as Latin American Spanish. While the Spanish of Spain itself can be referred to as Castilian Spanish. Castilian Spanish and Latin American Spanish vary in a multitude of ways. Latin American Spanish is generally considered to be spoken at a much slower pace and, due to this, is usually considered easier to learn. Pronunciation differs between them too. Noticeably, the sound Z and C makes when they come before either an I and or E changes across the Atlantic. In Castilian Spanish, it makes more of *a th* sound, while in Latin American Spanish, they sound a lot more like the S sound. Of course, there are all different kinds of words used in both forms of Spanish too. The South American delicacy of the avocado is called *aguacate* in Castilian Spanish. While in Cuban Spanish it is called *pagua*, in Venezuelan Spanish it's *cura*, and in Argentine Spanish it's *palta*. The different words in these languages stem from different outside influences, including the many native languages of the Americas, which now share their home with Latin American Spanish. These varieties of Spanish came into being all due to the mass migration of people from across the Atlantic, and it was the first truly huge global mass migration of this new age the world found itself in. Today, many of these Spanish speakers in the Americas are aware of the history that led to them being there today.

Varieties of Latin American Spanish are *número uno* across the Americas, especially in South America. Yet, it's only collectively that the Hispanic nations allow Spanish to outnumber all other tongues. The single biggest nation in South America doesn't use it as their go-to lingo. Instead, the neighbour of the majority of Spanish-speaking South American nations speaks the language of Spain's very own neighbour.

ALL THIS JUST FOR SOME TREES?

PORTUGUESE IN BRAZIL

Spain and Portugal have had an interesting relationship throughout history. These two Romance-speaking nations share the Iberian Peninsula and speak languages that are closely related to one another. Both are descendants of the Vulgar Latin which emerged across the Roman Empire. When Columbus arrived back from the Americas after his first voyage in 1493, it sent shockwaves across the peninsula. Both these nations wanted to claim the land for themselves but, instead of scrambling, the two nations came to an agreement. The year 1494 saw each kingdom sign the treaty of Tordesillas which split what they deemed the colonisable world into two halves. With an agreement over who was allowed to claim what, the two nations started to cross the Atlantic and brought their languages along for the ride to find their new homes. As we know, Spain spent the majority of the sixteenth century carving out the land bit by bit. Portugal, on the other hand, were a lot more succinct in their claim of the Americas.

In the year 1500, Spain had only just begun colonising the New World, with just the island of Hispaniola under their rule. Yet, this was also the year in which the Portuguese claimed what would go on to be the nation we now know as Brazil. Brazil is this huge marvellous exception in South America. Of the twelve countries on the continent, nine of them have Spanish as their dominant language. The three exceptions are Guyana who speak English, Suriname and their Dutch, and, of course, the behemoth of Brazil with their Portuguese. It's thanks to Brazil that we have the term Latin America, as Hispanic America only covers the Spanish-speaking nations. One of the most confounding things about the Portuguese colonisation of Brazil is the fact that it kind of happened by accident.

Portuguese explorer Pedro Álvares Cabral had intended to reach the south coast of Africa to claim land for his nation, yet, somehow, he missed his target and ended up on the wrong side of the Atlantic. Where he landed was, instead, close to what would become the grand city of Rio de Janeiro. This set in motion what would go on to become the largest nation of South America and overall fifth largest nation on the entire globe. A key reason as to why Brazil got so big was due to what became the nation's key export for the Portuguese. The Spanish mined their American claim for gold and silver. Sugar plantations were a key aim of the British in the Caribbean when they eventually arrived. What drew the Portuguese to the depths of Brazil, meanwhile, was something as simple as wood.

Wood is pretty darn abundant across the globe. Portugal itself is full to the brim with beautiful woodland and trees. One source indicates that around a third of modern Portugal is nothing but trees. So, why exactly did they feel the urge to form such a huge nation across the ocean from them in the name of trees? Were the trees here some special kind that couldn't be found anywhere else on the planet? Well, yes, actually. Across the Atlantic coast of Brazil, Portuguese explorers discovered a tree which they marvelled at. From the outside, it looked like just any other tree, but its sap shone bright red. This reminded the Portuguese explorers of another kind of tree found in Asia with a similar red sap. While this sap wasn't particularly edible, it could sell for a high price thanks to the fact that a

terrific red dye could be formed from it. In our day and age, the colours that grace
our clothes and possessions are often taken for granted. Most things are available
in a vast array of colours with minimal effort. In the past, however, the crafting
of colours required a lot more effort. They could not be made synthetically, so,
instead, pigments and the essences of these colours had to be found by natural
means. It's why purple became linked with royalty, as one of the key ways it was
formed was from sea snails of all things. Only the wealthy and affluent could
afford to extract purple in this process.

Red was another colour which proved tricky to come by, and its connotations
with power meant that there was demand for an easy source of red. For the
Portuguese and most of Europe, those trees in Asia were the best bet for acquiring
any red dyes, and this was expensive and long winded. Portugal now had their
own access to red dye, which not only made things way easier for them, but meant
they could monopolise the industry in Europe. This tree became Brazil's first cash
crop for the Portuguese and they dubbed it the *pau-brasil* which derived from their
words for wood, *pau*, and ember, *brasa*, due to the ember-like colour it produced.
This tree was so instrumental in the land that it lent its name to the country,
giving us the name Brazil. As the Portuguese harvested as much *pau-brasil* as they
could from the coast of the land, they ventured deeper into Brazil. This expanded
their claim in the continent, giving them more space to farm and harvest the trees,
which eventually expanded into them finding other important resources in the
land too. Yet, resources were not the only thing they found here.

Much like the rest of South America, the land that makes up Brazil was abundant
with native languages and peoples when the Portuguese arrived. It's thought
that around 1,000 languages were spoken here prior to colonisation. The most
significant Indigenous people that the Portuguese interacted with initially were
the Tupi that inhabited much of Brazil's coast. The Tupi were not one singular
tribe that spoke the same tongue. It is, instead, the collective term for various
groups that spoke a variety of tongues which all fall into the Tupian language
family. While these languages were first heard by the Portuguese on the coast, the
family is spread all across Brazil and even into other countries. One of the most
prominent native languages spoken in the Brazilian Amazon, Nheengatu, is even
a member of this family. For the sake of keeping this narrative as easy to follow as
possible, we will be referring to these natives as the Tupi on the whole.

Seemingly, relations between the Tupi and the Portuguese were good at first; what aided in this good relationship was the formation of the *língua geral* which means the general language. This was a kind of language which combined many elements of various Tupi tongues which gave the natives as well as the Portuguese an easy means of communication with one another. There's some evidence that, when it came to harvesting the trees, the Portuguese claimed the Tupi actually helped them out. Things took a turn in their relations, however, when *pau-brasil* trees dried up along the coast and the Portuguese wanted the coastal Tupi to come inland with them in their quest for more of this red wood. The natives were hesitant to traverse deeper inland. Brazil was and still very much is extremely wild in its geography, from mountain ranges and the deep unforgiven Amazon Rainforest. To this day, the coast is still far more inhabited than inland. The colonisers, however, did not have the same reservations. Their technologies made the more remote parts of the land less troublesome to explore. Yet, the Portuguese refused to take the Tupi's no for an answer. It's from here that the familiar tale of Europeans in the Americas starts to take palace. The Portuguese killed and enslaved many of the natives who wouldn't agree with them. This led to many of the coastal Tupi to delve into the heart of Brazil. Not out of choice but out of fear for what might have happened to them if found by the Portuguese.

The Tupi are just one of the many native peoples of Brazil, but the others also met this sad fate. The roughly 1,000 languages spoken in Brazil prior to the arrival of the Portuguese has now dwindled to somewhere between 100–200 languages. This means around 80 percent of the country's native tongues have gone extinct and many of those still around have just a handful of speakers. Yet, the expulsion of the Tupi into the depths of Brazil actually resulted in other languages arriving in Brazil. With the Portuguese unable to secure free labour from the natives, they turned their attention back over the Atlantic to their land claims in Africa. This opened the doors to the Brazilian slave trade of African natives. Slavery is one of the darkest chapters in human history and the slave trade in Brazil not only happened prior to the North Atlantic slave trade, but more slaves were exported to Brazil than any other nation. The Portuguese kidnapped humans in Africa from across the continent's Atlantic coast, likely from parts of the land they had either claimed at the time or would go on to claim, like the modern nations of Angola and Guinea-Bissau. These Africans would have spoken a selection of

Bantu languages. The tongues that migrated all across Africa in the far past were migrating once again, though this time not of their own choosing.

The cruel act of slavery was abolished in Brazil in just 1888, six years after the country declared independence from the Portuguese. So, the urge for a very specific kind of tree drove the Portuguese to form one of the largest countries on our planet and bequeath it with their tongue. When Portuguese first arrived in the land in 1500, it was in its modern form, meaning it was somewhat similar to how it is spoken to this day, at least over in Portugal, anyway. Brazilian Portuguese is very much its own thing in the same way Latin American Spanish is unique. European Portuguese is often seen as being far more guttural sounding when compared to the more nasal sound of Brazilian Portuguese. This has, in turn, made Brazilian Portuguese seem more musical sounding than the version spoken in Europe too.

Where they differ most, however, is in their lexicon. Various words are different between the two versions of Portuguese. Take the word "train"; in European Portuguese it is *comboio*, while Brazilian Portuguese goes with *trem*. Two of the biggest influences on Brazilian Portuguese are the various Tupi and Bantu languages which were native to the land and brought over to it. For example, Brazilian Portuguese has the interesting word of *caçula* which is from the Bantu Kimbundu language. It's a title for the youngest son in a family. I don't think European Portuguese has a term for this type of child specifically, nor do many other languages around the world. One of the words most deeply linked with Brazil is of African roots. The beloved samba, one of Brazil's cultural identifiers, is of African origins and so is the name. The Tupi languages, meanwhile, have not only influenced Brazilian Portuguese, but have gone on to form words in European Portuguese and various other languages. Take the name of a large rodent creature found in this part of the world. In Tupi languages it was dubbed the *capiuára* which means grass eater. Instead of giving it a whole new name, the Portuguese stuck with this one but adapted it in *capivara* in their tongues, which morphed into English as capybara. We really do have the Tupi to thank for the name of these adorable creatures.

Tupi words are most present, perhaps, to speakers of Brazilian Portuguese in the names of Brazilian states. A handful of the states of Brazil have names from Tupi origins, including Tocantins which means "nose of the toucan" due to the shape of two rivers in the land. Piauí is named after a fish found here. Acre translates into "green river." And Pernambuco, meaning "hollow in the sea," refers to the coral reefs along its shoreline. Tupi is not only alive and well in state names but in the mouths of speakers too. The language unto itself has been on its own evolutionary journey. The aforementioned Nheengatu language spoken in the Amazon is still around and it evolved from a lingua franca form of Tupi which was known as the Amazonian General Language. Many Tupi speakers ended up merging with Guaraní speakers in neighbouring Paraguay. Their languages merged together to form the Tupi-Guaraní branch of languages. The Guaraní language in this branch is still widely spoken in Paraguay with well over six million speakers.

South America might just be the continent most shaped and defined by the migration of languages and people. The travelling humans of Iberia took to this part of the world and everything they did there, both the good and the bad, allowed their languages to evolve in ways they never would have if they stayed home in Europe. While Spanish dominates most of the continent, it's the Portuguese-speaking Brazil that is the biggest and most populous single nation found here. This Portuguese-speaking island, floating in a sea of Spanish, really does all boil down to the fact that some people *really* liked the trees there.

THE TAEL OF MACAU

PORTUGUESE IN MACAU

Portugal's conquest of the world didn't see them just travel westward to the New World. The Lusosphere (the Portuguese-speaking world) ended up spanning across the Americas, parts of Africa, and even into a country that, on the whole, avoided the plague of European colonisation that struck other nations. Throughout its history, China, in its many iterations, always marched to its own drum. During antiquity, while Europe, North Africa, and the Near East were being conquered and divided by various powers. Over in Asia's Far East, a self-contained epic was playing out. The title of China's first dynasty is traditionally given to the Xia Dynasty which was established around 2070 BC. From this moment, other powers claimed the land and their ambiguous borders shifted in size and boundaries. From the Xia to the Shang to the Zhou to the Qin to the legendary Han.

Over parts of its history, the land would be ruled by multiple rulers; this is seen most clearly during the Three Kingdoms period from 220 to 265 BC when the kingdoms of Wei, Wu, and Shu Han duked it out for supremacy. Also, during the intertwined Five Dynasties and Ten Kingdoms period in the later stages of the first millennium. By the early sixteenth century, a majority of the land that makes up the modern nation was under the rule of the Great Ming Dynasty. This dynasty was a strong believer of isolationism, something China has dabbled in throughout its long history. This meant they wished for little interaction with the outside world in regard to trade and culture. Yet, in the early years of the sixteenth century, one small European nation with a hunger for an empire dared to claim a small slice of China for themselves, where not only they but their language could thrive.

In the later stages of the fifteenth century, as the New World was being torn open by European powers, Portuguese navigator Vasco de Gama sailed around the Cape of Good Hope in South Africa. This brought with it the possibility of maritime trade with Asia as opposed to traversing between Europe and Asia by land, the primary route until that point. The Portuguese were quick to act on this newfound potential. In 1513, Portuguese sea captain Jorge Álvares reached China and found himself at the Estuary of the Pearl River, where the booming modern Metropolis of Macau now resides. At this point in time, there was far less neon and gambling. The land was sparsely populated and not all that built up, with its main source of residency being the descendants of refugees who found the land a safe haven after the Mongol Conquest of China centuries ago. These people spoke one of the many languages that are now lumped together collectively as Chinese, called Cantonese. In reality, there is no singular Chinese language but, instead, Chinese is a branch unto itself which houses many languages and varieties. In the case of this land, Cantonese was the go-to tongue. The various Chinese languages form a branch of the large Sino-Tibetan family, which houses not just the Chinese tongues but languages like Burmese too.

This was land that the Portuguese felt would make a terrific trading post. It would not only allow them to trade with China but allow them to expand their operations across Asia. The Portuguese assumed that the Ming Dynasty would have no issues with letting them settle this small sleepy nook of their land. Yet, this Dynasty and their staunch opposition to outsiders felt otherwise. It would

take years for China to allow the Portuguese to even anchor their ships close to
the land, and even more centuries for the area to become anything remotely close
to a Portuguese colony. A huge amount of back and forth happened between
the Portuguese and Chinese in relation to the land. The Portuguese grew tired
of this politicking and attempted to claim their land by sheer force. This did not
work out for them as Ming Dynasty forces ousted all their attempts. It seems that
both sides grew tired of this squabbling by 1554. It was in this year that China
finally agreed to lease the land as nothing more than a simple trading post to the
Portuguese. All the Portuguese were allowed to do in the land was dock their ships
and build some simple storage sheds, no houses or fortifications. This came at a
price—as mentioned, China didn't give the land to them, they simply leased it.
The asking price was 500 taels of silver a year, with a tael being an old Chinese
weight and currency unit. In today's currency, it would be around $18,000, which
in all honesty is a bit of a steal for this amount of land in China.

This deal benefited both nations. Portugal now had access to the Far East like
they had dreamt about. In return, China got a hefty sum of money for renting
out a small chunk of their land. The deal also benefited China in other ways
too. While on the surface the Ming Dynasty were staunch isolationists, many
of the higher-ups in the land secretly craved goods from the outside world. The
Portuguese empire could bring those goods to them. By this point, Portugal's
empire spread into other parts of Asia and the New World. The idea of silver
from South America and spices from India finally making their way to China
sounded all too good, not that the Portuguese could know they were helping
China. The leasing situation made China feel like they had the upper hand. It was
part of their wider tributary system which involved other powers paying China for
the privilege of dealing with them. China would boast about how much they were
gaining from the relationship with the Portuguese, while the Portuguese were
under the pretence that their relationship was equal. Any relationship where the
participants aren't on the same page can be rocky at times.

The land was elevated from a simple trading post to a permanent Portuguese
establishment in 1577 when China (who still owned the land) allowed them to
build a settlement there. We aren't entirely sure as to why China finally agreed
to this. Some stories claim the Portuguese cleared the area of troublemakers.
I personally like the idea that China just gave up after decades of Portuguese

persistence. Finally, the land of Macau could be a Portuguese settlement away from Europe, and it only took some sixty odd years after Jorge Álvares first landed in the area back in 1513. Unlike their conquest of Brazil, there was far less bloodshed and destruction of native life when the Portuguese settled in China. The two powers had an agreement and trade deal. The Portuguese were not claiming the land with brute force, in fact, Macau was never really a colony in the way Brazil was. It was simply land leased to them by China which, over the centuries, they allowed the Portuguese to do as they wished with. This allowed more Portuguese people to come and live in the land and for Portuguese culture to plant roots here, but not at the expense of Chinese culture being stomped out. Instead, the two cultures, languages, and peoples flourished somewhat in tandem.

The Portuguese settlers in the early days of Macau would have been some of the first ordinary European people to live in China. Before this, it was nothing more than a far-off mysterious land to many Europeans. They would have experienced Chinese culture and, as the majority of these settlers were men, they would have met Chinese women. These Portuguese men and Chinese women in many cases would have gotten to know each other in an incredibly intimate way, producing children of mixed heritage. Yet, as the Portuguese by this point were seen as the authority in the land, it meant that the children would have grown up in a Portuguese lifestyle. Meaning they would be Catholic and, of course, speak the Iberian lingo. While Portuguese customs were placed on these kids, at the end of the day, they were still products of China, too, and lived their lives in the Far East surrounded by their mother's culture and tongue. This mixing of cultures and genes manifested in language too, with the emergence of Macanese Portuguese, a variation of standard Portuguese, as well as the creole language of Macanese Patois.

Macanese Portuguese is pretty much exactly what it sounds like, a variation of the Portuguese language spoken in Macau. From what I can gather, Macanese Portuguese and Iberian Portuguese aren't all that different, featuring many of the same words as one another. Macanese Portuguese does, however, feature influences from other Asian languages like Malay, due to proximity, and of course there's a Cantonese influence on the language too. Apparently, unlike Iberian Portuguese, the Macanese variation is far more tonal in its approach. Tonalism is a feature in many Asian languages, and especially present in the languages of

China. It means a word can change meaning depending on the tone it's said in. This isn't all that common in European tongues but Portuguese's migration to the Far East gave us a fantastic hybrid that can claim itself as a tonal European tongue. Macanese Patois, also known by its local name of *Patuá*, is somewhat like Macanese Portuguese, but is far more divergent from Iberian Portuguese and is a stronger mixture of the language with heavy doses of tongues like Cantonese, Malay, Dutch, and even Sinhala. *Patuá* is a kind of language known as a creole. Creoles are tongues that come into being when people who speak a variety of languages live within the same community, to compensate for their lack of understanding one another, naturally and overtime elements of all these languages come together so everyone can understand one another. Creoles have cropped up all across the world, and while this one was birthed in China, they grew to prominence somewhere else entirely, as well shall see later down the line.

Portugal's rule of Macau lasted centuries, while all the time the land technically belonged to China. It survived various dynasties, attacks from the Dutch and British—although the British would go on to claim a pocket of China for themselves in the future—a couple world wars, and even Mao's Communist revolution in the land. It was only in the mid-twentieth century after the fall of Portugal's very own dictator that things started to change for their holdings across the globe. The nation wanted to rid itself of their colonial past and, in turn, the Chinese too were more eager than ever to have all their land under their control. This culminated in an agreement between the two nations in 1999. By the turn of the millennium, there was a huge difference in the way Macau and the rest of China operated. China was now the People's Republic of China and under a Communist regime, while Macau thrived under the capitalist system the Portuguese placed on it. Portugal didn't want Macau to become like the rest of China and be under that regime too. So, an agreement was put in place stating that, while Macau would belong to China, it would still be allowed to operate under a capitalist system, for fifty years at least—this is known as the "one country, two systems" policy. What happens in 2049 is still a mystery to us at the time of this writing.

The Portuguese relinquishing Macau led to China being free from any kind of European influence. Funnily enough, the Portuguese were the first Europeans to claim land in China. They really were the first in and last out! Macau has

since evolved into a tourism hotspot. The amount of neon lights and casinos in
the city puts Las Vegas to shame. What isn't as common in the land these days,
however, is the Portuguese language. Portuguese is still technically an official
language of Macau, but around just 2 percent of the population actually speak it.
The majority, instead, speak the native Cantonese tongue. Just over 6,000 people
today can speak Macanese Portuguese and there's just a handful of *Patuá* speakers
left. Though, *Patuá* is having a revival of sorts. Many in the city wish to bring
the language back to life in a celebration of their heritage. The biggest impact
Portuguese has made in Macau is probably via street names. Most, if not all,
streets and roads in the city have names of Portuguese origins, often accompanied
by traditional Portuguese blue and white tiled signs too. This nook of China has
street names ranging from Rua Cidade do Porto, Avenida da República, and
Estrada do Campo, to name but three. These seem wildly out of place for the Far
East, but when you know the history of the land, they make all the sense in the
world. The rise and fall of Portuguese in Macau can also serve as a reminder that
while a tongue may migrate to a new part of the world, it may not always have the
sticking power to become the dominant language.

IMMIGRANTS, WE GET THE JOB DONE

ENGLISH IN THE USA

The beloved quote of "England and America are two countries divided by a common language" is contentious in its origins. Most sources attribute it to Irish playwright George Bernard Shaw, and he is the most likely candidate. Yet, another Irish playwright, one Oscar Wilde, is also linked with the similar quote of, "We have really everything in common with America nowadays except, of course, language." Even Winston Churchill's name is thrown into the mix at times when a quote of this kind emerges. Whoever truly said it first doesn't really matter, as the end result has stuck around and it's a perfectly succinct explanation for the difference English has in the USA and the UK. The United States of America is the greatest success story of English's migrations and evolution. It's the largest English-speaking nation on the planet with just over 95 percent of its population of over 300 million speaking it as their first tongue. English in the USA is more or less the poster child for immigrant tongues. Yet, as the aforementioned quote/quotes tell us, the English spoken in the USA is vastly different to the English spoken in England. In fact, it's resoundingly different to most other forms of English spoken across the globe.

American English and British English are different in multiple key ways. The first of those ways being the use of different words for the same things. "Pants" in British English refers to underpants, while in American English it is the go-to word for trousers. Then there's also "garbage" in American English and "rubbish" in British English, meaning waste. We also have "apartment" and "flat" in American and British English, respectively. And let's not forget "zucchini" and "courgette" meaning the long, green, somewhat cucumber-like vegetable. In this case, "zucchini" is American English while "courgette" is British English. That's just a sliver of the variety in vocabulary between the two dialects. There isn't really one defined reason as to why the two languages use so many different words. A prevailing theory is that American English actually uses more words of Older British English, the kind of English being spoken when the language first reached its shores. Then, over the years, the language changed in the UK but was left relatively untouched stateside.

Yet, even when words are the same in British and American English, they can still be different! This all comes down to their spellings. American English has remoulded the bizarre spelling of British English in many ways, so how the words are spelt is way more in line with how they sound. British English's spelling is confusing in many ways thanks to the huge mixed history the language has had, especially via French influence. This means that the R and E in the British English word "centre" have been swapped around in American English, with the word becoming "center," a spelling much more in line with how the word actually sounds. And, of course, there's the lack of U in American English's word "color." The British English word "colour," meanwhile, is a key source of pride across the United Kingdom. There's more concrete evidence as to why there's this difference in the spellings. When English first arrived in what would become the USA, spelling had not been finalised. People spelt words however they saw fit, as long as it got the job done. Spelling would be finalised in different ways across the pond. British English's spelling was standardised in the mid-eighteenth century when British writer Samuel Johnson released his now famous dictionary. American English's spelling, meanwhile, was standardised a few decades later in the early nineteenth century. By this time, the US was free of British rule and wanted to establish themselves as different from the UK as possible. This resulted in Noah Webster creating his own American English dictionary featuring many of the American English spellings we have today. These spelling were one of the many ways in which the US wanted to show how different they are to their former rulers.

English has changed so much in the USA that even smaller pockets of the country have their own versions of English. This can be seen on a state level with the likes of Texan and Californian English, or even by city with Philadelphian English. They aren't just bound by geography, however. As the USA is a melting pot of cultures, it means that different ethnic groups have acquired their own versions of the tongue from Blighty too. One of the most notable being African American English, spoken by many African American people in the nation. All these dialects and varieties of English spoken in the Land of the Free can even perplex other English speakers around the globe at times. It's truly remarkable that English not only managed to migrate and change from the UK to the USA, but continued migrating and evolving even once it touched American soil. While English has now travelled from sea to shining sea, it was far from the first European language spoken in what we now call the USA.

We know that from the fifteenth century onward, the land west of Europe had been deemed fair game by a variety of European powers wishing to plunder it for resources, land, and wealth. We also know that land to the north and south of the modern US was claimed across this period of time by the likes of the Spanish and the Portuguese. On top of this, nations like France and the Netherlands were intrigued about making a move here too. Ultimately, the first permanent European settlement in what we now consider the contiguous United States was established by the Spanish. San Miguel de Gualdape was a small settlement founded in 1626; it was located somewhere on the East Coast either in the present-day Carolinas or Georgia. The reason we aren't entirely sure is because, while this was the first, it only lasted three months. The Spanish had more success a few years down the line in what is now Florida with the settlement of Saint Augustine in 1565. A city that is still very much alive today.

By the mid-sixteenth century, the British were very much interested in taking a slice of this American pie for themselves. Their first attempt, while not successful, has gone down in history for an entirely different reason. In 1585, a group of just over a hundred English people set sail to the New World with the aim of establishing the first permanent English settlement in the land. Their target location was the island of Roanoke just off the coast of modern North Carolina. To start with, things were somewhat okay in this colony. The governor of the colony, John White, returned to England for fresh supplies a few years down the line. When he finally got back there in 1590, all traces of this colony had vanished. To this day, we still are not entirely sure what happened to them. The Lost Colony of Roanoke has made a lasting impact on the American psyche as one of the nation's biggest mysteries. This put a halt to any kind of British colonising of the land for over twenty years. Yet, by 1607, the British were willing to have a second crack at it and three boats, the *Susan Constant*, the *Godspeed*, and the *Discovery* set sail to a small nook on the east coast of this huge landmass. This land area was chosen for a variety of geographic advantages, such as being farther inland with ample water, as well as that water being deep enough for their ships to easily moor along the coast. Happy with the land, the passengers on these ships got to work building a town, which would be aptly named Jamestown in honour of the king of England and Scotland, James I. Jamestown was nothing shy of a success and, like Saint Augustine, is still around today, proudly declaring itself the first permanent English settlement in the nation. English had finally arrived in the USA, and things were just getting started for the language.

The settlement of Jamestown quickly expanded with more land being claimed by the British. This claimed land eventually became a full-blown British colony dubbed Virginia, in honour of the Virgin Queen Elizabeth I. While this was the first British colony, it was far from the last. The British would go on to claim land up and down the East Coast. A second popped up in 1620, founded by the passengers of the *Mayflower* which had sailed from Plymouth, England. The town they founded was also simply dubbed Plymouth and this cemented the founding of the second British colony of Massachusetts. As the seventeenth century rolled on, so did the British colonies; three years after the *Mayflower*'s tumultuous voyage, New Hampshire was established in 1623. The 1630s saw the additions of Maryland, Connecticut, Rhode Island, and Delaware. North and South Carolina came around in 1653. New York and New Jersey came under British rule in 1664. Pennsylvania was colonised in 1682 and, way later down the line, Georgia in 1732.

These thirteen colonies lay the foundation of what would become the United States of America and cemented English as yet another dominant foreign tongue in the New World, along with Spanish and Portuguese. Prior to the arrival of English and other European languages, ample tongues were spoken here by people who had called this land home (and still very much do) for thousands of years. These people are often lumped together with a single name that, in reality, isn't entirely fair. It would be like referring to people from France, Germany, and Poland all as just European all the time. Names they have been collectively called throughout the years include First Nationers, Native Americans, and (erroneously but consistently) Indians or Red Indias. A name that originates all the way back to Columbus and his belief that he had found a new part of India. These people arrived in the land the same way the native people of South America got there too. One of the earliest known civilisations we know of living in what we now call the USA is the Clovis culture. It is believed to have been a hunter-gatherer tribe whose remains have been found in New Mexico and are thought to have gotten there almost 13,000 years ago.

While these early settlers were hunter gatherers, that was far from the case for other Indigenous tribes as time went on in precolonial America. The Hopewell Tradition was an expansive trade route that various tribes east of the Mississippi partook in. And while many were nomadic in their lifestyle, they also founded permanent settlements too. Acoma Pueblo, a small village in New Mexico, was founded by Native Americans in the twelfth century. This is way before Columbus and co set foot there and the village has the true title of the oldest continuously inhabited settlement in the contiguous United States. A selection of notable tribes who resided within the thirteen colonies prior to and when the British arrived include the Wampanoag people. It was members of this tribe who were involved in the fabled and often misremembered story of the first Thanksgiving; they resided in Massachusetts and the Rhode Island area. In the northern state of Maine lived the Passamaquoddy people. And south of

them, in the region around modern Delaware and New Jersey, lived the Lenni
Lenape people. These tribes spoke/speak the languages Wôpanâak, Maliseet-
Passamaquoddy, and Munsee, respectively.

While these are all different languages, they are all considered a part of the Algic
language family. Algic is one of the largest language families native to North
America, with these being just three of the many within its branches. The most
widely spoken of the Algic languages, however, is Cree, which is spoken across
a huge part of Canada. This language family didn't just find a home in what
we now call the USA. Though, it is not the only language family of the Native
Americans. Languages belonging to the Iroquoian family were found throughout
the thirteen colonies too, most notably within the Iroquois Nation, a union of
different Iroquois-language-speaking tribes found in the state of New York and
the surrounding area. You could also find the Cherokee people, who spoke a
language of the same name, in more of the southern parts of the thirteen colonies.

Relations between these various native tribes and the early settlers fluctuated
overtime. Surprisingly enough, when they first met, things were seemingly pretty
good between the two. Natives and settlers would partake in trade with one
another. Not only did they trade in goods but also ideas. These tribes had lived in
the land for thousands of years, so had ample advice on surviving in their neck of
the woods to give to the settlers. Relations would eventually turn sour, however.
Sicknesses the natives had no immunity to were brought over from Europe and
killed many. Also, the settlers started to impeach far too much on their way of life.
Which, once again, was a lifestyle these people had been leading for countless
generations. These factors resulted in war between the colonists and the natives.
This, unfortunately, wouldn't be the last time native tribes would be thrown into
the warfare of outside powers in their land.

In 1775, enough time had passed in the land; no longer were the majority of
citizens here Brits who had travelled across the Atlantic to find a new home.
Instead, they were people who had lived all their life in these British colonies and
had built a unique identity for themselves. They were people who were born
and raised in a land called America, they were Americans. Yet, despite having
a unique identity for themselves, the land they called home was still under the
control of a small island across the ocean, and that island was demanding more

money from them and control over their home. Enough was enough, and a revolution broke out—a chance for these Americans to be free of British rule and be their own people. The natives of the land got wrapped up in all of this too, and they didn't all agree on whose side to take. Many tribes sided with the British under the rule of George III, while other tribes joined the rebels under the watch of George Washington. We, of course, all know the end result of this war. By 1783, the rebels had won the war and gained their independence from the British, Washington took the mantle of first president of this new nation, and the US as we know it today was off to the races. The language this burgeoning nation chose to use was, of course, English, despite the fact they had just spent years driving the originators of this tongue out of their country. While these new Americans wanted as little to do as possible with their former British rulers, dumping the language they had given them would have been a tad too excessive. The other option would have been deciding on a new language to use, either an established tongue or creating a whole new one, but expecting everyone to learn a new language in the midst of forming a new nation seemed a *little* unreasonable. They stuck with English but, as we know, over the years English has really become its own thing in the States.

The United States didn't go from being the thirteen colonies to covering the majority of North America overnight. The thin sliver down the East Coast of the continent expanded over the years into the shape it is today. As it expanded, English came along for the ride. By 1783, the land was hardly just those thirteen original colonies either, as the former British and then American claim on the land covered pretty much all the area east of the Mississippi. It wouldn't be until 1803 that the States really started to grow in size. It was in this year that the Louisiana Purchase took place. This saw then-president Thomas Jefferson purchase a huge chunk of land from the French who had previously claimed it. Jefferson wanted to expand the land claimed by the USA as he felt that the survival of the burgeoning nation depended on its people owning their land and taking pride in it. The people of the nation seemed to agree too and went on their merry way westward to find even more land to call home. This concept of the people taking the land into their own hands eventually became known as Manifest Destiny, and it's an idea that still resonates in the USA to this day.

Expansion continued in chunks and, step by step, English found itself migrating across this continent as it expanded westward. This expansion, however, did not always go smoothly. The US saw itself up against other European powers who had already claimed the land, natives who were already calling these areas home and, of course, it would butt heads with itself during the American Civil War in the 1860s, a war with the hugely contested subject of slavery at its heart. These are all subjects and issues that could and do have books written about them unto themselves, but remind us that the formation of the modern country we know today is pitted with darker moments. After the Louisiana Purchase in 1803, their next big expansion came in 1819. Here, the USA claimed the peninsular of Florida as well as the land to its west from the Spanish. The year 1845 saw the land that is now Texas, plus parts of some other states, come into their rule. Prior to this, Texas had been ruled as a breakaway state. The following year, in 1846, the US once again claimed land from the British. This time it was the Oregon Territory in the northwest of the modern nation. It was only two years later, in 1848, that the majority of the west coast came to the USA, as a concession from Mexico after the Mexican-American War. One final purchase (dubbed the Gadsden Purchase) from Mexico occurred in 1853. This saw a small region in the south that makes up part of modern Arizona come under US rule. This final small purchase saw all the land that now makes up the contiguous United States come under American ownership, though, as we know, that isn't quite the complete modern picture. The year 1867 saw the US purchase even more land, specifically the region that now makes up Alaska, which was brought from the Russians. Finally, in 1898, the islands of Hawaii, which were their own republic, came to be an American possession. It was also this year that the US ceded Puerto Rico from the Spanish too.

From here, the jigsaw was more or less complete. These areas of land that came under the US's control would over time morph into the fifty states that the stars on their flag represent. Though, Puerto Rico still hasn't reached statehood. In regard to language, each of the fifty states have English as their most prominent tongue, which dates all the way back to the fact that the British claimed land in the east, and that eastern land expanded westward once they were free from British rule but were still English-speaking. This expansion allowed English to be spoken from sea to shining sea. Yet, English is not the only language spoken in the States today, despite being the most popular. Other tongues of European origins are spoken in pockets in their own unique ways. Spanish can be found across the nation and especially in the south, close to the Spanish-speaking Mexico. Variations of French can still be found in the land the US got in the Louisiana Purchase. Even tongues like Polish, German, and Yiddish can be found in areas of the USA where speakers migrated to the land of opportunity.

Then, we have those native tongues. Despite the huge mistreatment natives of the land faced throughout the history of American colonisation, many of their languages have thankfully been able to stick around. Though, they have dwindled over the years. While there are still around 150 Native American languages found across the USA today, in the past there are believed to have been roughly double this amount. Their rights to land have dwindled too, in many cases it is only in their designated reservations where natives are allowed to practise a similar lifestyle to their ancestors. Even this doesn't always work out, with many modern Native Reservations being underfunded in a multitude of ways. Of the 150 languages still spoken, Navajo is by and far the most popular in the USA with over 170,000 speakers. Despite this, Navajo has no official status across the USA, but, then again, neither does English. While English is the most widely spoken and de facto language of the nation, it being the official language was never made law. This seems to stem from the American idea of freedom. People should have the right to speak whatever language they want without government interference. While on a nationwide level it may not be official, many individual states have made English their official tongue. A small handful of states have even gone a step further and given their native languages official status too. South Dakota has given the language of Sioux official status, and the Polynesian Hawaiian language of Hawaii has official status there too. Alaska really takes the cake in all this. Not only do they have English as their official language but also twenty of their native tongues, including the likes of Tlingit, Haida, Dena'ina, Yup'ik, and Deg Xinag, to name just a small portion.

The United States of America has gone on to become the world's dominant superpower. The voices of this nation have spread to every corner of the earth through their global influence as well as their popular culture. In most cases, that omnipresent American voice in our lives is speaking to us in English. We can only begin to imagine if those three ships who arrived in what would become Jamestown some 400 years ago truly understood the effect their actions would have on the world. It was an effect that resulted in the British planting their tongue there, and, eventually, the independent USA would cement it across the continent. It was also an effect that breathed a new life into the language and allowed it to change in ways no one really could have imagined. Ultimately, it's thanks to them that British and American people argue whether colour should have a U in it or not every time they meet each other.

LE GRAND NORD BLANC

FRENCH IN CANADA

To the north of the USA, during and after its freedom, a different story played out in the realm of language migration. We said that French, once upon a time, had a stronghold across a vast swath of modern US land—today the tongue in America is reserved mainly for small pockets and expats. The lingo of France, however, had much greater success above the forty-ninth parallel. The French language has become a key differing point between the US and Canada. While it's undeniable that French was able to find a home in the Great White North, the exact location of that home is often exaggerated. There's an assumption that French is spoken across the entirety of Canada, which is wildly inaccurate. While I have no doubts that speakers of the tongue of France are all across the nation, in reality, it is just one fairly sizable portion of the country where it is the go-to tongue.

The province of Québec is the largest of modern Canada's thirteen provinces and territories, as well as being its second most populated. It is home to around nine million people, roughly one quarter of the entire nation. While Montréal may be the most populous city in the province, it gets its name as a whole from its capital of Québec, often referred to as Québec City to save on confusion. The majority of the population of this province speak French, some, however, do speak English while others are fluent in both of these immigrant tongues.

We already know that France had a stronghold across North America—Thomas Jefferson bought a huge chunk of their claim to expand his own nation. France's claim in the New World started a few centuries prior to the Louisiana Purchase, and it started in land that is now firmly Canadian. In 1534, toward the early days of European exploration in the New World, France finally decided to enter the fold. Explorer Jacque Cartier was sent off to the west in the hope of finding passage across the Atlantic. This might sound familiar. Columbus was also instructed to do the exact same thing but ended up finding a whole new continent. Cartier took a different approach, while they now knew this land was here, there was still some hope that sailing over the top of it to reach Asia was a possibility. While that is technically possible via a trip to the Arctic Circle, that was something Cartier never achieved. Instead, he found himself sailing down what is now dubbed the Saint Lawrence River. It was during his second voyage that he travelled farther down this river and arrived in the land that would become Québec City. Cartier would end up exploring the land over three voyages. It was during these trips that he claimed the land for his home nation, where it received the title of New France, or *Nouvelle-France* in its native tongue, and set the foundation of French in the land. While it was now claimed by the French, Cartier didn't expand or build all that much during his visits.

Perhaps the biggest event to take place during this time was the coining of the name Canada. This title was formed when Cartier interacted with some of the locals in the land who told him they had a settlement nearby. Their word for settlement was *kanata* which Cartier mistook as their name for all the land. *Kanata* would eventually morph into Canada as we know it today. As we can see here, much like with the rest of the Americas, by the time Europeans started to colonise the area, people were already living here. The natives who travelled from Russia into the New World those thousands of years ago reached every nook of this land, Canada being no exception. The specific tribe who are thought to be pivotal in the creation of the name Canada are known as the Saint Lawrence Iroquoians. Their name is fairly self-explanatory. They were a tribe who resided by the Saint Lawrence River and part of the larger Iroquoian group of natives who span North America. Their language was known as Laurentian and part of the wider Iroquoian family, meaning it would have been related to other Iroquoian languages like Cherokee. The Saint Lawrence Iroquoians were not the only inhabitants. The Cree are one of the most dominant native tribes across all of Canada. Their native tongue of the same name comes from the other major native branch of Algic. Though, the most unique natives of the Québec region and Canada as a whole have to be the Inuit people. These are the natives of North America who live in the nation's far north. Due to the extreme conditions of the land, few European colonists interacted with them; to this day, there are very few non-Indigenous peoples living here. The northernmost third of modern Québec goes by the name of Nunavik and is home to around 14,000 people, mainly of Inuit origins. The most widely spoken language here is called Inuktitut, which is part of the wider Eskaleut family.

These Inuit people would have had minimal to do with Cartier while he was in the land. Aside from crafting the modern nation's name, he also set up the fur trade in the land. Fur would go on to become a huge business in New France, with beaver hides becoming one of the colony's key exports. During this time, all New France was really used for was the export of various furs back to Europe. It would take roughly seventy years after Cartier's first trip for a permanent French settlement to be established here. This came about in 1608 when French explorer Samuel de Champlain travelled farther down the Saint Lawrence River and arrived in a cliff-laden land, ideal geography for a well-fortified city. It was here that the city of Québec was finally founded, France's first permanent settlement in what would become Canada and the capital city of New France. The surrounding region grew under French influence too and became the province of Québec.

From here, New France grew in size and amassed a considerable chunk of North America in land that is not only Canada now but also the US. New France would eventually go on to be much larger than other European claims in North America, like Britain's thirteen colonies. Though big in size, New France lacked an equally grand population. The French Empire struggled with populating this claim. Many from Old France didn't really fancy a transatlantic voyage to the New World to live somewhere far colder and wilder than their home in Europe. Those who took the plunge, however, found themselves living a relatively peaceful life in New France and a distinct culture emerged in the land. With unique culture comes unique language.

Today, thanks to these migrations, there is way more than just one kind of French spoken in the land. There's Acadia French, spoken in the Acadia region which is now housed in New Brunswick, as well as the incredibly unique Métis French, a version of French spoken exclusively by the Indigenous Métis people. Though, the most popular version of French in Canada has to be Québec French, also known as Québécois. This, unsurprisingly, is spoken in the city of Québec as well as its wider province. While these varieties of French spoken in Canada are different to one another, they have enough in common to be grouped together and labelled as Canadian French.

They also all have differences to the French spoken back in Europe. Canadian French is seen as sounding far more archaic than the French in Europe, this may stem from the fact that it didn't have as many languages to be influenced by in the Great White North. French in France intermingled way more with its neighbouring tongues. Canadian French, however, did gain influence from English and the many Indigenous tongues of the land. I am sure it would shock many a Frenchman to hear their tongue entangled with English, but in Canadian French it is the norm. This is down to the fact that modern Canada is now dominantly English-speaking. Take a word like bicycle. In European French it is *vélo*. Canadian French, meanwhile, goes with *bicyclette*, which is far more in line with the English word. Then we have words of Indigenous origins. Snowshoes aren't particularly a mainstay in France, minus in its mountainous regions. Here, they are simply called *raquette*. Yet, in the harsh snows of Canada they have much more use, and they acquired a new name from the Algonquian word of *ababich*, being called *babiche* in Canadian French.

It is Québec French spoken by New France's population. Over the centuries, the land grew to be home to just 70,000 people or so. It was this small population that found themselves on the losing side of the Seven Years' War (which was actually just over six years in length) in 1763. This was yet another war fought between

European powers squabbling over land they had decided was theirs without the consent of the natives who had been living there for centuries. A plethora of nations were involved but, ultimately, this was France vs. Great Britain, and with Britain as the victor, the entirety of New France came under their control. You may be wondering, if Britain took over all of France's claims in North America in 1763, then how did Jefferson and the States purchase the Louisiana Territory from the French in 1803? It turns out, France secretly reclaimed this land in 1800, a few years prior to then selling it off to the USA.

While the Louisiana Territory switched hands multiple times, France's claim in what is now Canada stayed under British rule from 1763 all the way until Canada gained independence from the British years down the line. While the land was now under British rule, the Empire did not force English onto Canada's French speakers. Britain wanted to keep the people of their new claim on their good side, so allowed them to carry on living how they had been for centuries prior and speak the form of French they had spoken for so long. Taking away someone's tongue is a great way to really tick them off—Britain had no intention of doing that. This meant the Québec region could still speak French while English went on to dominate the rest of the nation as it expanded into its present shape. This has left us with a modern Canada which on the whole speaks English, minus one province that still gets to speak, quite literally, frankly.

STOLEN FROM AFRICA

CREOLES ACROSS THE CARIBBEAN

This book so far has revolved around languages and people that, on the whole, voluntarily migrated around the world. Speakers who purposely chose to uproot their lives and find new homes. Sadly, not every tongue that has travelled on our globe has done so consensually. History, tragically, has ample tales of people being taken away from their lives in one land and forced into a far more unpleasant life somewhere else. Forced migrations like these have been encapsulated in song form, perhaps none better than in the Bob Marley song "Buffalo Soldier." The speaker in the song recounts the experience of the real-life Buffalo Soldiers. These were all-Black regiments of the Union Army, supposedly named by Indigenous People of the Great Plains, as their thick curly hair reminded them of the buffalo they shared land with. Lines from this song extend to the wider African American experience in the New World. The character of the song explains how they were "stolen from Africa" and "brought to America" as well as saying they were "driven from the mainland to the heart of the Caribbean." These lines reflect the way in which many people of African origins arrived in the Americas, specifically the Caribbean, through the North Atlantic slave trade.

The trade of humans, treating them in the same way we treat things like spice and gold, is a grotesque part of our history. Declaring certain groups of humans lesser than others, designating them slaves, and selling them off reflects a wider sentiment of this period of time and one we look back on in disgust. It is, unfortunately, something civilisations have partaken in throughout history. By the Age of Exploration and the colonisation of the New World, European powers turned their eyes to the people of Africa to be the victims in their plans. Africans were unfairly plucked from their homes for a multitude of reasons. European powers, after picking the bones of the Americas dry of natural resources, turned to farming the land. Filling it with cash crops and other vegetation that grew unsuccessfully in Europe. These farms and plantations needed to be tended, and in their eyes more money could be made if those who were doing the work did it for free. Using Indigenous peoples of the Americas as slaves during this time was not a possibility. By the time these plantations sprang up, the native populations of the land had dwindled through disease or mass killings by colonial powers and those still alive wanted nothing to do with the new people in the land, and rightly so. To escape the fate many before them had, Indigenous peoples retreated into the wild depths of the Americas. It was land they knew but the Europeans didn't, and could act as a safe haven for the time being.

With native peoples out of the question, colonisers looked back across the Atlantic. Many powers like the British, French, and Portuguese already had small territorial claims in Africa, primarily down its west coast. The African locals were viewed by the Europeans of the time as inferior and less developed. Of course, this was far from the case. Yet, for the powers wanting to harness the soils of America, this was the outdated view they held. They figured they could easily out-power the African natives and shipped them in their millions to the New World. Around five million of these Africans sent to the New World found themselves across the islands of the Caribbean. Here, they would have worked the land, growing crops like sugarcane under the watch of whichever European power had claimed that island. Not only were these people taken from their home and shipped across the sea, but their native cultures were taken from them too. Many slaves were forbidden from partaking in things from their home. Songs, religion, and clothing from their home were banned. And of course, so were languages.

The people brought over to the Caribbean were not all from the same ethnic group nor did they all speak the same language. West Africa is full of languages and the first wave of enslaved peoples in the Caribbean would have spoken languages like Wolof and Yoruba, both part of the sprawling Atlantic-Congo family, which houses Africa's many Bantu languages too. There are also the many Mande languages spoken here too including Maninka, Bambara, and Susu. All these fantastic tongues were banned in many plantations across the Caribbean. While it's easy to remove the clothes off a person's back or even the songs from their mouths, forcing a whole group of people to all stop speaking the languages they had done their entire life wasn't as easy. This was exemplified by the fact that, beyond some basic phrases relating to their work, the colonists didn't teach them their tongues. This gave us a Caribbean that housed people forced into slavery who spoke a variety of African languages and colonial settlers with their European tongues. These two groups of people needed some way to communicate. This led to a mixing of tongues and languages evolving into languages we refer to as creoles.

We saw a creole come into being in Macau with the introduction of Portuguese a few decades prior, but the Caribbean is most likely the part of the world most linked with these languages. Creoles are tongues that come into being when two or more groups of people with different languages intermix and splice them together. Many creoles start their life as something known as a pidgin. Pidgins are creoles in their most basic form, when words and elements from different languages are used in conjunction with one another to achieve basic communication. They tend to graduate from pidgins to creoles when they are spoken for long enough that not only an entire group of people speak it, but their offspring also speak it as their go-to tongue too. Creoles are often viewed as lesser languages used by uneducated people, but they are just as much real languages as English, French, and Portuguese. These European tongues found themselves in the Caribbean in the name of colonisation and they became the foundations of many of the region's creoles.

Creoles of English concoction can be found across the Caribbean. While each has its fundamental basis in English, they picked up words and phrases from various other tongues ranging from Indigenous languages to ones brought over from Africa. Places like the Bahamas, Saint Kitts and Nevis, Grenada, and Antigua and Barbuda all have English based creoles as prominent languages. The most widely spoken English creole in the Caribbean, however, is the one that formed in Jamaica. The island of Jamaica across its history was ruled by both the Spanish and the British. It's why there is such a mixture of place names there. The capital's name of Kingston is of distinctly British origins, while place names like Port Maria and the aptly named Spanish Town are, unsurprisingly, of Spanish roots. In the realm of language, however, English clearly won out, as not only is English the official tongue of the nation today, but the local creole of Jamaican Patois is formed from English and widely spoken across the land. This form of English, along with the accent from the land, is one of their most recognisable exports. It's the language of much of Reggae music, such as from the likes of Bob Marley. It's easy to think that Jamaican Patois is just a corrupted version of English or one spoken with a heavy accent as, on the whole, it is somewhat compatible with the English spoken in places like the UK and the USA. Most English speakers will be able to easily translate the Jamaican Patois phrase of *lickkle more* into "little more" for example. But this truly is a language unto itself.

The language started to form across the seventeenth century. At this point, the island had been under Spanish rule for some time, but in 1670, it was seized by the British, who used it as a plantation operated by those forcefully brought to the land from Africa. This led to not only English and Spanish being spoken here, but the languages of West Africa and native tongues like Arawak too. This all intermixed with one another to form the language we know today. Take a word like *gizzada*. This is the name of a kind of cake originating from Jamaica. The word has its origins with the Spanish term *guisado*, meaning "to cook/prepare." This shows us that, while the Spanish haven't ruled the island for literal centuries, their influence can still be found on the language. *Poto-poto* is a Jamaican Patois word meaning "muddy." This obviously sounds nothing like the English word for mud, so it should come as no surprise that the term was lifted directly from the West African Yoruba language. Yoruba is not the only language that helped shape this creole, however. Terms like *himba*, the name for a kind of yam, *juk*, meaning "to poke," and *adure*, meaning a "medicine" or "drug," come from the

language of Igbo, Fula, and Akan, respectively. Words of Arawak origin that
are used in Jamaican Patois can be found in other versions of English too, like
hurricane and tobacco.

French didn't become the basis of all that many creoles in the Caribbean, but the
single most widely spoken one in this region is of French origin. That being the
Haitian Creole from the nation that now takes up the western half of Hispaniola,
the island Columbus first claimed on behalf of Spain. This island was once under
completely Spanish rule too, before the French claimed the western side of it
in 1625. The language began to develop in the latter stages of the seventeenth
century and into the eighteenth. It's easy to spot the French influence on this
creole from the get-go. Their word for "thank you," *mèsi*, clearly has its roots in
the French *merci*. Haiti is also the home of voodoo, the religion deeply linked with
dolls that can mirror a human. That word "voodoo" came into Haitian Creole
and then the wider world from African roots, with terms like *vódū* from the Ewe
language of West Africa. A less prominent French creole of the Caribbean is the
one spoken in Saint Lucia. This is, once again, based on French with influences
from tongues across the globe. What's interesting with this one is that, while their
creole is French in origin, the official language of the land is actually English.
This all comes down to the mixed colonial rule on the island. The creole began to
take shape while the island was a part of the French West Indies. By the time the
British claimed the island in 1814, the creole had planted its roots well enough to
stick around.

A similar case has happened with the Portuguese Caribbean Creole of
Papiamento. It is spoken primarily on the three islands of Aruba, Bonaire, and
Curaçao, also cleverly known as the ABC islands. These islands are actually
part of the Kingdom of the Netherlands. The Dutch also played a role in the
colonisation of the New World and these islands are a remnant of this time.
Papiamento is seemingly one of the more diverse creoles of the Caribbean. While
it is ultimately based on Portuguese, it has other European influences such as
English, Spanish, and Dutch. Beyond these, the usual West African influence
can be found in it too. Like the other creoles, it too came into being during the
seventeenth century. Something unique about Papiamento is that, while it is now
spoken in the Caribbean, it is not believed to have originated from there. Instead,

the tongue started life as a pidgin spoken in Portugal's West African claims before being exported across the Atlantic.

While the ruling classes barked orders at these enslaved people in their European tongues, at home and whatever private moment they could find, the languages of their old homes could once again be shared between friends and loved ones. The lines between their native tongues and the languages of their superiors became even more blurred as the years went by, eventually evolving into these creole languages. Thankfully, slavery would not last forever, and neither would foreign rule across these islands. Long after many parts of the Caribbean gained their independence from their colonial rulers, however, the tongues have stuck around. While these languages have populations of millions in some cases, they have not always had the best public persona. As mentioned already, they are often seen as lesser tongues and incorrect ways of speaking. In many cases, these nations will have one language as their official tongue while the creole will be far more widely spoken by the masses. This has led to speakers of creoles being shunned and higher-ups insisting they use a, quote unquote, "proper language." Thankfully, the stigma of creoles in the Caribbean is not as widespread as it was in the past. Many of these languages are far more celebrated, with dictionaries of creoles coming into being. Many even have official status too. In 1987, Haitian Creole was made an official language of the land along with French itself.

Despite all these languages, there's an odd emission, that being the lack of a Spanish creole of any kind in the Caribbean. Despite the Spanish being the first Europeans to really colonise this part of the world and their tongue becoming incredibly prominent in the land, it seems like it never really produced a creole during this period. This lack of Spanish creole seems to have come about for a myriad of reasons. One of the main reasons came down to the fact that the Spanish didn't have much of a land claim in Africa when these creoles were being formed. This meant that the language didn't intermix all that much in Africa like Papiamento did. While Spanish didn't get a creole of any kind in the Age of Colonisation, actual Spanish is spoken on these islands, noticeably in Cuba.

Today, the Caribbean is one of the world's most remarkable melting pots of languages. Tongues from Europe and Africa, as well as native languages to these islands, have been collected here and intertwined with one another to form new languages which otherwise wouldn't have come into being. As interesting as these languages are, the sad reality is that most only exist due to the barbaric actions of humans that came before us. These tongues were born regardless of if their speakers wanted them to be or not. This dark chapter of history led us to this linguistically diverse Caribbean. Traverse these islands today and you will find languages ranging from English to Spanish and even a form of French with African influences. It may seem strange to someone without a wider knowledge of this corner of the globe, but as Bob Marley said in "Buffalo Soldier," "If you know your history. Then you would know where you coming from."

Back in Africa, and a few decades down the line, what occurred in the Caribbean happened somewhat in reverse. Instead of African languages finding themselves in a land dominated by European tongues, a European language found itself in the depths of Africa, cohabiting with its many languages. This resulted in the birth of what is dubbed by many as the world's newest language.

SUB-SAHARAN DUTCH

THE BIRTH OF AFRIKAANS

The claim that Afrikaans is the youngest language on our planet is easily debated. New languages are emerging all the time. Whether that be through alterations on current tongues, with words and phrases picking up new meanings, or conlangs (short for constructed languages) being crafted by language enthusiasts. The reason Afrikaans often gets the title of youngest language is down to the fact that it is so unilaterally considered a language. Most sources see it as a wholly formed tongue, not a vernacular, pidgin, or creole. It even gets to sit on a branch of a language family. Afrikaans can be found in the Germanic branch of Indo-European along with the likes of English, German, and Swedish. If you couldn't guess from this language's name, it is primarily spoken on the continent of Africa. Specifically in the nation of South Africa, but it has pockets of speakers in other southern African nations too. While the rest of the Germanic languages have their ultimate home in Western and Northern Europe, the tongue of Afrikaans formed a great distance away from the rest of its siblings. In many ways, it is not entirely fair to even call Afrikaans a sibling to the Germanic languages. This is another tongue that has earned the title of daughter language, with its parent being the relatively smaller Germanic tongue of Dutch.

The Dutch language which has its roots in the Low Franconia language began to morph into the modern Germanic tongue it is today in around 700 AD. Today, it is seen as something of a middle ground between German and English. Speakers of either of these languages will be able to understand the tongue of the Netherlands to some extent. Dutch, on the world stage, has not made the greatest of impacts. It's spoken widely in the Netherlands of course, as well as in neighbouring Belgium. But on a global stage, it is only really a mainstay in the South American nation of Suriname, which belonged to their empire, and those aforementioned ABC islands. Dutch's migration in Southern Africa was so successful that it evolved into the completely new tongue of Afrikaans. While I say completely new, there are a huge number of similarities between them. Dutch and Afrikaans share roughly 90 percent of the same words. For example, a dog is called a *hond* in both Dutch and Afrikaans. Even when the words are not identical, they are very much alike. Their words for "breath" have just a one letter difference—*asem* and *adem* in Afrikaans and Dutch, respectively. Where their words do differ, we start to see many of the other influences on this Germanic language from Africa. *Hospitaal*, unsurprisingly, means hospital in Afrikaans, which is clearly inspired by the English word. This comes from English rule in the land as we shall see. Despite Dutch being so similar to English, their word for this establishment is, instead, *ziekenhuis*.

Another way in which Afrikaans is more like English than Dutch is through the features of the language as opposed to the words within it. Afrikaans has no grammatical gender much like English. Dutch, meanwhile, has three of them. These were probably stripped away from Afrikaans as the language developed. Aside from English, Portuguese is another European language that has shaped Afrikaans. This stems from a historic Portuguese settlement in the southern tip of the continent too. Portuguese influence on not just Afrikaans but South Africa as a whole can best be seen in the last name of Ferreira, meaning "iron mine." This Portuguese last name has become commonplace in the country and with its Afrikaans speakers and is definitely not of Dutch origins. Afrikaans' farthest afield influence comes in the form of the Malay language. This Asian tongue would have arrived on the shores of Africa down to the fact that, for the longest time, the language's homelands were ruled by the Dutch as part of Dutch East India. This meant that Malay speakers would have found themselves in other parts of the Dutch realm like Africa. Malay isn't too abundant in Afrikaans, but the name of the humble "saucer" in the tongue comes from Malay. The word is *piring* in the Asian tongue and *piering* in the African one. The Dutch term is far more in line with English, simply being *schotel*. Many native African tongues have found their way into the language too. From the informal term for "bugs," *gogga*, coming from the Khoe language, to the much-dreaded *babela*, the Afrikaans word for "hangover" which derives from Zulu.

While Afrikaans has been shaped by other languages, its influence on the modern tongue only really amounts to a handful of words—this is because the language is so chiefly shaped by Dutch. Dutch first reached the south of Africa in 1652. Prior to this, the land had been mainly inhabited by native Africans who spoke languages ranging from Zulu and Khoe, as previously mentioned, but also tongues like Ndebele and Xhosa from the Bantu branch, to name just a few. The Portuguese had already made some small claims in this land in the late fifteenth century, hence why their tongue shaped Afrikaans. It was in 1652 that Dutch navigator Jan van Riebeeck, on behalf of the Dutch East India Trading Company, landed on the tip of the continent and set up the Cape Colony. We can only imagine how completely foreign this part of Africa must have seemed to those first settlers who had left the Netherlands behind, swapping a flat windmill and tulip covered country for terrain far more extreme and wildlife far more dangerous.

This Cape Colony would eventually become Cape Town. The Dutch wished to have a base in South Africa for one main reason. At this time, the jewel of the Dutch Colonial Empire was their East Indian claim, which supplied the empire with valuable resources. The only issue was the fact that getting from the Netherlands itself to this part of the world was a long trek. The Suez Canal was far from being built, meaning the only way to easily get from Europe to Asia was sailing underneath Africa. What would make this trip easier, they thought, was having somewhere sailors could have a little break of sorts and restock their ships. A claim in Africa was the solution to this issue. The Cape Colony was established for this very purpose. It provided fresh water, fresh food, and dry land on the arduous journey from the Netherlands to East India.

For the Cape Colony to be a successful pitstop, it needed labour, and workers arrived in the land through two means. Many came over to Africa from the Netherlands itself, with the promise of free land to toil as they wish. Though, unfortunately, many others had little choice in coming to the colony. Enslaved peoples from the wider Dutch Empire were brought over to the land with no say in the matter. Coming from various places, including East India, was how Malay came to be spoken there. Just as we have seen many times over, the natives of the land were too treated poorly by the new colonial settlers. Various African natives (chiefly the Khoekhoe) could not match the manpower and the technology of the Dutch and found themselves enslaved or killed. Many Khoekhoe simply surrendered and offered to aid the Dutch in any way they could. These tragedies created a huge melting pot of people and languages in the Cape Colony, and eventually that new language of Afrikaans would emerge from it.

It's hard to pinpoint when exactly the language stopped being Dutch and became Afrikaans. Even 100 years after the Dutch founded the Cape Colony, the language spoken there was referred to as Broken Dutch or Kitchen Dutch. It was only in the nineteenth century that it started being called *Afrikaans Hollandsch*, meaning African Dutch, before it was shortened to just Afrikaans and gained recognition as its own thing. The language became deeply associated with the citizens of Dutch origins and white in skin colour. These people became known as Afrikaaners, or Boers, which comes from the Dutch word for farmers, as many of them came to the land to work it.

The land stayed under Dutch rule until 1795, when the British swiped it from them. For a few years after this, the land was juggled between each nation. The Dutch reclaimed it in 1803, but Britain got it back in 1806. It was in 1814 that the Dutch formally released all control of the land, and it became part of the British Empire once more. Britain's time as rulers of Southern Africa saw their claim expand beyond this one colony and allowed English to become a dominant tongue in the land too. Though, this didn't mean that Afrikaans all of a sudden vanished from the land; many of the Boers who spoke the tongue were unhappy to now be under British rule. In retaliation, a huge number of them migrated across the continent and left the British colony, in an event known as The Great Trek, to found their own republics known as Transvaal and the Orange Free State. The British and the Boers would butt heads in two wars across the late nineteenth and early twentieth century. It was these Boer strongholds that, in many ways, allowed the language to maintain relevance in the region while it was under British rule, and, ultimately, is a key factor as to why Afrikaans is still spoken today.

By the time South Africa gained independence from the British in 1961, English, Afrikaans, and many other native tongues were spoken in the nation. Despite this huge mixture of languages and ethnicities calling the country home, the nation was far from mixed unto itself. Prior to independence in 1948, new rules were introduced in South Africa, the rules of Apartheid. The former part of this name derives from the Dutch/Afrikaans term of *apart*, which means the same thing as it does in English. The latter part of it is a translation of the -hood suffix we see in English in terms like childhood, used to relate to states of being. Apartheid was exactly that, a state of being in South Africa in which people were forcibly moved apart from one another. Specifically, separation between the white and Black people of the nation. White South Africans of Dutch and English descent were the ones in power in 1948, and for a huge mixture of reasons involving the strugglers of workers, class warfare, and abject racism, they decided that pretty much every aspect of life in South Africa should be separated between whites (who were seen as the superiors) and non-whites.

This ranged from things like different parts of towns being segregated off for whites and non-whites, and even more simple things like park benches being labelled as "whites only." It's a truly heartbreaking period of human history and another case of Europeans migrating to a new land, making themselves the rulers, and subjecting the native population. It was compounded by the fact that white people in South Africa were, at the time, a minority unto themselves in that nation's population. Black people far outnumbered them, so this system kept the ruling minority in control while the majority faced worse living conditions and less rights, including Black people not being allowed to vote. Apartheid will still be remembered by many. It only came to an end in the early 1990s when Black people were given the vote and activist Nelson Mandela (who had spent the previous twenty plus years in prison due to his anti-apartheid activism) was elected president. Though, even in our post-apartheid world, issues between races are far from perfect in the nation.

While Apartheid was in action, language played a key role. Afrikaans was seen as the language of power as it was the main tongue of the whites who controlled the land. This gave the language far more prominence on the public stage and kept South Africa's many native tongues out of the limelight. This led to those native languages being discriminated against. This is, once again, compounded by the fact that Afrikaans was a minority language in the land. Even to this day, that is still the case. Modern South Africa is extremely celebratory of its linguistic diversity. The nation has no less than eleven official spoken languages. This includes Afrikaans as well as English, but also the native tongues of Ndebele, Sepedi, Sesotho, Setswana, Swazi, Tshivenda, Xhosa, Xitsonga, and Zulu. These languages are spoken across the country, with certain tongues having more prominence in specific areas. Zulu, for example, is spoken predominantly in the nation's east, while Tshivenda can be found more or less exclusively in the north. English, however, has become something of a lingua franca in the nation, with it even being used as the key language of schooling.

This brings us to Afrikaans in modern South Africa. This tongue born from Dutch migrating from mild Europe to rugged Africa is still something of a minority language with just over 13 percent of the nation's population of roughly sixty million speaking it. It can mainly be found in more urban areas like Cape Town, where the language was ultimately formed when it was merely the Dutch Cape Colony. The tongue's legacy today is mixed. It is remarkable that a Germanic tongue with origins in Europe was born on the tip of Africa, picking up words and rules from other languages along the way. The dark side of Afrikaans isn't so much the language itself but rather in how the language was used in the past. Afrikaans was the tongue of authority during Apartheid. Today, it is seen by many in South Africa (especially by those of Indigenous roots) as the language of the oppressors. The tongue which was placed upon them in place of the languages of their ancestors. Many even refuse to learn it. Undoubtedly, many Afrikaans speakers today, both Black and white, believe strongly that Apartheid was an awful thing. We can hope this language can and will move on from the atrocities that were carried out by its speakers in the past. So that it can be looked at as the curiosity of a tongue it is, as opposed to mainly being associated with segregation.

THE HOUSE OF THE RISING TONGUE

FRENCH IN LOUISIANA

By the early eighteenth century, languages were still finding their way around
the New World. Not only were tongues still being exported from Europe to
the Americas, but once in this new land many travelled even farther, going on
their own migrations. These kinds of migrations reflect the pockets of languages
that can be found across modern USA. One of the most prominent minority-
European languages in the States is the French spoken in Louisiana. We know
that the land which makes up the state was once French property, its name is a
remnant of the larger, former Louisiana Territory. While New France started life
in 1534, the empire wouldn't reach the Deep South for over a century. The land
we now call Louisiana in the USA only acquired that name in 1682 when French
explorer Robert Cavelier de La Salle named it in honour of the then French
king, Louis XIV. It would be easy to presume that the simple fact this land once

belonged to the French would explain to us why there is a version of the language spoken here. That is partially the explanation in this case. Louisiana French didn't just come into being from French people migrating from France to this state, what helped cement this language in Louisiana was, instead, a migration from within New France itself. This internal migration not only helped shape Louisiana French but also led to the formation of a group of people who call this state home. Their cultural identity, food, and language, has since become one of the things Louisiana is most deeply linked with.

Their story starts in pretty much the opposite end of New France in a region named Acadia. This colony of New France was founded in 1604 and on today's maps it roughly encompasses the modern maritime provinces of Canada: New Brunswick, Nova Scotia, and Prince Edward Island. This area of Canada is still sometimes referred to as Acadia, and the residents, especially those of French origin, as Acadian. While now the people of these provinces live fairly regular lives, those who called Acadia home in the past would have been tempted to migrate there from France with the promise of riches and land. This resulted in many farming the land and living their life through these means. It would have been tough, rigorous work, swapping the pleasantries of France for the cold of Canada, but many of them grew to be self-sufficient and satisfied. Many even created advanced water dike systems along the shores, which helped massively. So much so that, in some cases, Acadians were accused of being lazy workers. Acadia grew to be an idyllic little nook of New France, full of farms growing crops in abundance and cosy little settlements. In a rare scenario, the French settlers even lived fairly peacefully alongside the native Mi'kmaq people.

It was seemingly a small slice of paradise amongst the vast New France Empire in North America. Life started to become rocky for the Acadians in 1713, however, when the land fell into the hands of the British. Relations between the French-speaking Acadians and the British started off somewhat smoothly. They were allowed to carry on speaking French and generally go about their usual way of life. Over the decades, however, tensions between Britain and France started to rise and the Acadians were stuck in the middle of their squabbles. Britain's opinion on the Acadians slowly started to sour, their dislike of the French resulted in them being unhappy with having such a large French-speaking population in their land. This culminated in 1755 in an event known in French as *Le Grand*

Dérangement or in English as The Great Disturbance, The Great Upheaval, or The Expulsion of the Acadians. This was the forcible removal of the Acadians from their land. Their once idyllic life had been upheaved, with their homes destroyed, crops burned, and countless lives lost. Those who survived had to find new homes for themselves. Suddenly, they went from being happy peaceful people to exiles with nothing to their name. These exiled Acadians became looked down upon by the British, treated as second class citizens, and even sold into slavery. Once noble Acadian families were torn apart, never to see each other again as they toiled in colonies across the New World.

Not all found themselves dead or enslaved, many migrated across North America to find a new home where they could live in peace like they once did in Acadia. But their image as second-class citizens came with them as they ventured across North America looking for a fresh start. At this point, America was a patchwork of European powers, all of which treated the Acadians as though they were beneath them. Still, the Acadians wandered in an attempt to find somewhere to call their own. By the 1760s, one group of expelled Acadians reached as far as the Gulf of Mexico. At this time, the land was under Spanish rule, but on these shores, they found themselves at the Mississippi River Delta. The land that composed this delta was unforgiving, swampy marshland full of alligators and mosquitos. Yet, the Acadians saw the inhospitality of the land as a positive. It meant no one else (other than Indigenous peoples who had called the land home for so long) would be living here. It was here that these Acadians, who had travelled across the better part of North America, found their new home. They mastered the land and learned to work around it, fishing and farming in any way they could. Living in recluse from the world that had turned their back on them. They came to name this land the Bayou, which derives from the native Choctaw word of *bayuk* meaning "small stream."

Many of the descendants of the Acadians still live in this part of the world today and have a similar lifestyle. They are no longer known as the Acadians, as over the centuries that title got corrupted. The A at the start was dropped and the latter -dian part morphed into a different sound, eventually becoming just Cajun. The culture of the Cajuns, from their food to their incredibly unique accent, which sounds simultaneously both French and from the Deep South, is one of the defining features of the state on the global stage. It's these people who played such a vast role in bringing French to the land, as well as shaping modern Louisiana French. Though, in a twist in the tale, many Cajun people now speak their own variation of English known as Cajun English.

The various Louisiana French dialects spoken by Cajuns and many other people across Louisiana are fairly similar to other forms of the language found across the globe. Where they are at their most unique is with words born into this form of French which have gone on to be used in wider language. When we look into these words, we start to notice many of the other influences of Louisiana French too. Bayou has already been covered and this is a concept very linked with the Cajuns and the state. We saw the word come from Indigenous roots. Various native tongues of this nook of America helped shape Louisiana French. Though, another huge factor was West African tongues too. These languages arrived in Louisiana the same way in which they found themselves in the Caribbean, through the inhumane slave trade that plagued this corner of the globe. Like the Cajuns, many slaves fled to this swampy land to seek refuge and came to live side by side with the exiled Acadians. Their language's influence can be seen best in the name of one of Louisiana most celebrated dishes, gumbo. The name of this meal comes from the Bantu tongue of Mbundu and their word for okra, *ngombo*. Other European tongues influenced Louisiana French too. A popular kind of canoe linked with this neck of the woods is called a "pirogue," which comes from the Spanish *piragua*. This makes sense as, when the Cajuns settled the land, it was under Spanish rule.

Louisiana French is a reminder of just how resilient people and their languages can be. A language like French, born in the tame lands of Europe, has been able to survive and evolve in the swamplands of the USA's Deep South. Spoken in large part by the descendants of people who were banished from their comfortable lives in modern Canada. People who trekked thousands of miles across the continent, dodging persecution and being sold into slavery, before ultimately finding a new home in thick swampland many other people would have deemed uninhabitable. It's a fantastic example of a non-English European language finding a home in the USA, but it is far from the only one.

AMISH PARADISE

THE BIRTH OF PENNSYLVANIA DUTCH

When languages migrate, something that tends to not change about them is their names. English is still called English whether it's being spoken in the UK, USA, or Australia. This would lead you to believe that Pennsylvania Dutch is a form of the Dutch language, the same one that evolved into Afrikaans in South Africa, spoken in the US state of Pennsylvania. Naturally, you'd be wrong. Pennsylvania Dutch is, instead, a version of German. The reason it is referred to as Dutch comes down to the fact that, in the past, Dutch was a more ambiguous term in English to collectively refer to Germanic speakers of continental Europe. The Dutch, as we know them today, would have been called Dutch, as would those who spoke German. The term Dutch has its ultimate origins in an old Germanic word which more or less just means "people." It's even seen in Germany's own native name of *Deutschland*, which simply means the land of the people. More accurate names for this language would be something like Pennsylvania German or its native name of *Deitsch*, but the folksy antiquated name of Pennsylvania Dutch has stuck around as the go-to moniker.

With the nomenclature confusion out of the way, we can actually look into this fascinating language. This evolution of German in the USA came into being thanks to a very specific group of people migrating to that titular northeast state. This is a tongue deeply linked with the Anabaptists groups who call Pennsylvania and the surrounding area their home. Anabaptism is a division of Christianity. Their core values include things like separation from wider society and government control, minimal adoption of modern technology, and simple living. There are various Anabaptists found across the globe and they are often also known as the Plain People due to their plain lifestyle and clothing. The Anabaptist group that are seemingly the most known in the USA, and the key speakers of Pennsylvania Dutch, are the Amish. The Amish are deeply linked with the Anabaptist ideals previously mentioned and known for their image of raising barns, churning butter, and large communal meals. This stereotype isn't exactly what modern Amish life looks like. Many Amish people have more integration with larger society then you may expect, some even use phones and computers. In the modern USA, there's just shy of 400,000 Amish people, with the bulk of them living in the state of Pennsylvania. Many of them are still fluent in the language of Pennsylvania Dutch as well as English.

The Amish and Anabaptists in general came into being as a wider extension of the Protestant reformations. These kicked off in Europe in 1517 when monk Martin Luther grew tired of the operations of the Catholic church and wanted a form of Christianity which put less emphasis on money and the establishment itself and more focus on the word of God written within the Bible itself. By 1525, this ideal had morphed into Anabaptism in Switzerland. By 1693, another Swiss man, Jakob Ammann, adapted the beliefs even more so, putting a huge amount of value in simple living and supporting one another in the community. His form of the religion took, and those who followed it were named the Amish, after their founder Jakob Ammann. Despite Jakob being Swiss, the birthplace of the Amish is seen to be the Alsace region which now resides in Eastern France, as Ammann moved there and formed his beliefs in the land. From here, Amish beliefs spread and took off, proving popular with neighbouring German lands. At this time, Germany was not a singular nation like we know it today. It was more a patchwork of smaller tribes and kingdoms. While all these German groups spoke a language that can collectively be called German, many of them spoke smaller varieties of the tongue which would have had varying degrees of intelligibility with one another. The German-speaking region east of Amish's homeland Alsace is called the Palatinate, or *Die Pfalz* in modern Standard German. Here, the people spoke a variety of German dialects known collectively as the Palatinate German Dialects, for self-explanatory reasons.

The Palatinate German Dialects are still spoken in the region. While all these dialects are different unto themselves (with two of the more widely spoken ones being called *Westpfälzisch* and *Vorderpfälzisch*), they do all have similarities. These include similar accents as well as some words being different to Standard German. In Standard German, the simple word of "stone" is *stein*, while in the Palatinate dialects it becomes *schdää*. *Beine*, meaning "legs" in Standard German, becomes *bää* in the Palatinate dialects. While "potato," which is *kartoffel* in Standard German, is *grumbeea* in the *Vorderpfälzisch* dialect and *grumbeer* in the *Westpfälzisch* dialect. On the whole, it's not completely indecipherable from Standard German or the many other dialects found in the country, but it certainly has its unique quirks.

It was this version of German that many Amish people spoke in Europe when the movement started out. In time, the Amish way of life started to become scrutinised. This scrutiny came down to the simple fact that the Amish were different to other Christians in the way they lived their life; as history has repeatedly shown us, when groups of people are different, it's the smallest group which often get judged and punished for it. By the early eighteenth century, many Amish people were being persecuted for their way of life. Fed up with how they were being treated in Europe, the Amish wanted a fresh start in new land, a land full of religious freedom so they could live as they pleased. Luckily enough for them, a land founded on religious freedom had been doing its thing for a few centuries across the Atlantic.

William Penn was born in London in 1664 into a wealthy and influential family; it meant that he had sway in the land with those in power. He was also born into a Quaker family. Quakers are another subdivision of Christianity which have a long history with persecution. As a young man, William Penn was too fed up with the hatred he and his fellow Quakers received and decided to do something about it. Due to his prestigious background, he was able to have a word with the king himself, Charles II at the time. Penn demanded land in the British's claim to the New World, a section of the World where he could be a Quaker in peace and free of religious intolerance. Charles II was in a bind. He owed William Penn's father the sum of £16,000 for various reasons, and as Penn's father had died, that debt had moved onto William. Instead of paying the money back, Charles, instead, gave Penn a huge tract of land in America. Penn was more than happy with this offer and the land was proclaimed his in 1681, being dubbed Pennsylvania in ode to his family name. From here, William Penn got to work on forming his utopia of religious freedom. On the whole, this worked out, especially to begin with. When the land came under Penn's ownership it was far from empty. The natives of the land, the Lenape with their Unami language, were at first hesitant with the coloniser's arrival. Many Indigenous Americans at this point had already fallen victim to Europeans. Penn, however, took a different approach with the natives, and for some time the European settlers and the Lenape lived in peace. It was only after the death of Penn that relations wore down and the culture and the religion of the Lenape started to become demonised. A sad fact for a land built on religious freedom.

The Lenape struggled in the land which was once theirs to enjoy, meanwhile, faiths of other kinds (mainly different forms of Christianity) did indeed enjoy religious freedom. By the time the Amish were wanting to leave Europe in the early eighteenth century, Pennsylvania was still a British colony and was making a splash on the world stage for its liberal approach to religious practices. It must have seemed like a dream come true for the Amish. With their eyes set on a land where they could live how they wanted, the Amish arrived in their droves to Pennsylvania. Over the course of the eighteenth century and into the nineteenth, thousands of Amish people left Europe for the state. Across this migration period, Pennsylvania would shift from being a colony of the British to a state of the independent USA, being one of the thirteen founding states. The land they found there was remote, vast, and empty. Meaning it was perfect for them to live their ideal reclusive life away from wider society. Churning butter to their heart's content. Many of these Amish people who left Europe were speakers of those Palatinate German Dialects, which cemented these forms of German in

Pennsylvania. Land that, just a few years prior, was a hub of Native American activity and languages quickly shifted to being a hub of Amish life, with an archaic form of German evolving in the land.

To many, it might seem odd that not only can this tongue be found in the USA, but the Amish are still there living in a similar way to those ancestors of centuries past. These people and their language have been able to live relatively undisturbed, mainly down to the sheer scale of the USA. Pennsylvania alone is over 46,000 square miles in size—that's larger than whole nations like Portugal, the Netherlands, Malawi, and Jordan. There was ample room in the burgeoning New World for a group of people from another nook of the earth to find a small slice for themselves and be left to their own devices.

The Amish would go on to settle in more than just this single state. Today, Amish communities can be found all across the state, but the largest concentration is still found in Pennsylvania. It was here that they found the most religious freedom; they also had linguistic freedom too. The Amish, on their arrival in the New World, didn't have to learn English, they were allowed to carry on talking the tongue they had back home. For the majority of them, it was the Palatinate German Dialects. As they lived in such isolation from the wider world, it meant the dialects could carry on changing and evolving, morphing into those Pennsylvania Dutch dialects that we have today. Modern Pennsylvania Dutch isn't all that different to the various forms of German spoken in Germany. One of the biggest differences is the use of English words in the language. As English has become the mainstay of modern Pennsylvania and the USA, it's no surprise that the language has crept in, especially as the lines between isolated Amish life and standard American life have become more blurred. Occasionally, Pennsylvania Dutch speakers will throw in the odd English word while communicating. This goes the other way too, seemingly. While Pennsylvania Dutch is a form of German with an English influence, Pennsylvania Dutch English is a form of English with a German influence. A majority of Amish people are able to speak both Pennsylvania Dutch and English, so it only makes sense that the tongues would become intertwined and birth this unique form of English too.

English has very much become a key language for the Amish, especially as they start to integrate more into the wider USA. Some supermarkets in the country have specific spaces for horse drawn buggies in their car parks and those same buggies can even be seen ordering fast food from the drive through. While many may speak the tongue of the English, Pennsylvania Dutch is the tongue of their old home. One that has stuck around to this very day, even though it's not technically Dutch.

DO YOU SPEAK-A MY LANGUAGE?

ENGLISH IN AUSTRALIA

The land we now call Australia has a human history dating back way further than the arrival of the British or any European nation's knowledge of the land's existence. The first people to arrive in the modern nation are believed to have migrated from various parts of southeast Asia, traversing the waters, around 70,000 years ago. These initial settlers didn't make themselves at home in the bulk of the land we call Australia, but instead on a chain of small islands along the land's north coast. These are now dubbed the Torres Islands. Tens of thousands of years later, a different group of people arrived on the Australian mainland, also from Southeast Asia, and became the first known humans to inhabit this great land mass. It's these two groups of people who are the Indigenous inhabitants of Australia, and today they are most commonly referred to as the Aboriginals and the Torres Strait Islanders. They are not lumped under one title, as these are two very different groups of people with different ancestry and different histories. They can, however, all be labelled as Indigenous Australians today.

As the islanders spread across the Torres Strait and the Aboriginals found homes in every possible nook of Australia, including its surrounding islands like Tasmania, they started to splinter into unique groups and tribes. The tongues they spoke started to change too. In Australia, prior to colonisation there were thought to be hundreds of Aboriginal languages thriving across the continent. Many of these languages even had smaller dialect forms too. A majority of these languages belong to the large Pama-Nyungan language family. This huge family has its origins with the hypothetical Proto-Pama-Nyungan language which arrived with the Aboriginals, before planting its roots in the majority of the land and spinning off into many different languages. The name of this language family derives from the word for man in its two key branches. The Pama branch uses that word of *pama* for "man," and, unsurprisingly, the languages of the Nyungan branch use that word.

Pama-Nyungan languages include the likes of Mangarla, spoken by the Mangarla people in Western Australia, Turrbal spoken by the Turrbal people of Queensland, and Warumungu spoken by the Warumungu people in the Northern Territory. That's just three of the many Pama-Nyungan tongues found in the nation. Non-Pama-Nyungan languages are found in Australia too. The majority of which are found in the far north, such as the Nyulnyulan languages, the Wagiman Languages, and even some isolated languages which belong to no wider family. A notable language isolate in Australia is Tiwi, spoken on the Tiwi islands off the northern coast of Australia. Languages are not as abundant on the Torres Strait Islands, there are three key tongues native there. The language of Kala Lagaw Ya belongs to the Pama-Nyungan family. Meanwhile, Meriam Mir belongs to the Trans-Fly languages, which have their origin in the island of New Guinea, which makes sense as these islands are neatly nestled between Australia and New Guinea. The third is a creole that came around much later. It's based on English and is simply called Torres Strait Creole, or natively *Yumplatok*.

Australia's extreme isolation from the wider world in the past allowed these many languages to thrive and follow their own path, making them some of the most unique tongues on the planet. The Land Down Under wouldn't be left to its own devices forever. The urge for more land, resources, and power grew in Europe, resulting in sailors and explorers travelling to the farthest corners of the earth in their quests for global domination. Australia was first discovered by Europeans in 1606. By this point, the Indigenous people of the land had been there for tens of thousands of years and their languages had spread across the continent. It was the Dutch who took the crown of first Europeans to land in the country, specifically the sea captain of Willem Janszoon. Yet, despite this, they didn't do all that much with the land. They never settled it nor colonised it in any way. That first landing in 1606 saw the deaths of Janszoon's men when they explored. This seemingly put them off claiming Australia in any meaningful way. The biggest impact the Dutch had in Australia was in giving it its first name. *Nieuw-Holland* simply translates into New Holland. This is the oldest known name we have for the land as a whole as, while the Indigenous peoples had names for their respective parts of the country, they didn't really use a collective name for it.

This name didn't stick around, but the name the nation has today actually predates the European notion of the nation itself. The name Australia derives from the concept of *Terra Australis*, which means Southern Land in Latin. This was originally the name of a hypothetical landmass in the Southern Hemisphere dating back to the ancient past. The belief was that, if there was a large mass of land in the north of the globe, then surely the same would apply for the bottom of the earth. When Australia came to wider knowledge in Europe, this name was applied to it. It was chiefly the British who really got the ball rolling on the name Australia. For the rest of the seventeenth century, the Dutch left Australia relatively untouched. The British and French, meanwhile, often ventured down there to explore the land and figure out its potential for their grand schemes. It wasn't until the late eighteenth century that European settlement truly began, and it was the British that planted their flag first. This was partly done out of fear the French would claim the land, but Britain also realised that Australia might be the solution to a problem they were facing back home.

It's become something of a joke at this point, the notion that Australia is a nation founded on convicts and criminals, and that, to the British, the nation was little more than a dumping group for its most dangerous citizens. While that is partially the reason why English became the dominant tongue in the land, there is, of course, a lot more to it. It was also in the late eighteenth century that the Industrial Revolution burst into Britain. The old ways of working were fading away and fierce steam powered machines took their place. Work which was once spread across the nation became centred on major cities like London, Manchester, and Birmingham. This drove those who lived in rural Britain to the cities as their old way of life came to a crashing halt. As machines had taken so many jobs, it meant that there wasn't enough work to go around for everybody. Many of those who now found themselves away from their pastoral homeland, living in the smoke billowing cities, struggled to live without work, and turned to petty crimes.

The UK was unnecessarily tough on these people committing relatively minor offences for means of survival and their prisons quickly filled up. Despite overflowing prisons, the UK didn't let up in their conquest to punish those simply trying to get by. It was here that they realised that there was land unclaimed by Europeans in the Southern Hemisphere which they could utilise as a solution to their prison problem. These petty criminals started being shipped down under, even for things as minimal as stealing a loaf of bread. It was these people, the new struggling lower class of the UK who had been replaced by contraptions of the Industrial Revolution, unable to work and who turned to petty crime, which made up the majority of Australia's initial English-speaking peoples. It wasn't Britain's worst and most deadly criminals, as the stereotype persists.

The first fleet of British convicts arrived in 1788 in Botany Bay in the land's south. This quickly led to the founding of Sydney as Australia's first European permanent settlement. When those first settlers arrived off the boats, they were transported to a land which was literally and metaphorically the complete opposite of Britain. The months in which they usually expected a harsh cold winter were replaced with a scorching summer, the cows and chickens of Britain's fields were replaced with kangaroos and emus, and the rolling green hills and countryside of home were replaced with huge empty swaths of land which would range from jungle to desert. These convicts came from all across the island of Britain, from the tip of Scotland to the heart of London.

Britain is well-known for having a huge variety of dialects and accents across its shores, you can travel a few miles on the island and find yourself surrounded by people speaking in a completely different way. Around this time in Britain, most residents stuck to their own patch of the country and didn't integrate or interact that much with others. This changed down under. Australia brought people from across Britain together and the land quickly became a melting pot of British dialects and accents. Cockneys would have lived alongside Glaswegians, Scousers would work in tandem with Janners, and Geordies would break bread with Cardiffians. This level of intermixing between British dialects didn't really take place in such a concentrated manner in Britain. These people, forced to live alongside one another on the other side of the world, were brought together. All these people would have spoken English, but the versions of English they spoke could greatly differ. To make communication efficient, they would have compromised bits of their speech so they could make sense of one another. Likewise, over the generations, their accents would have merged together too. This huge mixture of British accents and dialects came together and birthed Australian English as well as the Australian accent. When this accent first emerged, some decades after British colonisation of the land, it was deemed by linguists of the time to be English in its purest form, a version of the tongue free from any kind of accent or regional dialect. The irony in all of this is that today the Australian accent is one of the most unique, recognisable, beloved, and poorly imitated on the planet.

Obviously, these convicts didn't appreciate the fact they were making linguistic breakthroughs in those early days of Australian settlement. Life was incredibly tough for them and made tougher by the fact that they were there for punishment. While these first convict settlers would end up having their own homes unlike the cells back home, the majority of them were sent to work manual labour jobs, like gathering wood and mining. All made harder by the sun, storms, and spiders of Australia. Amongst these convicts and settlers were the Aboriginal people, trying to live their lives as they had done for thousands of years. They camped on the outskirts of the freshly minted town of Sydney, some even became locals in the town and partook in trade there. This peace would, unfortunately, not last forever as the British claimed more territory in the land. This resulted in the displacement, imprisonment, and death of countless Aboriginals and Torres Strait Islanders. These actions have ramifications on Australia's Indigenous people to this day, as many still find themselves sidelined from the wider nation, in a similar manner to the Indigenous populations of other parts of the world European powers claimed as their own.

This land would not stay under European power forever. Australia gained independence from the British in 1901. By this point, English was firmly the dominant tongue in the land and the number of Indigenous people and languages had drastically fallen. Today around 3 percent of the entire nation's population are Indigenous. While there are still hundreds of Indigenous languages, most of them have incredibly small speaking populations. The three most spoken are called Warlpiri, Murrinh-patha, and Tiwi, which each only have around 1,000–3,000 speakers each. The speaking population of other Indigenous languages range from a few hundred to a mere handful.

While Indigenous tongues shrink, Australian English continues to grow and evolve its own unique identity. As well as the Australian accent and the unique tone it has given English, many words and phrases have become commonplace in this down under form of English that aren't really heard anywhere else. Many of these have become staples of the Australian identity. Terms like "struth," "bonza," "drongo," and "ripper" are deeply Australian. These entered the Australian lexicon in various ways. "Struth," for example, came into being as a phonetic spelling of someone saying "it's truth" with an Australian accent. This is a word that could only come into being thanks to the accent formed in the land. "Drongo," which is used to call someone an idiot, has its origins in the name of a species of bird which can be found all across the world. The reason it has stuck as an insult in Australia is down to the fact that a racehorse in the country carried this name in the 1920s. The horse Drongo was supposedly one of the best for their time, but when they failed to win many races, they were deemed a bit of an idiot horse, with this horse's name of Drongo going on to be used for idiots as a whole. The origins of "bonza" and "ripper" are a tad more disputed but they are seen as equally Australian to the masses.

When Australian English isn't making up whole new words, they are shortening them. A defining feature of Australian English is its love of shortening words and ending them with an EE sound. A tin has become a "tinnie," a swimming costume has become a "cossie," and a barbeque has become a "barbie." Many words of Aboriginal roots have found themselves used in not only Australian English but in other variations of English too. In most of these cases, they relate to the natural world, things the Indigenous people knew about and had named for centuries, which the English speakers adopted when they arrived. Terms like "dingo" and "koala," names for some of the nation's most famous creatures, come from the Dharug language. Billabong, meanwhile, comes from the Wiradjuri language and is used as the name for a body of water also known as an oxbow lake.

English's arrival in Australia is equal parts heartbreaking and astonishing. Heartbreaking down to the devastating impact it had on the Aboriginal and Torres Strait Islanders, destroying much of their way of life. Astonishing down to the simple fact of how far away from English's homeland the language has planted its roots. While the world is now more connected than ever, Australia is still an incredibly long way from Britain. A nonstop flight from London to Perth still takes more than a staggering sixteen hours. If one is to make this voyage, whether that be in the luxury of a plane or via a ship like it was done by those first settlers, you will be greeted on the other side to a place vastly different. Though it is connected by a common tongue, the British colonisation of Australia saw English travel farther than it ever had done, but the Age of Colonisation wasn't quite wrapped up yet. Across the Tasman Sea, another chain of islands could be found, ones that, like Australia, had flourished with their own identity for many years. It was this land that would go on to be the last major European claim during this period of world altering history.

OFF THE MAP

ENGLISH IN NEW ZEALAND

New Zealand is widely believed to be the last major landmass on Earth to be settled by humans. For so long, the islands that make up this nation would have been left off of maps charted by other parts of the world. In fact, even to this day, map makers have a reputation of forgetting to include New Zealand, a phenomenon that has become something of a recurring joke in the nation which many Kiwis today take on the chin. The first people to step foot on this land and chart it in some way happened around 750 years ago. While that might seem like a pretty long time ago, that's nothing in the grand scheme. For context, by the time New Zealand was first settled by humans, Western Rome had already been and gone, spreading Latin across Europe, the Norsemen had started to find a new home for their tongue in Iceland, the ancestors of modern Hungarian and Turkish speakers had migrated across Asia to Europe, and Europe as a whole was on the cusp of realising the potential of the New World. The short time that New Zealand went from being uninhabited to one of the most developed countries on the planet is nothing short of remarkable. What's perhaps more remarkable is the fact that, if you take the roughly twenty-four-hour flight from London to Wellington, you will be hearing pretty much the exact same language being spoken when you arrive that you heard when you departed. In 750 short years New Zealand has blossomed into one of the most known of English-speaking nations. Yet, it wasn't English speakers who landed on its shores more than seven centuries ago—that language would get there a tad later down the line.

Who, instead, first called these islands home were the Māori, a Polynesian people who still make up a large portion of the New Zealand population to this day. When they first made a landing here, they did not have this name—they didn't really have a collective name at all. To themselves, they were just ordinary people. This is why they referred to themselves as Māori when they came into contact with the outside world, as the word simply means "ordinary" in their language. How they arrived in this land is a story of migration just as wondrous as the many covered in this book so far. The Māoris travelled in canoe-like boats known as *waka* which were simply paddled with oars, no wind-based sails or motors here. They didn't, seemingly, stumble upon New Zealand by accident. The Māori reached this land as part of a planned navigation to find new lands in the Pacific Ocean. They navigated the sea by using the stars in the sky as well as the currents of the ocean, which is blisteringly incredible for such primitive boats.

This migration leans into mythology. As the story goes, the legendary Polynesian explorer Kupe was the first person to discover New Zealand, and he supposedly came from the island of Hawaiki. This is the part of the story that bewilders people the most. A modern map of Polynesia shows us no island by this name and no one has ever been able to truly pinpoint what island Hawaiki may actually be. One of the leading theories is that it's Raiatea, an island which makes up part of French Polynesia close to Tahiti. This is only a theory, maybe Hawaiki vanished from the seas once Kupe and his people left. Whatever the truth of Hawaiki is, this is the go-to legend for how the Māori arrived on the islands, though retellings of it vary from tribe to tribe.

The language the Māori speak is also simply called Māori, also known as *te reo Māori* in the language. It is a part of the Polynesian branch of the Austronesian language family with one of its closest relatives being the Tahitian language spoken in Tahiti. This could partially explain to us why it's thought that the true Hawaiki is the island of Raiatea, as it is close to Tahiti and Tahitian speakers. Kupe and his people were, of course, talking prior to their arrival in New Zealand. It's not like they were mute until the moment their feet touched the shores. Yet, the language they were speaking 750 years ago wasn't quite the same Māori language we know today. It would have been some kind of Proto-Māori language we don't know all too much about. What we can be surer of is that this Proto-Māori carried on evolving and shifted into the Māori language we know today as its speakers migrated across the islands we now call New Zealand.

The Māori would not only migrate around the two main islands that make up modern New Zealand but also the farther afield. Roughly 200 years after they first arrived in New Zealand, a small group of them set sail. They found a small cluster of uninhabited islands over 400 miles away from New Zealand's South Island, which are now known as the Chatham Islands. These Māori lived in such isolation and changed so much from those in New Zealand at the time that they became their own group of people, the Moriori. Not only did they change, but their language did too. The Māori they spoke evolved and became its own unique Moriori language.

They were able to live peaceful lives on these islands at the edge of the earth for some time; yet, unfortunately, that changed in 1835. In this year, members of two Māori tribes descended onto the islands, killing a huge amount of the Moriori people and enslaving the rest of them. As subjects to the Māori, the Moriori were banned from celebrating their own culture, including using their language. This horrific chapter in history is known as the Moriori Genocide and it's one of the darker tales in New Zealand's history. The Moriori never fully recovered from this genocide. Today, there are thought to be just around 1,000 Moriori people alive, their unique language is all but dead. It has just about been saved by a small group of people trying to revive the language. These actions by the Māori may seem out of character with the image they have today, but at the time this genocide was carried out, the Māori were in a vastly different living situation then they had been for the centuries prior. As, by the time of this event, the English had reached their home and so had their language.

The English were not the first Europeans to come across New Zealand, that name alone should make it abundantly clear. There's nowhere in the English-speaking world named Zealand for these islands to be the "new" version of. The Netherlands, on the other hand, is home to the region of Zeeland which makes things a tad clearer in regard to which Europeans found the islands first. In December of 1642, the Dutch explorer Abel Tasman sighted the islands while exploring this little-known nook of the world at that time. His visit was brief and not all too eventful. He and his crew left the following month after a brief encounter with the Māori which saw four of his team killed. While not the most eventful of encounters, this was a key moment in the history of New Zealand, as it had finally been discovered by the wider world. In turn, it received that name from the Dutch Tasman in ode to the region back home it reminded him of.

While he was Dutch, the Netherlands seemed to have little interest in doing anything with New Zealand or claiming the land as their own. As the years went by, after this first encounter, the islands grew a reputation for themselves of being a wild place filled with savage people; obviously, the Māori are not mindless savages. At this time, they were simply panicked people as invaders, who looked nothing like them, appeared in huge vessels unlike anything they had seen before. With one of these alien vessels appearing in October 1769. It was called HMS *Endeavour* and on board was the British explorer Jame Cook, part way through the first of his three world voyages. The Dutch may not have seen all that much potential in New Zealand, but Cook certainly did. Cook is seen by many as a legendary explorer who helped shape the modern world, but in the same way we now view Columbus' legacy, the reality is far from that simple. Across his various expeditions, Cook and his crew sacked, raped, and killed many Indigenous peoples in the lands he "discovered." Most of his activity was done in the name of the British Empire, to expand their land and their resources. What he saw in New Zealand was a land rich in goods that could grow the empire. He kept a record of his time in New Zealand and shared it back in the UK. This attracted the attention of whalers and traders as well as missionaries who thought it was more land to spread Christianity through. The floodgates opened and New Zealand was now open to the wider world whether it wanted to be or not.

Although their first contact with Europeans ended in the death of some of Tasman's crew, further interactions between the Māori and Europeans went smoothly most of the time. Yet, unfortunately, many Europeans who found their way there were more than happy to harass and even kill Māori who stood in their way. This tragic tale that persists through the Age of Colonisation repeated here yet again. The European advancement in New Zealand culminated on the twenty-second of January 1840. It was on this day that the Treaty of Waitangi was signed, which made New Zealand officially part of the British Empire. This treaty proved controversial, however, with one of the main issues about it revolving around language. The Māori version of the treaty claimed that they would still have possession of the land while the English version claimed that it belonged to the empire outright. This led to an explosion of violence between the British and the Māori and, while the Māori outnumbered the colonisers, they struggled deeply against the more brutal weaponry of the British. This culminated with the British cementing their place in this land with the founding of Wellington, the first permanent English-speaking settlement in the land which would, of course, grow to become the nation's capital. The British didn't stop in Wellington, and from here they founded more towns and cities across the islands. As the British expanded their settlements, the influences of English grew in conjunction with the dwindling Māori population who were either cast aside or unfairly killed. Before too long, Māori was no longer the dominant tongue of New Zealand, instead replaced with English.

By now, this is a story we are all too familiar with, a tactic which the British first used in Ireland and proved effective for them centuries later. For those on the opposing side, it heartbreakingly ended the same way, in most cases. The systematic destruction of their old way of life and the people who once controlled the land finding themselves as outsiders in their own homes. This domination over Indigenous peoples resulted in English not just being the dominant tongue of New Zealand, but in many parts of the globe the empire stuck their fingers in. These events from centuries gone by proved instrumental in defining us and the world we live in today. Of course, the world is not a one for one duplicate of how it was in the nineteenth century. A key change for New Zealand is that, like many other former British colonies, it too found independence years down the line. By the time New Zealand was in control of its own fate, English had been cemented as the key lingo. The tongue had also evolved into its own unique dialect by this point too.

The main reason this change occurred in the language was due to the variety of English people who came to the land. In similar events as to what happened in Australia, British English speakers from all across the UK found themselves in this land. Intermixing and forming what we now call New Zealand English. There's a variety of words used in New Zealand English that wouldn't really be found in British English. A key influence on this Kiwi lingo is the variety of English spoken in Australia. These two nations have a long-shared history with one another, with migration between the two common. Terms like "dairy" for a small local shop, "togs" for swimwear, "pants" instead of trousers, and phrases like "sweet" for something that's good or "yea nah" for no and "nah yeah" for yes are all shared between the two lands.

New Zealand English is at its most unique through its integration with many words from the language of those who first called this land home. Ample damage has been done to the Māori people since the dawn of European colonisation of New Zealand. Thankfully, now things are starting to become more rectified in the land and the voices of the Māori are louder than ever. This voice is heard in quite a literal way too, with the abundance of Māori words that are now regularly used in New Zealand English. One of the most recognisable is the phrase *kia ora* which is simply Māori for "hello." There's also the term *pakeha*, word for a New Zealander of non-Māori, usually European, origin. On top of this, many native animals in the land have maintained their Māori names. Like the tūī bird and the kiwi, which has become a symbol for the nation as well as a demonym for the people of the land. Though, perhaps the most important word of Māori is the one still fighting for recognition. This land was only dubbed New Zealand in the seventeenth century and the Māori had been there way before that. They, of course, named the land they called home, dubbing it *Aotearoa*, meaning the land of the long white cloud. And it is not only the nation as a whole which has a Māori name, as the two main islands do too. *Te Ika-a-Māui* and *Te Wāipounamu* are the Māori names for the North and South Island, respectively. These are names that many in New Zealand, Māori and pakeha alike, argue the country should be officially known as. It would be a move that would help New Zealand identify more with its native history than its colonial past. But at the time of writing, this country is still firmly called New Zealand.

The Māori voice today can not only be heard but seen too. For the longest time, Māori was purely an oral language with no written form. While oral storytelling is still a huge tradition amongst the Māori, the language was eventually put to paper. In the nineteenth century, Europeans settlers helped adapt the language into a written form with the use of the Latin alphabet. This was to help ease communication between the peoples during these early days of New Zealand colonisation. It may seem sad to some to know that languages as far removed from each other as Latin and Māori share a script, but efforts have been made to change this. A unique Māori alphabet has been created and its use has been proposed. It features beautiful, curved characters which heavily feature the swirling patterns linked so deeply with these people.

The story of the Māori receiving more recognition in their homeland in modern times is thankfully reflected in other parts of the world that had immigrant tongues placed on them during the Age of Colonisation. In many former colonial countries, the voices of the Indigenous peoples are becoming louder and more listened to. It has taken centuries to undo so much of the damage that colonisation did to the ancestors of these people. Hopefully, today the speakers of both immigrant tongues and native tongues can coexist, speak, and listen.

In many ways, the European settlement of New Zealand is seen as the final large event during the Age of Colonisation. With the land fully chartered, the world map was more or less complete. The end of this period of history, however, didn't mean languages and people were going to stay put. While Earth was mostly uncovered, it was far from completely claimed by European powers. In fact, by the late eighteenth century, many former European colonies had found their freedom. This led to the next stage in the mass migration of tongues and people. A period of time which would cement the world in shape and its languages as we know them today.

PART III

NEW IMPERIALISM & BEYOND

NINETEENTH CENTURY TO NOW

THE OTHER LAND OF THE RISING SUN

JAPANESE IN PALAU

New Imperialism, in layman's terms, was the successor to the Age of Colonisation. It's a time period linked with the late nineteenth and early twentieth century, but by the dawn of the nineteenth century we can spot some of the foundations of this time period. A defining feature of this era is the emergence of both new and returning global powers claiming land already identified but not under any kind of foreign rule. These new powers chiefly included the USA, a few decades post-independence and on their way to becoming the world's next superpower. Yet, another country also started to see its power rise.

While Europe had been claiming land and in turn losing that land, Japan had been bubbling away, going through its historic periods such as the Jōmon, Asuka, and Muromachi Periods. By the early eighteenth century, it was in the midst of its Edo Period, where the land was ruled by the Tokugawa Shogunate, a military centric government founded by Shogun Tokugawa Ieyasu. This Asian island nation had decided to follow its own path and develop somewhat independently. Isolationism has been a core belief in Japanese culture for periods of its history. An over-200-year time period dubbed Sakoku literally forced Japan to be isolated from the wider world from 1603 until 1868. This isolation had many drawbacks but allowed Japan's unique culture to flourish into what it is today. It was also far from concrete, seemingly, as people from outside the nation did venture into the Land of the Rising Sun. Likewise, some native to the country explored the seas around them, bringing their customs and language along for the journey.

Language is another thing that thrived during Japan's isolation. The Japanese tongue does not belong to any of the major families we have covered thus far but is instead the principal language of the Japonic language family. Other languages of this family include the various Ryukyuan languages spoken on the nation's Ryukyuan Islands to its south. The ultimate origins of this language are hard to deduce. A leading theory is that this language arrived on the islands of Japan in the fourth century BC, coming from people who migrated from the Korean Peninsula. Despite this, the language is not related to Korean, which too is in its own Korenic language family. The two tongues have something in common, a logographic writing system that has its ultimate origins in China. These different languages call these symbols different things. Japanese calls them Kanji, Korean calls them Hanja, and in Chinese they are called Hanzi.

On the islands of Japan, the language evolved throughout the centuries. It started simply as Proto-Japanese before evolving into Old Japanese and Middle Japanese. By the early nineteenth century, it was in its Early Modern Period and on its way to becoming the tongue we all know now. Around the world today, there are around 123 million speakers of Japanese. This makes it the eighth most widely spoken native language. Yet, the vast majority of those Japanese speakers make up the population of Japan unto itself. While it is spoken by a huge number of people, the tongue hasn't travelled all that far. There are, of course, pockets of Japanese speakers across the globe in smaller communities, there's only one nation that recognises the language in any official capacity. That country isn't even Japan itself, as the language has never needed official status there. Instead, Japanese became an official language in the tiny Pacific Island nation of Palau. This came into being thanks to the Japanese finally breaking free of isolation in its own homeland and planting itself in new areas, like European tongues before them had. An added bonus about Palau is the fact that it lies within the same time zone as Japan itself. Meaning that, not only is Japanese an official tongue here, but it is also *technically* the Land of the Rising Sun too.

Not many people know this fact about Palau being the only country that has Japanese as an official language, because not many people know about Palau full stop. The country isn't the most renowned on the world stage, it doesn't have the loudest voice in the UN, and it hasn't even won an Olympic medal. It's hard to even pinpoint on a world map down to the fact it is so incredibly small. For those still struggling to locate the nation, it lies around 2,000 miles south of Japan. It's composed of over 300 islands but has a humble population of just over 18,000. It's thought to have first found a human population well over 4,000 years ago. People who are thought to have lived in modern Indonesia made their way to the islands in 2500 BC. Here, they developed their own way of life and their own tongue. Palauan, the Indigenous language of this country, falls into the Austronesian family of languages, and is more specifically part of the Malayo-Polynesian branch. This makes it a relative of languages like Indonesian, Samoan, and Māori, albeit a fairly distant cousin. The people of Palau were widely left to their own devices until the eighteenth century, when those in Europe found their way to this part of the world. The British are seen as the first Europeans to land on the island when captain Henry Wilson and his crew found themselves shipwrecked here in 1783. In an unexpected twist, the British didn't actually claim it as a colony but instead set up trade deals with the locals.

Japan's relationship with Palau, meanwhile, came into being roughly forty years after the British found themselves stuck here. Funnily enough, the stories are somewhat similar. The Japanese discovery of Palau is too a result of a ship journey not going to plan. In December of 1820, a ship called the *Jinja Maru* captained by Shokichi, along with his small crew of eleven, set sail from the Iwate prefecture in north central Japan. The planned destination was the city of Edo, a city that would later down the line become the nation's new capital, Tokyo.

It was meant to be a relatively straightforward journey, but a strong unexpected wind blew them completely off course. Without the Japanese coast or any other land in sight, the *Jinja Maru* traversed the expanse of the Pacific in the hopes that they could find some sort of land. Land would finally come into view in February 1821. The crew of the *Jinja Maru* found themselves on the island of Palau.

It seems the Japanese were treated kindly here, as Shokichi and his crew would eventually stay in Palau for four years. This event over 200 years ago is seen as the true start of relations between the nations. Though, once again, like the British, the Japanese didn't take claim over these islands. It's quite remarkable how long Palau went without having another nation claim it as their own. Many other parts of the wider world were being swept up by the likes of Britain and France in this period. Palau was more or less free to do its own thing while making friends and dealing with the likes of Britain and Japan. It was only in 1885 that Spain decided to assert that the islands were theirs and seemingly got their wish. Yet even Spain didn't have claim to Palau for all that long, as just a few years later in 1899 they sold it off to Germany who were finally on their way to building their own empire.

Germany's plans were going smoothly until a certain war came up, the Great War. We have come across wars many times across these migrations and, while each and every one is tragic, none harmed the entire globe quite like this First World War. We don't know the total amount of lives lost, but the estimate is somewhere between fifteen to twenty-two million people. While much of the war focus was on Europe, fighting took place across the planet, and in the Pacific, fighting broke out between Germany and Japan, who were on the side of the Allied Powers along with the UK, France, and USA. During this bloodshed, Palau's old friends of the Japanese would seize these islands from German rule, and, in 1920, they were formally put under the rule of Japan by the League of Nations along with many other nearby small islands which were formally under German rule. Germany lost a huge amount of its holdings as a result of losing this war. Collectively, under Japanese rule, it was known as the South Seas Mandate.

While Japanese contact and influence in Palau had its origins in 1821 when the *Jinja Maru* went adrift, it was here that the language really started to sink its teeth into the islands. Many Japanese people found their way to Palau to set up shop. They lived and worked amongst the natives in the land. Despite Japan and Palau having a long-standing relationship with one another, things were not always harmonious. In the same way European power squashed the liberties of Indigenous peoples in the Americas and Pacific, this Japanese rule in Palau led to great damage to the local culture of Palau. People from Japan, as well as subjects of Japan's empire which they had built up by this point, descended onto the islands. Eventually, expats greatly outnumbered the native Palauan people. Over 20,000 Japanese people found themselves in Palau.

This would have entrenched Japanese as a key language of the nation, but, as quickly the Japanese appeared on the island, they disappeared. The upheaval of Japanese culture came about due to the Second World War. This is the only war on our planet that has topped the first in regard to lives lost and damage caused. The ramifications of the Second World War in many ways set in motion the world we live in today. This war wasn't a repeat of the first in regard to who was on which side. This time around, Germany and Japan fought side by side as part of the Axis Powers. Once again, Palau saw itself as an unexpected epicentre of this conflict. The Battle of Peleliu took place on these islands, starting on the fifteenth of September 1944. Fought between Japan and the US, it is seen as one of the bloodiest battles in this war. The US would go on to be victorious here and in the wider war, along with the Allied Powers, yet again. Aside from the Battle of Peleliu, Palau saw tremendous industrial and economic damage during the Second World War while under Japanese control. So much so that, in defeat, Japan lost many of their claims across the globe, like Germany did in the previous war. The country came under US control and many of the Japanese who lived on the islands found themselves going back to Japan. This allowed the Indigenous Palauan people to become the dominant group in the nation yet again. By the 1980s, Palau gained its own independence, refusing to join other nearby islands to form the one large nation of Micronesia.

The Japanese did not completely abandon the islands, however. By the '80s, when Palau found its independence, many Japanese people and their descendants still held positions of power there. This is what led to the Japanese language receiving official status in the nation. Many of Palau's islands are their own states. With one of the nation's more southern islands, Angaur, being one of those states. In 1982, they wrote into their constitution that the official languages of this state were to be the native Palauan tongue, English, and Japanese. This comes down to the fact that it was Japanese speakers in Palau making many of these rules. Japanese still has official status here to this day. This is how the state/island of Angaur in Palau became the only place in the world where Japanese is an official language. Though, a relatively small number of people actually use Japanese as their go-to language in Palau in this day and age.

Today in Palau, the most widely spoken languages are their native tongue of Palauan as well as English. English became a dominant tongue while the nation was under US control post the Second World War. Palau English is even its own unique form of the language. Words of Japanese origins, however, can be found commonly used amongst the people of Palau. Terms like *daijobu*, meaning "OK" or "alright," and *denki*, meaning "electrical," are shared between Japanese and Palauan. In modern times, Japan and Palau seemingly have a happy relationship together. It's a popular spot amongst Japanese tourists for holidays and a bridge which connects two of Palau's islands is dubbed the Japan-Palau Friendship bridge to signify the ties these nations have. In 2021, the two nations had a collective celebration of their 200 years of friendship, as it had been 200 years since the *Jinja Maru* ran adrift and connected these two islands together. This ship ultimately led to one of the world's most spoken languages having a small outpost in a relatively isolated and unheard-of corner of the globe. What this all shows us is that, across the nineteenth century, New Imperialism started to shape the world in new ways, and that planet Earth was far more than just Europe's plaything.

IMMIGRANT HANDS

SIGN LANGUAGE IN THE USA

Sign languages are a unique branch of linguistics where spoken words are replaced by hand movements and facial expressions, usually to aid those hard of hearing. In many cases, sign languages have gone on their own journeys too, finding homes in new places and evolving along the way. This is perhaps best seen in the sign language used in the United States. As the USA uses English as its go-to tongue, it would be easy to presume that the sign language here is akin to the sign language used in other English-speaking parts of the world, like the UK or Australia. It's here that your presumption would be wrong.

One thing the two most popular versions of sign language have in common is the fact they are indeed fully formed languages. They are far from simple tools that allow you to translate English into a different form. Sign languages have their own unique grammars and rules in the same way spoken languages do. Where they differ is in how they are communicated. The dominant sign language of the United States is called American Sign Language, ASL for short. Here in the UK, it's British Sign Language, BSL for short. The defining area in which they differ are the number of hands used in each. Fingerspelling is a part of sign languages that allows users to spell out specific words. Each letter has its own gesture. The finger spelling of the letter A in ASL simply requires you to hold your hand up in a fist and this is because all fingerspelling in ASL requires just one hand. BSL meanwhile uses two hands for finger spelling. This can be seen with their version of A which sees the index finger of one of your hands touching the thumb of your other hand. Words have completely different gestures too. To say you are hungry in ASL, the hand takes a C like shape and is dropped down your abdomen. In BSL it's the simple act of rubbing your stomach which tells people you are ready to eat. A sign that is also pretty universal.

BSL is very much a homegrown concoction. Its origins are incredibly murky. It's very likely that people on the island of Britain have been using simple hand gestures for centuries as a means of communication. Especially considering the huge linguistic upheaval the land has faced over the years. Going from Celtic-speaking to Latin-speaking to Germanic-speaking to Norman-speaking before English finally settled and morphed into what it is today in Britain. Our earliest evidence of a more organised sign language being used in Britain dates to 1576. A wedding record from this year in Leicester details that a ceremony was partially performed in sign language in aid of the Deaf groom. Signs would carry on being used in Britain, but they were not formally recognised as a language until the nineteenth century. This recognition came at a cost. Many higher-ups in the education of children, especially Deaf children, deemed sign language to be inferior to lip reading. This resulted in the teaching of the language being heavily downplayed. Thankfully, it was not outright banned and small pockets of people carried on using it. BSL would stay out of vogue until the 1970s, with the formation of the British Deaf Association and their promotion of it. It was only in the year 2003 that the UK government finally recognised BSL as an official language of the nation.

Despite its ups and downs, BSL is very much a product of Britain. The sign language of the States, however, does not originate on American soil, but neither is it an export of the UK. As the USA likes to pride itself as a nation made of migrants, it only makes sense that their sign language is something of an immigrant too. ASL is not the offspring of BSL nor any kind of English sign language. It is instead the product of France's sign language. Sign language in France is recorded as far back as the seventeenth century, and since then it has flourished in its own unique way. By the dawn of the nineteenth century, it had morphed into a kind of sign language different to the one found across the channel. It would be at this time that French Sign Language would travel across the pond in large part due to one man and a young girl he met by happenstance.

American Thomas Hopkins Gallaudet was spending time with his family in Connecticut in 1814. While checking on his younger siblings, he realised that there was another child out there his brother and sister weren't playing with. He checked on this young girl to ask why she wasn't joining in the fun only to find no response; the young girl was Deaf. Gallaudet was a curious man and always ready to learn and engage with others. Prior to this fateful encounter, he had studied in a variety of fields ranging from law to trade. He eventually found out the young girl was named Alice Cogswell and initial attempts to communicate with her included pointing to his hat and then writing the word hat in the dirt. This tickled Alice immensely and also gained the attention of her father, wealthy Doctor Mason Cogswell. Dr. Cogswell wished for Gallaudet to help his daughter with her communication and had the finances to back it up. Cogswell paid for a trip to Europe for Gallaudet with the aim being he found a suitable means of communication for the Deaf across the Atlantic. Until this point, there hadn't been one universally adopted sign language in the USA. There were some basic signs in pockets of the nation and Indigenous people had been using simple signs for centuries to communicate with tribes and eventually colonisers, but none of them had caught the zeitgeist.

His first port of call was England which makes logical sense. The USA and the UK share a common spoken language, so perhaps their sign language could benefit the US too. While England did have its own sign language, it wasn't accessible to Gallaudet at this time. We know that during the nineteenth century in Britain, BSL was looked down upon in favour of lipreading. With a lack of information in England on their sign language, and those who *did* know about it refusing to lend a hand, Gallaudet felt defeated. Not all hope was lost, thankfully.

In England, Gallaudet met three Frenchmen. Abbe Sicard, the lead at Paris' Royal Institute for the Deaf and Mute, and his two colleagues, Laurent Clerc and Jean Massieu. The French were more on board with signed communication than the English, much to Gallaudet's delight. He went back to France with them to study. Here, Gallaudet came to grips with the basics of French Sign, how the hands and face were used to express words and communicate as easily as spoken phrases. Gallaudet eventually hit a snag in his research. While his financier Mason Cogswell was a wealthy man, the money couldn't last forever. With his funds depleted, Thomas Hopkins Gallaudet caught a ship back to the USA, but he didn't go back home alone. One of the Frenchmen he met in England and studied with in France, Laurent Clerc, came to the US with him. This migration from France to the USA in the early nineteenth century wasn't as seamless as it is now. Travel via ship could take multiple weeks depending on what kind of boat you had. While steamships had come into being, they were still relatively new, so Gallaudet and Clerc might have had to let the wind be their engine. The two new chums didn't just sit around on their voyage back to the Americas. They helped each other out for life in the USA. Gallaudet taught Clerc spoken English and Clerc taught Gallaudet signed French.

By the time they both arrived back in Connecticut, they were ready to teach not just Alice Cogswell who had initiated this quest, but many people in the USA how to sign. The final hurdle was the fact that, while French Sign was good, it wasn't quite perfect for the hands of America. Certain features and gestures had to be altered, which led to the creation of American Sign Language as an adaptation of French Sign Language. The two are very similar to this day, with many of the finger spellings in French being similar if not the same in ASL. In 1817, the two (along with Mason Cogswell) opened the American School for the Deaf to teach kids and adults alike the new sign language. The school is still open to this very day and led to the eventual spread of this sign language across the US, entrenching it as the go-to form of communication amongst the hard of hearing.

Sign languages really have immigrated across the globe just like spoken languages. Another way in which they are like spoken languages is that they are grouped together in related families. ASL is not the only child of French Sign Language. They both belong to the wider Francosign Family with Old French Sign (which evolved into modern French Sign) as the great grandparent of them all. In addition to giving birth to ASL, French Sign was also the inspiration for other sign languages in Europe, like Danish Sign and Italian Sign. These two had offspring unto themselves. Danish sign was the foundation of Norwegian and Icelandic Sign while Italian Sign was the basis of the sign language used in Tunisia. ASL unto itself has gone on to form other versions of sign language too, like being the basis for Nigerian Sign, Bolivian Sign, and Thai Sign. There are even specific dialects of ASL used by groups within the USA, like Black American Sign used amongst the African American community of the USA. BSL, meanwhile, was the impetus of its own language family, which goes by the catchy name of BANZSL. This is an acronym for British, Australian, and New Zealand Sign Language. From that name alone, you should have a good idea as to what sign languages this family contains. It makes sense as to why these signs are related, as all these lands were once a part of the British Empire. In the same way they share a common spoken tongue, it makes sense why their sign languages would relate to one another. South African Sign is also part of this family too, despite not being referenced in its name.

Before the wider introduction and acceptance of sign languages, the world was a place void of language to many Deaf people. A sad fact as, by this time in history, the world was now brimming with tongues in every corner of the earth. From native languages to immigrant tongues. But there was still one spot, in fact a whole continent, which was devoid of tongues of any kind. That would swiftly change during this time of New Imperialism.

PENGUIN WHISPERS

LANGUAGES IN ANTARCTICA

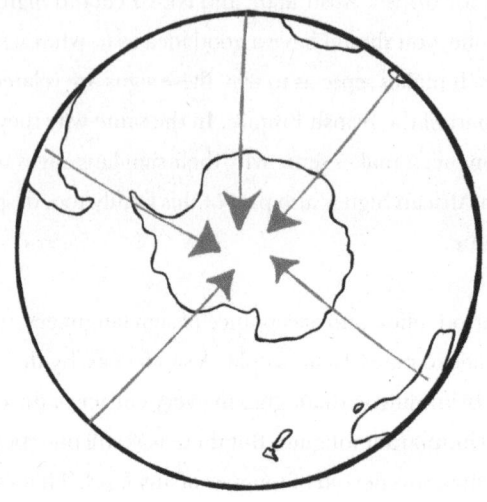

Millions of years ago, flightless birds native to Australia and New Zealand found themselves adrift in the waters of the Southern Ocean. Their lack in flying abilities was more than compensated for in their swimming capabilities. Between their swimming skills and the ocean's currents, these birds found themselves in a new home. A home at the very bottom of the world. The birds evolved into the various penguin species which populate the world's most inhospitable continent, Antarctica. From the mighty emperor penguins to the tiny rock hoppers. The squawking and chirping of these birds were the dominant tongue of this continent for millennia. That all changed in 1821, when American fur trader John Davis claimed to have been the first person to set foot on the continent. This is heavily disputed. Prior to his supposed landing in Antarctica, we had known of its existence. The Ancient Greeks theorised that there must be a huge landmass at the bottom of the earth, and the continent had been sighted multiple times prior to 1821. In the late eighteenth century, James Cook, on one of this many expeditions, crossed the Antarctic Circle. While we don't know if John Davis really was the first person to walk across the Antarctic wasteland, we know for sure he was not the last. In the years after 1821, people from all across the globe made their way to the continent in the name of discovery and research. They, of course, brought their languages along for the journey. Since then, the penguins of the continent have had to share their conversations with a variety of languages.

Antarctica was a blank canvas, meaning it has never had any kind of Indigenous peoples, minus the penguins of course. A lack of native tongue to the land has allowed other languages to (somewhat) thrive on the continent. As the nineteenth century waned on after that supposed first landing by American John Davis, the wider world yearned to plant their flags (both metaphorically and literally) in Antarctica. By this point in human history, all of Earth's major land masses had been opened up to the wider world to varying degrees. Antarctica was the final challenge of sorts. It was more than just an untapped nook of the earth, but an entire continent devoid of human interaction. What lay across the snow-covered plains of Antarctica was a mystery. There was one thing that people knew was definitely lying in wait somewhere in the land—the legendary South Pole, the very bottom of the earth. The race was on to uncover Antarctica and be the first human to reach the South Pole. Whether that be to tap into any potential unknown resources that lay in the land or simply for bragging rights.

In 1839, the British naval officer James Clark Ross made a solid attempt to reach Antarctica's frozen core. His two ships HMS *Erebus* and *Terror* were kitted out in the latest equipment in preparation for conditions few humans had ever encountered. While they ultimately failed in reaching the South Pole, the expedition gathered a huge amount of information on Antarctica. They uncovered things like the kinds of animals and plant life that could survive there. They surveyed a huge amount of the land too, including the largest ice shelf on the continent which has gone on to be named after the man, the Ross Ice Shelf. It was in just 1887 that the name we know for this land first appeared on maps. The name means the opposite Arctic, which is fairly self-explanatory. Toward the end of the nineteenth century and the early twentieth century, more nations sent expeditions down there to uncover more information on the land. Inch by inch, nations like Belgium, Germany, and Japan chipped away at the continent, unravelling more information about the land, which for millennia had been untouched by humans. These tongues were some of the first to be uttered in this wasteland.

In 1910, things really picked up. Finally, with enough knowledge of the land and lessons learned from previous failures, humans were prepared to uncover that fabled South Pole. The first exhibition with eyes set on reaching it departed from Cardiff on the fifteenth of June 1910. The *Terra Nova* was a former whaling ship led by Captain Robert Falcon Scott. Scott had spent most of his life up to this point uncovering the globe for personal satisfaction and to bring pride to his home nation of Great Britain. Being the first man to reach the South Pole in the White Continent was his own personal White Whale. Finding the South Pole would not have only been the jewel in his crown but doing it on behalf of Britain would have given the nation bragging rights on the world stage. Scott was on his way to the bottom of the earth for around two months when he received a message that he was not alone in this quest. On the sixth of September, on a ship named *Fram*, fellow explorer, the Norwegian Roald Amundsen, set sail from Madeira. Amundsen was another seasoned explorer and somewhat a rival to Scott. Upon hearing Scott was planning to reach the South Pole, he felt compelled to beat him to the finish line. The race was on.

The two crews spent months not only sailing to Antarctica but also on the continent itself. They made temporary bases and survived across the extremely harsh winter months. It wouldn't be until the following December in 1911 that one of them would be the victor. After months of meticulous planning as well as organising rations and manpower to not only reach the South Pole but to get back home, it was Roald Amundsen who planted the flag for Norway into this pole first. The crew to reach the pole consisted of five men, four sleds, and fifty-two dogs to power those sleds. Just over a month later, in January 1912, Scott and his crew reached it. They were devastated by the sight of the Norwegian flag. Nevertheless, Scott left the Union Jack alongside the flag of Norway. While Amundsen made it off the continent, Scott and his crew were not so lucky. Unable to escape Antarctica, Robert Falcon Scott and his crew froze to death in the land.

The race between Scott and Amundsen caught the zeitgeist of the time, and suddenly Antarctica was open for business. From a language perspective, this shows us that two of the first major tongues to be spoken in the land were English and Norwegian. Those two languages would go on to find a more permanent home in the continent too. A few years after the race to the pole in 1917, Britain made the first territorial claim on Antarctica. Why Britain wished to have any kind of claim over a harsh uninhabited wasteland is debated. Theories range from the land being in a somewhat strategic location, to the potential of resources under the continent, to the idea they claimed is simply because they could. Britain was at a point in its history when it was one of the world's dominant superpowers. They planted their flag in land like a child places stickers in a sticker album. Britain's claim of land in Antarctica worried other nations. Not too long after Britain, the nations of Argentina, Chile, Norway, and France claimed parts of Antarctica too. Argentina and Chile claimed land, as geographically they are some of the closest countries to Antarctica. Norway claimed land due to their historic ties. France, meanwhile, has been the nation to keep an eye on Britain throughout history, so it's no major surprise to see them there too. This was a period of history where more land equalled more power. With the majority of the world's landmass already claimed by one place or another, Antarctica was one of the few untapped corners of the earth where nations could claim more land for their empires.

As the twentieth century carried on, claims in Antarctica started to get messy. Countries squabbled over who had rights to what in the continent and what exactly they could do with the land. During the Second World War, tensions grew so much that the Nazis actually flew over Antarctica, dropping flags onto the land, claiming it as their own. It was after this war that things finally cooled down with Antarctica, when the Antarctic Treaty was signed. This declared that no one nation could formally claim the land but only have territories there. It also set in stone that Antarctica could only be used for scientific purposes. Meaning no military bases or mining. Today, seven countries have territorial claims in Antarctica. The five previously mentioned—the UK, France, Norway, Chile, and Argentina—as well as Australia and New Zealand. These two tagged along as, like Argentina and Chile, they are relatively close by. As we know, the first residents of Antarctica migrated from these two southern countries thousands of years ago.

From a linguistic perspective, this means that today we can expect to hear four
languages here. The English of the UK, Australia, and New Zealand, the Spanish
of Argentina and Chile, the French of France, and the Norwegian of Norway. In
reality, this is just the tip of the iceberg in regard to language in Antarctica, pun
intended. While these territorial claims do exist, they don't really mean all that
much. What is more concrete in regard to languages spoken in the continent are
the tongues of the research centres in the land. Antarctica can only be used for
scientific reasons and many nations from across the globe have set up shop here
to study the wilds of the land. Around forty different nations have set up around
seventy research centres on the continent. Each station speaks the language of
the nation it represents. These research stations have allowed languages like
Japanese, Korean, Russian, Ukrainian, Italian, and Polish to be spoken here.
This gives Antarctica a surprising amount of linguistic diversity, especially for
a continent that around 100 years ago had no human habitation at all. While
many languages from around the world have made themselves at home here, they
are only spoken by small groups of people. Antarctica's population is small and
not permanent. People spend a chunk of time researching there before heading
somewhere a tad less cold. In the summer months, the population hits a peak of
around 5,000 people, and in the winter, it dwindles to just 1,000 or so.

Of all these languages, one has to reign supreme, and unsurprisingly that title
goes to English. Spanish and Russian, meanwhile, tie in a close second due to
the amount of research stations Russia and Spanish-speaking nations have in
the land. English dominates Antarctica because of the vast amount of English-
speaking research stations out there. Countries such as the UK, the USA,
Australia, and New Zealand all have stations there. English also wins, as it is
the world's lingua franca, so it only makes sense that that title would extend to
Antarctica too. What's perhaps most incredible is that, even in the depths of
Antarctica, English has been able to morph into its own unique form. In the
same way we have American English and Australian English, we also have a
dialect known as Antarctic English. This dialect is nowhere near as fully formed
or unique as other English dialects out there. Nor is it as well researched, though
a dictionary of Antarctic English is available. Antarctic English is ultimately
composed of a collection of slang words and terms coined for things relating to life
down in the deep cold south. Antarctica itself is simply referred to as "The Ice"
in Antarctic English. Picking up rubbish is known as a "fod plod." "Snotsicle"

is the name for frozen snot hanging like a stalactite from your nose. And "good weather" (if good weather can exist in Antarctica) is simply known as "dingle."

This Antarctic vocabulary is often paired with a unique accent which has formed on the continent too. Like Antarctica's form of English, this accent isn't too noticeable. It has been studied minimally and its most noticeable features are longer vowel sounds and the *ou* sound being produced from the front of the mouth rather than the back. It's only really been heard in people who have spent a considerable amount of time down there. It really goes to show that special vocabularies and accents can form and evolve in the most unexpected of places. While Scott of the Antarctic might not have reached the South Pole first, and even met his end in Antarctica, I am sure he may rest somewhat happily knowing that the language of his home country is now widely spoken in its own unique way in the land that has become so deeply linked with him.

TEA LEAF

ENGLISH IN HONG KONG

By the 1840s, Britain's claim in the New World was a thing of the past. The United States of America was its own independent nation following its own path. The loss of this territory would have been a huge blow to the British Empire, but it marched on. An ever-expanding world during the time of New Imperialism gave Britain more opportunities to find new claims. It was in this decade that Britain stopped looking westward and turned their eyes to the East. Britain followed in the footsteps of another European empirical power, albeit a good few centuries later. In the same way that the Portuguese found themselves a small enclave of China in the shape of Macau, the British found themselves ruling in Hong Kong, a small island/region of China near Macau, in 1841. The small region of Hong Kong, while under British rule, quickly morphed into one of largest commercial hubs in eastern Asia and of deep importance to the empire. Modern Hong Kong is still a thriving metropolis. Despite its small size—it's noticeably smaller than

Greater London—it has a population of over seven million. The people of Hong Kong have erected towers and reclaimed land from the sea to fit everyone in.

While no longer under British rule, influence is still seen in the region, especially in regard to language. Modern Hong Kong has English as one of its two official tongues. This means that the vast majority of official paperwork and signage found across the land will be written in English and the language is spoken to varying degrees in the region. In the city's core, English is pretty much guaranteed while toward the outskirts the language isn't as well spoken. The English spoken in Hong Kong today is once again a unique variety of the language known as Hong Kong English. This dialect of English sounds different to tongues like British English or American English. Words like *dim sum* and *siu mei*, which are both names for popular Hong Kong dishes, first arrived in Hong Kong English before becoming popular around the world. Yet, Hong Kong English also features words of neither native nor English origins. Thanks to the city being a vital part of the empire as well as being a port meant all kinds of tongues came and went from the city, making varying impacts on the languages there. The Hindi word of *chit* meaning a "note" has found its way into Hong Kong English via trade with relatively nearby India, as has the Malay word of *godown* meaning a "warehouse." Even a Portuguese word like *amah*, translating to a woman who works as a housekeeper and nanny, can be found in this dialect, most likely via nearby Macau which was under Portuguese rule during the entire time Hong Kong was under British rule.

While English is a co-official language in the land, in reality, only a small number of its citizens have it as their first tongue. Just under 5 percent of all modern Hong Kong residents have it as their native language. The vast majority, instead, speak the other co-official language of the land, Cantonese. The same Cantonese that is spoken natively in Macau. This is the language that would have been spoken here in the centuries prior to British rule. The land area has evidence of human civilisation spanning over 7,000 years. That long string of dynasties which ruled over China in the past all had control over the area. During these times, the area wasn't of any particular importance. Hong Kong's residents of the far past lived simple farming and fishing lives and would have kept mostly to themselves. This idea of keeping to themselves is somewhat reflective of wider China and Asia in the far past. For example, while there was contact between the Romans and China during the age of Rome, they didn't trade too much with each other. China had pretty much everything it could need or want at its own front door, so the desire to barter with outside European powers just wasn't really there. This was also a reason why China and other Asian powers didn't partake in the colonising of the New World like Europe did. Throughout this time, much of Asia just kept to themselves, as they didn't need to seek new lands to extract resources or power from. As we know with Portugal's jaunt in Macau, while China didn't reach out to the rest of the world, the rest of the world came to China.

Over the course of the seventeenth and eighteenth century, many European nations started trading with China for goods like silk and jade, which they simply could not get anywhere else. At this point, China was ruled by the Qing Dynasty, also known as the Great Qing, which encompassed much of modern-day mainland China and is seen by many as the last imperial dynasty of the land. One of the European powers which traded with China was Britain. While China had a myriad of goods Britain could barter for, there was one thing in particular that the island nation craved the most from China. It wasn't any kind of precious mineral or even exquisite silks or spices. Instead, it was a simple leaf that the British got quickly hooked on when dried and boiled.

The British and their tea go hand in hand. A cup of tea, infused with milk with a biscuit on the side, is one of the most definitively British images on the global stage. The plant in which tea leaves emerge from, however, are not native to the isles. China has been drinking a huge array of teas way before the British started sipping the stuff. Tea started spilling out of China around the dawn of the seventeenth century when Dutch traders with a base in what they were dubbing the "East Indies" brought crates of the stuff back to Europe with them. By the middle of the century, it had found its way to Britain. To start with, it was something of a gimmick—coffee was, surprisingly, the hot drink of choice in Britain at the time—but it built up a small fan base. Tea is seen to have hit its stride in Britain specifically in 1662. It was this year that King Charles II married Catherine of Braganza, daughter of the then King of Portugal, John IV. Accustomed to tea back in Portugal, the soon-to-be queen received a chest of leaves from Iberia as a wedding gift. Knowledge of this tea trickled down the nobility of Britain before finding its footing with the masses. From there, tea mania in the UK began and the country knew it had to go directly to the source, China, if it wanted to keep up with demand.

Across the rest of the seventeenth, eighteenth, and early into the nineteenth century, Britain sailed directly to China to secure the leaves that kept their island going. Initially, tea was a high commodity item, only available to the wealthy— this led to tea smugglers sneaking the stuff into Britain! This smuggled tea, along with some tax cuts, allowed the brew to reach the mouths of more people, and finally everyone could drink it. Yet, the taste of tea in more people's mouths meant that Britain would have to buy even more from China. China under the Qing Dynasty had proved tricky to trade with. Britain had nothing to offer them in exchange for their tea. China's masses of fertile land offered them pretty much anything and everything they could wish for. China would only part with their tea for one thing—the same thing they bartered with Portugal for all those years ago: silver. Britain accepted the trade to meet the demand tea had back home. This amassing of tea heavily depleted Britain's own silver reserves. Britain needed some way to recoup their losses. This led the British Empire to do something incredibly devious, even for their standards.

As Britain got hooked on tea, the higher powers in the nation decided that they would get China hooked on something too, with the aim of recouping their losses. Except, what the British introduced to China would be a lot more potent than simple tea. In another part of Britain's sprawling empire at this time, a flower called *papaver somniferum*, which is more commonly referred to as a poppy, grew in abundance. A fluid produced by this flower prior to its full blooming can be processed into an incredibly strong drug, opium. When consumed (usually via smoking the stuff), opium creates a euphoric high which sends the user into an unparalleled relaxation. This is countered, however, with users often becoming quivering pools of their former selves and finding themselves both mentally and physically dependent on the drug to survive. Opium use can cause seizures, comas, and even death. It's a horrifyingly addictive, life destroying drug. It was this drug that Britain decided to trade with China to reclaim their lost silver. Britain really did get a nation hooked on a highly addictive and highly destructive drug simply in the name of profit, it was an empire that showed horrifically little mercy at times. China had no desire to see this drug reach their shores. This led to

Britain itself becoming the smuggler, secretly selling the stuff at the ports of Hong Kong in exchange for masses of silver.

This silver would ping-pong between Great Britain and China as tea and opium flowed into opposing nations. This illegal selling of opium in China via the British had been going on since the eighteenth century and, by 1839, the Qing Dynasty were sick of it. China tried to stop Britain from exporting this plague of a drug into their country that had already ruined so many lives, but Britain refused to back down. This drug smuggling stalemate culminated in war between the two nations, breaking out in 1839. A war now fittingly dubbed the First Opium War, as it was this drug which sparked the battle in the first place. The epicentre of this trade war (turned real war) was the Canton region of China. It's from this region where the language gets its name from, and the islands of Hong Kong and Macau can be found off its coast. Today, the region is more commonly known as Guangdong, a more correct translation of its native name. This part of the world was the theatre of combat for this war, and it was a war which saw Britain come out as the victor. With a victory in battle comes reward. In this case, that reward was the island of Hong Kong. Britain formally claimed Hong Kong from the Qing Dynasty in 1841 in the midst of the First Opium War. This gave Britain land directly in China itself that they could use as they saw fit and trade through without China getting in the way. This would not be the last of their wars. From the name of the First Opium War alone, it should not come as a shock that there was a second one. It took place from 1856 to 1860, with the horrendous drug still at the heart of the matter. China faced yet another defeat. This saw Britain claim even more territory in China, including part of the Kowloon Peninsula on mainland China itself by the island of Hong Kong.

Britain's claiming of Hong Kong gave them unparalleled access to a land which was once supremely closed off to the wider world. The tea leaves they craved so much were now at their fingertips. As the drink went down their throats back in Blighty, their language came tumbling out in Hong Kong. The war had given the English a permanent residence in the land, well, until 2047 anyway. In the same way Portugal handed back Macau, the UK peacefully handed Hong Kong back to China in 1997, after over 150 years of rule. The UK returned Hong Kong back to what was now the Communist People's Republic of China, and it was placed under the same "one country, two systems" policy that Macau saw itself under when it, too, was handed back over. Once again, this system is only in place for fifty years—what happens beyond 2047 is unwritten history at the time of this writing. It's possible that nothing in the special administrative zone will change at all and Hong Kong will carry on functioning in the same way it has been for over 200 years—the length of time that will be applicable at that point anyway. Yet, there's the potential that Hong Kong will become more like the rest of the People's Republic. This could be the final nail in the coffin for that unique, official, dialect of English which grew in the land. A version of English formed in the Far East which has its origins lying in Britain's unquenchable thirst for tea.

Britain's thirst for tea would carry on growing. While Hong Kong gave them something of a footing in the tea industry, what they really needed was more land and the right climate so they could grow the plant themselves. Bypassing China entirely. Evidently, Britain already had somewhere in mind.

HOBSON-JOBSON

ENGLISH IN INDIA

Since 2023, India has had the title of world's most populated country. It is home to just under a staggering one and a half billion people. That's more people in one country than who live in the entirety of Europe. With such a large population of people, expecting the nation to have any kind of linguistic cohesion would seem impossible, yet that isn't entirely off the table. India is home to over 100 native languages. Of these Indigenous tongues, when combining languages by their quantity of first, second, and third speakers, Hindi is undoubtedly the most spoken with just under 700 million speakers. This means well over half the population understand the tongue to some degree. This has allowed India to use Hindi as a sort of lingua franca for large portions of the nation. The second most spoken language in the land isn't one of those many native tongues, but instead a language hellbent on migrating and sticking its teeth into every corner of our globe. English has an odd presence in the modern nation. A humble quarter of a million use it as their first tongue, but well over 120 million in the nation use it as their second or third language. Collectively, just under 130 million in India can understand English to some degree. This technically makes India the second largest English-speaking nation on the planet behind the USA and they aren't even really trying.

Between the native tongue of Hindi and that immigrant tongue of English, India gets by fairly well in communication across the vast nation. It's remarkable that a nation stocked with well over 100 native languages uses a tongue that has its origins on a tiny windy island thousands of miles away as their second most popular lingo. What's even more remarkable is the fact that English has been spoken in India in a meaningful way for a relatively short time. For millennia, the land that makes up modern India has been a playground for people and their languages to thrive in. When it comes to the question of India's oldest language, there is a fierce debate, with two languages duking it out over the title: Sanskrit and Tamil. While we are unable to pinpoint which one is the oldest, we can universally agree that they are some of the oldest languages on our planet that are still actively used. While both are spoken it is worth mentioning that Sanskrit isn't widely spoken by a community of people but instead more used for ceremonial reasons. The language holds a similar position in India as Latin does in Europe. Tamil, meanwhile, is thriving with over eighty million speakers across the globe, with the majority found in India and neighbouring Sri Lanka. Sanskrit and Tamil in India represent more than just a debate over the nation's oldest language. It represents the larger split in languages of the nation as the vast majority of the nation's tongues fall into one of two language families, with Sanskrit and Tamil somewhat being the poster children for each of those families.

Sanskrit belongs to the Indo-Aryan branch of the much larger Indo-European language family. This is a family that has cropped up multiple times across this book and we are finally delving into the Indo side of it. Sanskrit came into being thousands of years ago, and since then it has passed from being a widely spoken tongue to one mainly of historical importance, but many of its descendants are still spoken today. Sanskrit's biggest legacy is most likely the two Hindustani languages. One of these we have already mentioned multiple times, Hindi, but there is Urdu too. Hindi and Urdu are both spoken in India, albeit Hindi is far more popular. Urdu is found more in neighbouring Pakistan. These two languages of Hindi and Urdu are, in reality, more or less the exact same language but written in different scripts. India's Indo-Aryan languages dominate much of the nation's north, centre, east, and west. The nation's south, meanwhile, is a much different story. It's down here where the majority of the nation's Tamil speakers can be found. Tamil does not belong to any branch of Indo-European. Tamil belongs to the wider Dravidian language family which is native to this nook of the world. Other Dravidian languages found in Southern India include the likes of Malayalam, Kannada, and Telugu, which is the most widely spoken of all Dravidian languages.

It's these two language families which are most deeply linked with India, but they are not alone here. Languages of other families, such as the Austroasiatic and Sino-Tibetan, can be found across the country too. India even has language isolates too, like the small Nihali tongue, which has around just 2,000 speakers and is not related to any other major family. India's linguistic diversity is unlike most other nations. In many ways, the country is more comparable to a continent than a single country due to the large mixture of peoples, languages, and cultures which call it home.

The idea of India being a single nation is a relatively newer one too. For the majority of this land's history, it was not ruled as one but instead belonged to various empires and dynasties, many of which coexisted with one another on the land at the same time. Take the ancient Sanskrit-speaking Maurya Empire with its origins in the fourth century BC. It was replaced by the also Sanskrit-speaking Shunga Empire which lasted until 73 BC. The first major empire in AD times in India was the Gupta Empire. They, too, spoke Sanskrit, with the Gupta Empire being seen as the Golden Age of Indian history. The nation still looks fondly back on this time period to this day, with Gupta artwork and architecture being deeply revered. The Gupta Empire stuck around until the mid-sixth century and was followed by the likes of the Pala and Chola empires. The early thirteenth century saw Islam find its way to India in a meaningful way with the emergence of the Delhi Sultanate. This was an extension of those Muslim conquests that spread across North Africa centuries prior. The Delhi Sultanate not only introduced Persian to the land as a language but also intermixed Persian with Sanskrit—which was spoken by the masses at the time—and started the formation of the Hindustani languages. The end of the Delhi Sultanate in the early sixteenth century saw the start of the even larger Muslim power in India of the Mughal Empire. This empire's first ruler, Prince Babur, descended from central Asia to India and overthrew the powers in Delhi promptly in 1526. From here, the Empire went on to claim not only much of modern India but Pakistan and Afghanistan too. The Mughal Empire's reign lasted hundreds of years from this point onward and it shaped so much of what we understand of India today. One of India's most iconic landmarks, the Taj Mahal, is a product of the Mughal Empire.

The start of the Mughal Empire's reign in 1526 ties in neatly with the period of history in which Europe was exploring and claiming wider parts of the world. As we have seen, Europe was picking the flesh off the bones over in the Americas, but they had started turning their attention to old friends in the East too. India and wider Asia was not an unheard of or undiscovered part of the world in the eyes of Europe. Alexander the Great conquered land which is now Indian as far back as 330 BC and Rome had trade deals with Indian powers on the subcontinent too. In the sixteenth century, as the world became far more globalised and people in Europe craved goods that were only produced in places like India, it meant that European powers had to plant their flag in the East as well as the West. By 1498, the Portuguese were the first Europeans to arrive in India via a sea route, traversing below Africa's Cape of Good Hope. This trip was led by one Vaso Da Gama and the result of this Portuguese exploration of India led to them being the first European nation with bases in the subcontinent. Portuguese forts could be found all across the coast of India.

This opened the land up for European operation, and many other nations like the Netherlands, Denmark, Austria, Sweden, and France followed Portugal's suit and either claimed forts in the land or set up trading companies who solely focused on the import and export of goods in and out of India. In this time, India didn't just refer to the nation we know today but a region known as Greater India which was often split into smaller regions like the East Indies. This included nations like Indonesia and the Philippines and even extended somewhat erroneously into the West Indies with the Caribbean. To start with, a lot more attention was given to the land being dubbed East India. This was a land thought to be rich in resources and goods for the wider world to enjoy. Britain, yet again, wanted a slice of this pie and in the year 1600, the East India Company was established and approved by Queen Elizabeth I herself. This was a hugely powerful, but private, company set up by a myriad of British merchants with the aim of collecting goods such as spices, cotton, and dyes from East India and selling them back in Britain.

This was the plan, at least—it didn't prove all too fruitful. The East Indian market had already been gobbled up by the likes of France, Spain, and the Dutch. With little to no wriggle room in East India, the trading company set up by the British looked to central India and the wider subcontinent for business. Despite still being dubbed the East India Company, it was here in India proper that they gained way more traction and success. It was in 1608 that the first British ship arrived in India, landing in the port city of Surat in India's west. While the Portuguese had small operations in India, the land was relatively untapped in the eyes of the British. A Mughal-run India, while in many places on the cutting edge of arts and technology, was on the whole a fairly rural agricultural empire. This made things much easier for the British to trade with them, and at first the Mughal Empire was more than happy to cooperate. This was not a one-way deal, the British got their dyes and spices from India and, in return, India received British goods and silver to bolster their own economy. As the seventeenth century carried on, the East India Company gained more land and control in the subcontinent. Their first British fort in the land, Fort St. George, located in India's southeast, was constructed in 1639. This is just one of the many British forts which would appear in the country. Over the years, the British would erect many more, such as Anchuthengu Fort in the southwest and Sion Hillock fort in the city now dubbed Mumbai. The British even established trading posts and factories in the land too. This would have seen English make its first proper steps into the subcontinent.

Britain was able to establish so much claim in India for multiple reasons. A chief reason was India's Mughal Empire was (as previously mentioned) more than happy to have the British there. To start with, they had a good working relationship with one another. The East India Company, however, also had a trick up their sleeve—private armies. Any kind of resistance the Company met in India was quickly quashed by their own private military might. The use of these armies hampered the good relations the Mughal Empire and the East India Company had established. Upset with how the Company was treating their land and their people, the Mughal Empire refused to do any further business with them. The East India Company retorted by blockading ports in India, if they couldn't trade then, in their eyes, no one could! All this led to the Anglo-Mughal War kicking off in 1686 and lasting all the way until 1690. This was a private company raging war with one of Asia's most powerful empires, so, unsurprisingly, the Mughals came out as the victors. While they won this war, their choices in the aftermath, in many ways, led to their eventual downfall. The Mughals didn't see Britain as much of a threat. They were way more concerned with the rising Maratha Empire to their north. The Mughals could have banned Britain from India forever. Instead, they simply asked them for a fine and an apology, the equivalent of a slap on the wrist.

Post this war, Britain and their East Indian Company became just another European power operating in India. By the middle of the eighteenth century, the number of Europeans trading with India had dwindled, there were just two major players. Britain and their East India Company, and France with their *Compagnie Française Pour Le Commerce des Indes Orientales*. These two companies came to butt heads and duked it out in 1757 at the Battle of Plassey in India's east. Unlike their last fight, the British East India Company were actually the victors this time around. This victory had a huge consequence for India. It removed France from the equation, making the British the dominant foreign power in the land. They could single handedly dictate what came in and out of the nation. It also allowed Britain to put people in power to access parts of India too. This meant the East India Company could place puppet rulers in most places that took their liking in India. Fundamentally, after this victory in 1757, Britain had control of the land. And with control comes language. But this control came with a huge caveat. The Mughal Empire was still technically a thing in India and was in power, but its control had been greatly minimised by the East India Company. We must keep in mind, of course, the British government/crown were not the ones calling the shots here. It was, instead, the privately owned East India Company.

Life for everyday people under the East India Company's regime proved tough. Many fell into deep poverty as their earnings and assets were claimed by the British and forced to sell what they could produce to the British for a very low price. Lots of the individual princes who ruled smaller parts of India were removed from their positions of power; those who kept their seats had to pledge loyalty to the East India Company. What India lost, the British gained. The East India Company's domain over India was incredibly prosperous for those back in Britain. New exotic goods, like spices and silks, made their way to the island, as well as the huge amounts of funds India generated for Britain. Much of the burgeoning Industrial Revolution was paid for via the plundering of India. India also finally gave Britain something they had been craving ever since their aforementioned run-in with China and their wars over Hong Kong: ample land in the right climate to produce their own tea. Much of India was farmed for tea via seeds stolen from China. Today, India is deeply linked with tea, even though it's *not technically* native to the land. British dominance in the land also led to English becoming the dominant language. Not only was it spoken by the British expats in the land, but many native Indians who sided with the British would have learned the language too. Those natives who learnt English, meanwhile, probably would have just used it for business reasons; between friends and family, their native tongue of choice would have been the go-to.

Many of the Indians who sided with the British were soldiers in the East India Company's private army. They became known as Sepoys, and it was via them that Britain's control over India went to the next level. 100 years after the Battle of Plassey, in 1857, the Sepoys started rebelling. This rebellion is thought to have originated due to a rumour that the new rifles being given to them had cartridges covered in cow and pig's blood as a means of lubrication. The consumption of these animals was against the beliefs of many native Indians, so they felt that the East India Company was not respecting their way of life. The fact this was even a possibility shows us just how little regard the British had for the native Indians they now ruled over and their customs. Understandably, this led to the Sepoys revolting against their rulers. This rebellion was an abject failure. Not only did it see the ultimate demise of the Mughal Empire, but it also gave the British metaphorical ammunition to use against the natives. The British used these events to paint the local people as unruly and in need of stricter governing.

This led to the British government themselves stepping in and taking direct control of India, instead of the East India Company calling the shots. It was that same year, in 1857, that India finally became undoubtedly British. From this point, India became known as the British Raj. This also included land that constitutes modern Pakistan, Bangladesh, and Myanmar, as well as modern India. Life in the British Raj brought along with it many of the same challenges as life under the rule of the East India Company. Poor living and working conditions for the locals, for example, along with English being placed as the language of power. Thankfully, the British didn't outright ban the native tongues, to some degree they embraced them. A huge debate broke out in the British Raj over what should be the standard tongue of the people, Hindi or Urdu. As we can see today, Hindi won out in this debate while Urdu instead took off in Pakistan. English became the language of work and bureaucracy, while many stuck with their native tongue at home.

After just shy of 100 years of rule under the British Raj, in 1947 India finally found its independence. This freedom came after decades of pressure and actions from the people of the nation, most famously one Mohandas/Mahatma Gandhi. The freedom saw the British Raj partitioned into multiple countries. The bulk of the land would go on to become India as we know it today while smaller sections would eventually become the nations of Pakistan and Bangladesh. It was then that India easily could have removed English entirely from its vocabulary but, in a strange way, it was at this time it needed English the most. The language was well and truly ingrained into the nation at this point, yet it was also a moment when India found itself completely independent for the first time in around 200 years. The nation had to stand on its own two feet, to barter and debate with the world without the safety net of Britain. To do this, they had to have some means to communicate with the wider world and English was the answer to this problem. Not only because English was spoken by countries like the UK and USA, but also because it was quickly becoming the world's global tongue. While the nation has hundreds of Indigenous tongues, not many of them would serve as a good lingua franca for communicating on the global stage. This has led to English being seen as something of a prestigious language in India. The ability to speak it is a good skill to help you progress in life and in work.

This is why English is not only a co-official language in the nation today, but also so well spoken as a second or third tongue in India. While many can speak it to some degree, they mainly use it for business reasons or to communicate with tourists. Indians rarely speak to one another in this immigrant tongue. Even the version of English that is used in India is somewhat different to other varieties. Words like *karma*, *biryani*, and *tala*—which mean "action," "rice," and "rhythm," respectively—are all words of various Indian language origins which can be heard in Indian English. Indian English has also produced some strange terms.

Terms like *kitty party* refers to a social gathering with the aim of raising funds. Interestingly, just "kitty" or "the kitty" is a term for a metaphorical piggy bank of sorts used in British English; the two are likely related. Indian English is also full of other unique features too, like the common reduplication of adjectives in sentences. For example, an Indian English speaker would more likely say, "We have a big, big problem," instead of just "We have a big problem" or even "We have a huge problem." Indian English also contains this unique quirk known as fronting. Fronting is when certain words are placed at the start of a sentence instead of where they are normally found in other versions of English. Someone in British English might say, "We will see each other tomorrow," while Indian English speakers may say, "Tomorrow, we will see each other." This is, of course, akin to the way in which a certain Jedi master speaks. As far as I'm aware, Indian English was being spoken in this way long before Yoda ever uttered a single word.

The relationship between India and English, however, goes both ways. In the same way English has taken a hold on the subcontinent, many words from this part of the world have found themselves being used in wider English. Words like bungalow, pyjamas, jungle, and chutney all have their origins in Hindi. Not every word which reached English from the shores of the subcontinent has stood the test of time, however. Hobson-Jobson was once a fairly popular term deriving from India and could be used to refer to any kind of religious observation in India. Today, using this catch-all term for the many celebrations of India is seemingly a little outdated but, once upon a time, it was so popular that an entire dictionary of Anglo-Indian words was published under this title in 1889. More specifically, it had the title of *Hobson-Jobson: A Glossary of Colloquial Anglo-Indian Words and Phrases, and of Kindred Terms, Etymological, Historical, Geographical and Discursive*.

English's position as a lingua franca in India has thankfully not led to the extinction of the countless native languages in the land. While not every language in India has stood the test of time, many are still spoken to this day. Hindi and English are the official languages of India but a further twenty-one have varying degrees of official and protected status across various parts of India. These twenty-one languages are Assamese, Bengali, Bodo, Dogri, Gujarati, Kannada, Kashmiri, Konkani, Maithili, Malayalam, Meitei, Marathi, Nepali, Odia, Punjabi, Sanskrit, Santali, Sindhi, Tamil, Telugu, and Urdu.

This has allowed India to become one of the most multilingual nations on the planet. Many citizens can speak two or three languages depending on where they live. These languages can range from some of the more widely spoken like Hindi or Tamil, a smaller more local language like Bodo, or even that immigrant tongue of English—a language that, as we know, found itself slowly taking more and more control in the land. So, it went from being a language used solely by merchants and traders in the land, to a tongue that had a smattering of influence as the East India Company gained more traction. Then, from it being the language of the authority during the British Raj, to the current situation English finds itself in in India. It is a language a vast amount of people know but rarely use with friends and family. English's journey in the world's most populated country is quite unlike any other journey the language has undertaken. In a lot of ways, English in India is seemingly everywhere and nowhere.

ARGENTINE DRAGONS

WELSH IN ARGENTINA

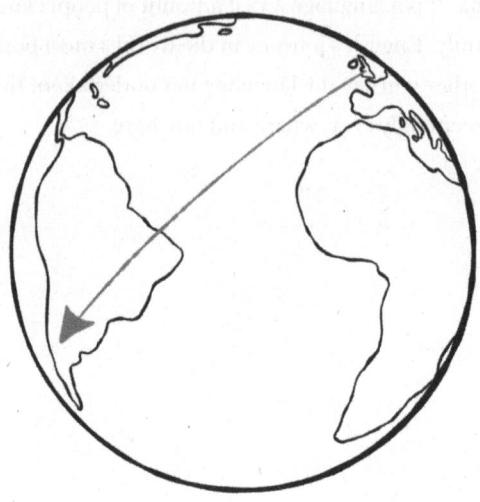

We have seen how rapidly the English language became quite possibly the United
Kingdom's most successful export. From the Americas, to Australia, to Asia.
Despite its success, English is not the only tongue of Blighty to have stretched
its legs. One of the most fascinating language migrations to have ever been
undertaken on our planet has to be the journey of a small Celtic tongue finding
itself at home toward the bottom of the world. Imagine exploring the depths of
Argentina, a land full of rugged terrains and unpredictable weather. A country
where, thanks to the exploits of Columbus and co, Spanish reigns supreme. Yet,
as you find yourself off the beaten track and in one small nook of the nation,
suddenly those speaking to you aren't saying words in the Romance language of
Español. Instead, the singsong, consonant-clustering, Brythonic language from

the valleys and hills of Wales are coming out of their mouths. The language of the land of the dragons has been able to take a small stronghold in this land of silver.

With well over half a million speakers, Welsh takes the title of most widely spoken Celtic language on our planet still around today in the aftermath of Rome wiping out the majority of Europe's Celtic tongues as they spread their Latin lingo. Of the Celtic languages still around, Welsh has the most in common with Cornish spoken in the Cornwall region of England to its south, and Breton found across the channel in the French region of Brittany. This gives us a clear idea as to how the Welsh language arrived in Britain to begin with. The ancestor of Welsh, along with those two languages, is believed to have arrived on the island of Great Britain around 600 BC. This was way before the Romans arrived on the island, let alone the emergence of the Anglo-Saxons in the land. This makes Welsh one of the (if not the oldest) language of Britain which is still being spoken. Its predecessor language was certainly in the land way before English's. The speakers of the Proto-Welsh language would have travelled across the channel. While some would have remained in the island's deep southwest and formed the Cornish language, others of this group ventured farther along this island. Just north of what is now Cornwall and the Southwest of England, over the Bristol channel and Severn Estuary, lies a growth of land which looks remarkably like a pig's head, something that you are unable to not see once it's pointed out to you.

This land area has much more inhospitable natural geography, ranging from deep valleys to rolling hills. It was here that Celtic speakers found themselves at home and, thanks to the isolation the land provided, the way they spoke could morph and shift independently from the wider world. Even once Rome claimed this corner of the island, the language spoken there could still maintain and flourish thanks to its isolation, unlike the Celtic languages, which were born in modern England and have since all died out. Old Welsh, one of the language's earliest forms, came around sometime in the eighth century AD. The land this language was spoken in would eventually form its own identity. Becoming the home nation of *Cymru* or Wales as it is called in English.

Fast forward just over 1,000 years to the nineteenth century, and Wales as well as its lingo had changed substantially. By this point, the language was more or less in its modern form and being spoken in a similar way it is today. While the language might have sounded similar in the nineteenth century as it does today, a huge difference was found in the amount of people speaking it. While records were not being kept, it is believed that at the start of this century a majority of Wales natively spoke Welsh, with there being little to no native English being spoken there. By the end of this century, however, people realised it may be a good idea to keep track of things like the number of speakers. The first record of this kind for Wales dates from 1891 and it sees just half the population using Welsh and their main language and only a small number of people had absolutely no knowledge of English. During the course of this century, the popularity of the language plummeted. That decline has somewhat maintained since then; however, thankfully, revival efforts have been put in place in more recent years. The Industrial Revolution tore through nineteenth-century Britain and impacted pretty much all aspects of life across the island, including the Welsh language. Prior to this period, Wales was primarily a farming nation formed of rural communities. This revolution, however, needed to be fed by coal, steel, and slate—all things which could be found in ample supply across Wales. The green of Wales was torn up and in its place stood many mines, burrowing deep into Britain to harvest precious minerals. Wales would go on to become deeply linked with mining and it has since become a proud part of their culture, but during the initial period when these mines were formed, it destroyed so much of the Welsh way of life at the time.

This industry introduced more people from outside the nation to Wales. Suddenly, more English was being spoken here, which kicked off the Welsh language's decline. The industry also pillaged the rural settlements of Wales and threw life in the land into disarray. This is even seen in the reputation that Wales picked up in the wider UK at the time. In the midst of the nineteenth century, riots and discontent broke out across Wales. Those in power in London wanted to know why Wales was becoming such a seemingly lawless place and, for some reason, many felt it was the Welsh language which led to this. The more accurate reason was most likely the fact that the Industrial Revolution kicked off by London had in many ways sucked the very soul out of Wales. To those in London, it was simply easier to blame the different language they spoke as the reason why they were so restless. The UK cracked down on Welsh, forcing children in Wales to learn English and ostracising those who spoke Welsh. This too led to the rapid decline the language faced in the nineteenth century. Between the Industrial

Revolution and the actions of the British government, Wales' way of life had been completely upturned by the mid-nineteenth century. Understandably, many Welsh people were deeply saddened by what had become of their homeland. Many wanted to go back to the pre-Industrial Revolution way of life in Wales, yet this was fundamentally unachievable. The land had changed too much. Instead of simply yearning for Wales to go back to how Wales once was, a small group of Welsh people decided to instead settle in a new land where they could live their life like they did in the Wales of yore.

A handful of Welsh expat communities had already started to crop up across the Atlantic in the USA. Notable examples are within the town of Utica in New York State and Scranton, Pennsylvania, which has historically been seen as the Welsh capital of the US. While the Welsh were more than welcomed in these parts of the world, it tended to just be that, welcomed. They still had to integrate with the wider community they lived in and learn their lingo, and in the case of Utica and Scranton that was English. The Welsh of the mid-nineteenth century wished to migrate to escape English entirely. This meant that they couldn't just move into an established town and find a little corner to dub New Wales. They would instead have to find somewhere completely devoid of life. A blank canvas to shape in their own image and grace with their own language. Their initial idea was actually to go to the Canadian island of Vancouver, which still has Welsh descendants to this day. Yet, those wishing to move from Wales stopped searching for somewhere in North America. Instead, they drew their attention much farther south, to a land vastly different to the one they had called home for so long.

The nineteenth century was something of a roller coaster for Argentina. The land had been claimed by the Spanish a few centuries prior and spent the majority of this time as part of Spain's Viceroyalty of the Río de la Plata. It was in just 1816 that Argentina finally declared independence from Spain. While free from Spanish rule, the nation had held influence long enough on the land for Spanish to become the dominant tongue, ousting many of the Indigenous languages as the number one tongue. The Spanish here has even taken on its own unique form. The Rioplatense dialect of Spanish is the go-to in not just Argentina but neighbouring Uruguay too. It contains a variety of words not really found in other forms of Spanish like *gaucho* which comes from the Quechua language family and is the title for Argentina's cowboys. By 1861, Argentina had been its own independent nation for just shy of sixty years, doing its own thing and speaking its own form of Spanish, all while trying to find its own two feet on the global stage. The last thing the government of Argentina needed in this moment of need was a plea for help from across the Atlantic but that's exactly what they got.

In a small house in North Wales in 1861, a group of Welshmen discussed the idea of relocating to the Patagonia region of Argentina. From what they had heard, it was a large empty land abundant with good natural resources. It would be perfect as a New Wales of sorts for them. It was seen by them as a land where they could live and speak as they wished to. A letter was sent to Argentina and, despite some hesitancy, the rulers of the South American nation agreed to allow the Welsh rights to live in the land. This might have been due to the kinship they felt with the Welsh, they were, after all, a group of people trying to break free of an oppressor in the same way Argentina had freed themselves from Spain just a few decades prior. This was far from a quick fix—after years of negotiating with Argentina, the first 100 or so Welsh settlers finally set their eyes on their new home in 1865. It was in this year that a ship dubbed *Mimosa* departed from Liverpool on an eight-week voyage to the depths of Argentina. Upon arriving on the eastern coast of South America, the Welsh quickly realised that Patagonia wasn't exactly what they had in their collective minds. It was less like the fertile lowlands of Wales and far more inhospitable, barren, and desolate then they had all expected. There was no forest to harvest building supplies from and, perhaps more worryingly, there was no fresh water supply either.

What saved these Welshmen was a mixture of help from the local Tehuelche tribe and an emergency supply mission sent to them. With this help, they could just about manage and carve out their first permanent settlement—the town of Rawson which was founded in 1865. From here, more Welsh people arrived in the land after hearing word of the quality of life those who made the trip experienced. More Welsh-speaking settlements were established across Patagonia like Gaiman, Dolavon, and Trelew, which all collectively became known as *Y Wladfa* which simply means "The Colony." Today, around 70,000 people live across the settlements of Argentina with Welsh origins. The Welsh language can be found all over these towns. From signs written in Spanish and Welsh to even traditional Welsh Tea Rooms located here. Perhaps the biggest remnant of Welsh settlement here is the unique dialect of Welsh spoken in Argentina to this very day.

Patagonian Welsh is spoken by a few thousand people in this region of Argentina. We lack defined numbers but estimates ranging from 1,500 to 5,000 speakers. While this version of Welsh is fairly interchangeable with the Welsh of Wales, it has some unique features. Entirely new words of Welsh have been formed in South America, often words of Spanish origins. In standard Welsh the word for bank is simply *banc*. In Patagonian Welsh, meanwhile, it is *arianfa*, which derives from the older Welsh word for silver *arian*. As silver was a driving force behind Argentina (the country is literally named after the stuff), it makes sense as to why their version of banks would be named after the precious metal. There's also the Patagonian Welsh word of *Ymdrochfa*, which means a "bathing spot," "spa," or "beach." In British Welsh, this would more likely be a word like *sba* or *traeth*, which mean "spa" and "beach," respectively. The Patagonian Welsh word comes directly from the Spanish word of the same meaning, *balneario*. This makes Patagonian Welsh an immigrant tongue which has, in turn, been shaped by the fellow immigrant tongue of Rioplatense Spanish. Welsh might seem like an odd relic of a language, but even it has moved across the globe and found a new lease on life. Even if that fresh start is toward the very bottom of the earth.

BELGIANS IN THE CONGO

EUROPEAN LANGUAGES ACROSS AFRICA

By the mid to late nineteenth century, Europe had lost the Americas, and the majority of the land there—once ruled by the British, Spanish, and co—was now following its own path. What small chunks of Asia Europe could get a hold of, they had done already with the likes of Hong Kong and Macau. Even the farthest reaches of the world in the South Pacific had European flags placed on them. A large majority of the world by this time had either been plucked by Europe to be part of their larger operation or were formerly part of this system. Only one continent lay predominantly unaccounted for, one quite literally under Europe's nose. When they realised the potential this land had in their worldwide conquests, Europe quite literally scrambled for it.

During that peak Age of Colonisation from around the fourteenth to seventeenth century, when the New World and the Southern Hemisphere were starting to fall under European control, Africa remained resoundingly unclaimed. Europe did interact with Africa during this time. Most infamously plundering the land of resources, and even people, to cruelly work as slaves in their new land across the Atlantic. During the time of the slave trade, Europeans didn't settle all that much in the continent. There were some European settlements in the land dating back through the centuries; if we go far enough back in time, we will encounter the time when Rome claimed North Africa! By the mid-nineteenth century, most European claims in Africa were found dotted along the continent's vast coast. The Cape Colony initially founded by the Dutch was now under British rule in Africa's southernmost point. The remains of Dutch rule in this area were now residing in the Orange Free State. The Portuguese claimed what would become the nation of Angola down Africa's west coast in the fifteenth century. France had small pockets of control in parts of Western Africa. There's even the unique case of Liberia. This West African nation was established in 1822 by the USA as a land that freed slaves could live in, whether they were once kidnapped from Africa or if they were born in the USA. The idea of Liberia might have sounded good to those at the time but, in reality, their true intentions were mixed at best. Liberia still resides in this corner of Africa today. Its name is a reference to the liberated status of the land's initial settlers—even their flag looks similar to the USA's.

These claims accounted for small patches of the continent's coast. The majority of the land, especially its deep inner core, remained more or less colonial free. At this time in the mid-nineteenth century, Africa was a patchwork of much smaller Indigenous kingdoms, tribes, empires, and states. Powers like the native Lunda Empire toward the centre of the continent, the Sultanate of Geledi founded on the horn of Africa, and even Ethiopia existed in some form during this period of African history. Ethiopia is widely seen as the birthplace of modern humans. It's where we all started before spreading ourselves and our languages across the globe. These various native African powers spoke a myriad of languages. The continent is believed to be home to over 3,000 languages! While a lot of these have since gone extinct, many are still spoken by millions to this very day. The large majority of Africa's native languages belong to four families.

Afro-Asiatic is a transcontinental language family with native origins across
Asia's Middle East and Africa. It's the family of languages which contains Arabic
which, centuries ago, came to be the de facto tongue of North Africa. Yet, it also
contains languages like Oromo, Amharic, and Somali. The family is also home
to the ancient language of the Egyptians, a tongue long dead by this point but
its memory surviving through its hieroglyphs. The Atlantic-Congo family is the
dominant group of sub-Saharan Africa. It contains the many Bantu languages
like Zulu and Swahili which migrated across the continent millennia ago. It
also contains non-Bantu tongues like the Mande languages of North Africa, or
the Gbaya tongues found in modern Cameroon and the surrounding nations.
Khoisan languages can be found in the southwest of the continent. These tongues
all contain the incredibly unique "clicking," consonant sounds used for speech.
Languages which feature clicks are more or less isolated to this part of the world
and they can help us understand just how different languages can be. A notable
language of this branch is Khoekhoe which can be found in modern Namibia and
South Africa. Finally, we have the Nilo-Saharan family. This language grouping
is often debated and many dub it as something of a dumping ground for African
languages that don't fit into any of the other families. They can mainly be found
just north of Africa's centre somewhere between the Nile and the Saharan, hence
the family's name. The most widely spoken tongue of this supposed family is
Dholuo, which can be heard mainly in Kenya and Tanzania.

Not every African language belongs to one of these families, with a really curious
example being the native language of Madagascar. This African island/nation
is home to the tongue of Malagasy. Malagasy is not Bantu, or Afro-Asiatic,
or even a click-based language. Malagasy is, instead, part of the Austronesian
language family—a group of tongues which are primarily located in southeast
Asia and the southern Pacific. Malagasy is part of the Malayo-Polynesian branch
of Austronesia. Meaning, it has more in common with languages like Māori
and Indonesian found on the opposite side of the Indian ocean then it does with
languages found across the channel it shares with Mozambique. Then there are
also the Indo-European languages of Africa that were around at this time. Most
noticeably Afrikaans, that form of Dutch which migrated and evolved in the land
centuries prior. Not all African tongues belong to a family, though. This land
is also home to a handful of language isolates. The tongue of Sandawe has no
relationship to any other tongue, has around 60,000 speakers, and it's found in

Tanzania. Then there's also the less spoken Shabo found in Ethiopia, and Laal found in Chad.

What this shows us is just how incredibly linguistically diverse Africa truly is. The continent is home to the second highest number of languages, only being beaten slightly by Asia. These are tongues deeply important to the native people of the land and their cultures. Despite some of these tongues being spoken in their millions, many go unheard of to the wider world and lack the global appeal other languages spoken in these quantities have. This mainly comes down to the fact that, in most cases, these Indigenous languages were vastly overshadowed by immigrant tongues which came to be the languages of authority when they moseyed into the land in the late eighteenth century. Today, a country like the Ivory Coast is often thought to be a French-speaking nation rather than a Baoulé-and-Sénoufo-speaking one. European languages dominate this entire continent.

But from around the fifteenth century, when Europeans first started taking baby steps into Africa, all the way until the late nineteenth century, languages in the land stayed pretty stationary. We had a small smattering of European influence on the continent, but Africa was still natively speaking on the whole. There's one specific decade which is seen as the turning point of African history and colonisation of the land: the 1880s. The New World was now more or less entirely free of European rule, with nations like the USA, Canada, Mexico, and Brazil all doing their own thing. The issue for nations like Britain, France, Spain, and Portugal, however, was that they still needed the resources and sway these formerly claimed lands once gave them. In the quest for resources (especially resources to fuel the Industrial Revolution), many nations turned their attention to Africa. The continent was finally on the radar of Europe for multiple reasons. A key reason was down to the abolishment of the slave trade. While this was a wildly good event in world history, the sad reality was the capitalist machine still needed to be fed in Europe. With the trade of people thankfully now out of the picture, Europe became much more interested in trading and selling other resources Africa had to offer, as well as using the land to grow cash crops, like sugar and coffee, as they had once in the New World. Technological advancements also made the exploitation of Africa's inner core easier too. Steamships, which didn't rely on wind to move, could manoeuvre the many rivers of Africa more easily and access the continent's deeper land. By this point in world history, locomotion had become a mainstay in the world too. Rails could be planted across Africa and huge trains could carry the bounty of these empires directly across the lands. There was also a deep sense of exploration in the air across the nineteenth century. Europeans were on a quest to reach each and every nook of the planet, and Africa was one of the final blank areas of the map by this point.

Technological improvements, the urge to fill in the blanks of the map, and the greed for money and power kicked off a historical event known as the Scramble for Africa. This was pretty much exactly what it sounds like—a chaotic dash for land and resources by European powers across Africa. Calling this period a "scramble" really highlights just how erratic this conquering of land was. Minimal thought was used when nations chose where to plant their flags. Across the first half of the 1880s, familiar nations like Britain, France, Portugal, and Spain had plucked parts of Africa; in Portugal's case, they had had land there for centuries. Yet, the former part of this decade also saw some other nations who hadn't made big waves in the realm of colonisation stake claims in Africa too. Germany, for example, who had done little to no empire-building during the Age of Colonisation, pinched areas in the southwest and east of Africa, as well as the land which forms modern Togo. Likewise, Italy, the home of Latin, whose offspring tongues have since gone on to migrate across the globe, started claiming land yet again by placing their flag in modern Eritrea, in Africa's east. One of the more unique European holdings in Africa came in the form of a vast area of land around the Congo River. The land came under European rule prior to the 1880s and, technically, it didn't belong to a nation, but instead one man. That one man, however, happened to be the king of Belgium.

Leopold II became King of the Belgians in 1865 and, from that moment, he wished to make his country the epicentre of a grand empire. An empire similar to the one his cousin, Victoria, across the channel, was ruling over. To build his burgeoning Belgian empire, Leopold looked to Africa and hired explorer Henry Stanley to explore the area on his behalf. Stanley's explorations took place in the 1870s and were instrumental in setting off the Scramble for Africa. Leopold liked what he saw in Congo (today known as the Democratic Republic of Congo) and claimed the area, but not on behalf of Belgium. The nation unto itself lacked the finances to run an overseas colony. Instead, King Leopold II and a group of investors claimed the land privately, with Congo becoming something of his own personal playground. Playground is putting things extremely jovially. In reality, Leopold devastated the land for its natural resources and brutalised the natives of the land. From overworking them for his personal gain to killing them in their hundreds for sport and pleasure. These atrocities were happening during the 1870s and, by the 1880s, the wider world was finally starting to catch wind of what Leopold was actually doing in the Congo for his own personal gain, and once again, not for wider Belgium.

Between Leopold and his horrific treatment of the Congo and its people, as well as the other European powers picking off Africa willy-nilly, something needed to be done. It was the German chancellor, Otto Von Bismark, who stepped up. On the fifteenth of November 1884, he set up the now infamous Berlin Conference. This meeting brought together some of the world's most dominant powers to figure out what to do with Africa and who was granted what land. Fourteen countries/powers were present at the Berlin Conference. This included two non-European powers in the form of the USA and the Ottoman Empire. The remaining twelve were Germany, the Austro-Hungarian Empire, Spain, Denmark, France, Britain, Italy, the Netherlands, Portugal, Russia, the United Kingdom of Sweden and Norway, and something called the International Congo Society. This was the private company headed by Belgium's King Leopold II. This collection of powers covered a huge chunk of the world, yet there was a significant attendee absent. None of these nations spoke for the people who lived in Africa natively. No power or representative from the continent itself was invited to the Berlin Conference—the conference that was set up to seal their fate.

After over three months of negotiating, the Berlin Conference concluded on the twenty-sixth of February 1885. The end result saw Africa's land split between other nations with the intention of putting the entire continent under foreign rule. Despite there being fourteen nations present in Berlin, just half of them were granted Africa's bountiful lands. Those were Britain, France, Portugal, Spain, Germany, Italy, and the International Congo Society. Africa was more or less arbitrarily split into different colonies for these seven nations to claim as their own. There was little to no rhyme or reason as to where the borders of these colonies were drawn. They didn't respect things like the boundaries of African tribes, linguistic groupings, or even natural geographic borders in some cases. These borders placed on the land by Europe split up communities and devastated

lives in Africa. With hypothetical borders for the continent in place, Europe got to
work on making them a reality. This was done by sending out explorers to these
parts of Africa to sign treaties with local leaders. The treaties offered supposed
European protection for these lands. In reality, these scam treaties offered Africa
very little protection and, in many ways, were schemes to remove control of the
land from the natives. By the early twentieth century, these borders had come to
fruition and those seven nations were each granted various parts of Africa. It was
these incredibly underhanded tactics which led to the borders and languages of
Africa we know today. The land these nations acquired in relation to the modern
countries of Africa are roughly as follows.

> **Britain:** Egypt, Sudan, South Sudan, Uganda, Kenya, the northern area
> of Somalia, Zambia, Malawi, Botswana, South Africa, Eswatini, Lesotho,
> Nigeria, Ghana, Sierra Leone, the Republic of The Gambia, the Seychelles

> **France:** Morocco, Algeria, Tunisia, Mauritania, Mali, Niger, Burkina
> Faso, Senegal, Guinea, Ivory Coast, Benin, Chad, Central African Republic,
> Gabon, the Republic of the Congo, Djibouti, Madagascar, Mauritius

> **Portugal:** Angola, Mozambique, Sao Tome and Principe, Cape Verde,
> Guinea-Bissau

> **Germany:** Cameroon, Tanzania, Namibia, Togo

> **Italy:** Remainder of Somalia, Eritrea, part of Libya

> **Spain:** Western Sahara, northern part of Morocco, Equatorial Guinea

> **The International Congo Society:** The Democratic Republic
> of the Congo

As we can see, Leopold was able to hold onto his Congo claim in the aftermath of
the Berlin Conference, despite one of the key reasons it was set up in the first place
was to deal with Leopold and his actions there. He managed this by persuading
the rest of the conference participants that he was actually doing good in the land.
He claimed he was using the region for philanthropy and making trade tax free

in the land, as well as abolishing slavery in the region too. These lies worked and Leopold was able to formally make the region his own private land, dubbing it the Congo Free State. Only two parts of Africa did not fall under European rule after the Scramble for Africa. Liberia was off limits as, by this point, it had been a long-established nation set up by the US. Ethiopia was the other area. Italy actually had it on their docket to be theirs. Yet, when it came to actually claiming the land, Italian forces were met by the powerful army of Ethiopia. This led to the Battle of Adwa in the land which saw the Ethiopian forces victorious over Italy, allowing Ethiopia to remain independent. It is widely seen as the only African nation to never be fully colonised in any way. Though a region of the country was eventually claimed by Italy way later down the line, in 1936, it was only under Italian rule until 1941.

While Liberia and Ethiopia remained free of Europeans, the rest of Africa was set up to be harvested by the northern continent. Its land was turned to farms to grow valuable crops tended to by the locals who now found themselves as subjects to foreign powers. What lay beneath the continent, valuable minerals like gold and even diamonds, were extracted from the earth too. Europe found tremendous wealth in Africa, but it came at the price of the devastation of the land and lives of the natives. Nowhere was this more apparent than in the Congo Free State. Leopold "legally" owned this land and continued to ruin it like a child with a magnifying glass pointed at an anthill. When it finally came to light just how awful Leopold had been in the Congo in 1908, the land was taken from his private control and became a formal colony of Belgium itself, dubbed Belgian Congo. Today, the atrocities carried out by King Leopold II in the Congo Free State are seen as some of the most horrendous crimes against humanity in our history, with Leopold himself seen as one of history's biggest monsters.

This colonisation of Africa saw a huge number of European languages dig their claws into the continent too. People from lands like France and Britain arrived in their respective colonies in authoritative roles, using their native tongues to dominate the locals. These immigrant tongues became the superior languages of the land while Indigenous tongues were neglected, banned, and even died during this period. The average locals in this continent would have seen the languages they and their families had been speaking for generations become second class tongues, while anything deemed of note would have been written out in one of these European tongues. Native African languages like Seroa, Ajawa, and Horo became extinct across the late nineteenth and early twentieth centuries during this period of European rule in Africa.

The Scramble for Africa saw a huge upheaval to geopolitics in a relatively short time. This period of African colonisation kicked off in the late nineteenth century and changed the foundations of the land, introducing new powers and new languages. Yet, by the mid-to-late twentieth century, most of these colonies had found their independence as the modern nations of Africa today. Countries like Algeria, Kenya, and the Democratic Republic of the Congo (DRC), found their freedom from France, Britain, and Belgium, respectively, in the 1960s. The decolonisation of Africa mainly came down to the two bloody and brutal World Wars which took place across the twentieth century. These wars eroded so much of the power these nations had and meant they could no longer manage their overseas colonies. This ultimately equates to around 100 years of European rule in Africa. In the grand scheme of human history, this really is not that long. Yet, it had a resoundingly deep impact on Africa. Many of the nations on the continent are direct products of this time period. European influence is seen in their borders, customs, and, of course, languages. The immigrant tongues which were introduced during the Scramble have had varying degrees of success in the continent. The most noticeable successes in Africa are English and French. French has official status in over twenty countries in Africa, with the former Belgian-ruled Democratic Republic of the Congo having the continent's largest speaking French population. Seventy-two million people in the DRC speak French, that is more French speakers than there are people in actual France. The French spoken in the Democratic Republic of the Congo is seemingly very similar to the French spoken in France itself. One of the big differences is the slang used in the DRC, which derives from various native languages.

Another twenty or so nations have English as their official tongue. Nigeria alone has almost 180 million English speakers. That's well over 100 million more people than there are in England itself. Nigerian English has flourished in its own unique way, with words appearing in the dialect of native origins. A term like *buka* is used in Nigerian English as the name for a small roadside restaurant. The word has its origins in the native Yoruba language. Other European tongues which belonged to former ruling powers in the land like Portuguese, Spanish, German, and Italian haven't had as much staying power in Africa. Angola mainly speaks Portuguese today, but Namibia barely speaks German. Likewise, there's little to no Italian in modern Eritrea and just the one nation of Equatorial Guinea has Spanish as an official language. In these countries that haven't really held on to the tongues of their colonisers, native languages have stuck around as the dominant lingo. In modern Namibia, which was once under German rule, the most widely spoken language is the Bantu tongue of Oshiwambo. Likewise, in Nigeria, despite its 180 million or so English speakers, the native languages of Hausa, a Chadic tongue, and Yoruba, a Volta-Niger tongue, have eighty million and fifty million speakers, respectively. Africa is a continent of two halves when it comes to language. Immigrant tongues are spoken in the millions up and down the continent due to the quick and brutal colonisation of the land in the late nineteenth century. Yet, unlike the Americas where a large majority of native languages have dwindled in populations significantly, Africa's native tongues have survived. The likes of Britain, France, and Belgium's tyrannical Leopold II were unable to silence these tongues. Home grown languages like Yoruba, Swahili, and Hausa are still spoken in their millions.

The Scramble for Africa is seen as the definitive event in the age of New Imperialism. The second wave of colonisation powered by the Industrial Revolution is widely seen to have come to an end at the start of the First World War. Yet even though New Imperialism was done and dusted, the movement of language across our globe didn't come to a halt.

MOTHER OF EXILES

YIDDISH IN NEW YORK

Not like the brazen giant of Greek fame,
With conquering limbs astride from land to land;
Here at our sea-washed, sunset gates shall stand
A mighty woman with a torch, whose flame
Is the imprisoned lightning, and her name
Mother of Exiles. From her beacon-hand
Glows world-wide welcome; her mild eyes command
The air-bridged harbor that twin cities frame.
"Keep, ancient lands, your storied pomp!" cries she
With silent lips. "Give me your tired, your poor,
Your huddled masses yearning to breathe free,
The wretched refuse of your teeming shore.
Send these, the homeless, tempest-tost to me,
I lift my lamp beside the golden door!"

—"The New Colossus," Emma Lazarus

These are the words inscribed on the Statue of Liberty's podium. This poem is a rallying cry, a message to the world which reflects the image the Statue of Liberty has. It is a beacon of hope to migrants from around the world who made the journey to New York City to start a fresh life. Countless in the past arrived in New York, New York via arduous ship journeys and one of their first sights would have been Lady Liberty herself. New York is a city which has come to be defined as a hub of migration. Many communities have arrived in the city and brought along their customs, cultures, and, of course, their languages. From Chinatown to Little Italy. New York City is also home to a certain community of people and their language who have throughout history become just as linked with travel and migration as the concrete jungle itself has.

Judaism is a resoundingly ancient religion, the oldest of the Abrahamic religions. These religions all have their roots with a man called Abraham who God revealed himself to, supposedly at some point in the second millennium BC, somewhere in the Levant region of western Asia. From Abraham, this Jewish religion arose and one of the defining traits of Judaism is its severe lack of deities. At this time, most religions had a whole pantheon of gods. A god for the seas, a god for the skies, a god for fertility, a god for wine. We see this in the likes of Norse mythology and Greek/Roman myths. Judaism, however, has just one god, one almighty, all-powerful god who is in control of everything. A religion with just one god is correctly referred to as monotheistic. Judaism is seen as the oldest still widely practised monotheistic religion in the world. Today, monotheistic religions are incredibly popular, with two of most widely followed religions in the world being monotheistic. Those other Abrahamic religions are Christianity and Islam, which were born out of Judaism later down the line. In the far past, when Judaism was the only major monotheistic religion, the wider world marked the Jews as different to them. It wasn't just the singular god which made Jews different to other people in the ancient Levant and wider Europe/Asia. Many of their practices were different too, like how they worshipped and what they ate. Another thing that differentiated Jews from others was the language they spoke. The language of Hebrew is seen as the traditional tongue of Judaism and emerged amongst people of this ethno-religious group in the third century BC. It is found in the Semitic branch of the Afro-Asiatic language family, making it a relative of Arabic.

These differences are in no way shape or form negative nor even incorrect ways of practicing religion, they were simply different. Yet, all these differences culminated in the eyes of non-Jews in this part of the world. A general distaste and distrust of Jews started to emerge. This is now referred to as antisemitism and it is (like most forms of hate) wholly unnecessary. Antisemitism arose in the far past when people who were somewhat different to others were greatly mistreated and ostracised. It has somehow painstakingly manifested itself in many forms across history, and even to this day an unnecessary dislike of Jewish people can still be found. This historical mistreatment and the eventual persecutions of Jews in their place of origin caused them to flee the land. Notably, in the first century AD, the land of the Jews, Judaea, was claimed by the Romans in a brutal war which saw many killed and their second temple (which was already a replacement for a previously destroyed one) torn down.

This hatred Jews faced across history has led to its practitioners becoming incredibly adaptable, being able to live in communities within other countries and empires. During antiquity and the Middle Ages, Jews migrated away from the Levant area of western Asia and all across Europe. The ins and outs of their migrations have been poorly recorded, meaning many of the finer details remain a mystery to us. The general consensus is that toward the end of the Middle Ages, around the mid-to-late fifteenth century, a community of Jews had settled long enough in Central to Eastern Europe that they acquired their own identity. These Jews became known specifically as the Ashkenazi Jews. Something that made this Jewish group different from others is the language they spoke. While Hebrew was the traditional language of Judaism at the time, the Ashkenazi found themselves at the forefront of another language—one that would go on to be just as distinctly Jewish as Hebrew is.

We lack a definitive count for the number of Yiddish speakers on the planet today. Estimates range from a few hundred thousand to a million at best. If we are conservative with estimates and put the number to around a quarter of a million, it makes Yiddish one of the less popular languages of the Germanic branch of the Indo-European family. It contains much fewer speakers than languages like English, German, Dutch, and Afrikaans, but is somewhat on par with Icelandic. It's a descendant of Old High German, meaning that the language it is most akin to is probably modern German. This is reflected in the similarities amongst many of their words. Take their words for "waste," which are *abfall* and *opfal* in German and Yiddish, respectively. Yiddish is far from a carbon copy of German. The language emerged supposedly in the tenth century when Jews living in modern France and Italy migrated toward the Rhineland which makes up much of modern western Germany. These Jews would have spoken various Romance languages like Old French, but their move to Germanic-speaking lands meant their language got intermixed with various Germanic languages. This saw the emergence of Yiddish in its earliest form. There's still a Romance influence on Yiddish today, with many terms in the language stemming from Old French. The title for the son of a monarch, "prince," comes from the Old French *prince*, which also gave us the Yiddish *prints*.

Over the centuries, the speakers of Yiddish continued their migrations across Europe, seemingly going eastward. This movement is seen to have been a result of Jewish persecution as well as plagues that swept Europe. Venturing eastward, Yiddish speakers started to interact more with speakers of Slavic languages. This makes Yiddish a Germanic language with strong Romance and Slavic influences. It's something of a Swiss Army knife for European tongues. Its influences even go beyond the branches of Indo-European. The language is written using the Hebrew script, though it can be adapted into the Latin alphabet too. In the culture of the aforementioned Ashkenazi Jews, Yiddish is the language of day-to-day chit-chat, while Hebrew and another tongue called Aramaic were used for religious and educational reasons, respectively. The Ashkenazi who lived in Eastern Europe from the fifteenth century onward would have primarily lived in small Jewish towns known as Shtetls. These communities valued their religion along with family and the ideals of helping one another out. Life for Jews would have been pleasant within the Shtetls, while hardship could emerge from the outside. Shtetls would have been established in other kingdoms and empires that Jews would have to live in, among Christians and people of other religions. While many got along with one another, ideologies could collide at times.

A huge amount of strife came for the Ashkenazi Jews of Eastern Europe in the 1880s. Much of this part of the world where these people resided was land under the rule of the almighty Russian Empire. A predominantly Christian empire, they wanted to remove all traces of Jews living in their land. Persecution against Jews, unfortunately, repeated itself once again as state-sponsored murder and destruction of them and their life—an organised massacre known as the pogroms—were ordered. This happened at this time period due to the 1881 assassination of Russian Emperor Alexander II. For no particular reason, the blame for this death was pointed solely at the Jews. These people were most likely framed in all this to give Russia a supposed valid reason for their actions during the pogroms. These persecutions were a breaking point for many Jews in Eastern Europe. Like their ancestors had done before them, these people, too, searched for a new home where they could live their life free from the plague that is antisemitism. This new home came in the form of a country across the Atlantic, somewhere that had historically taken in those who wished for the freedom of religious expression like the Amish had centuries prior. This country had one city in particular which was building up a reputation for itself as the bastion for those fleeing their old life and wishing to start a new one.

The land we now refer to as New York City has a long history with people arriving from other parts of the world to call it home. The first humans to reside here would have been the Indigenous Lenape people. The chief island of NYC, Manhattan Island, was sold by the natives to the Dutch in 1626. The Dutch already had a small colony in this part of the world fittingly dubbed New Amsterdam. This small settlement was transferred over to their new island claim where it thrived even more. New Amsterdam would only remain Dutch for two more years following this, since New Amsterdam was captured by the British in 1664, when it acquired its current name of New York. By the time it was named New York, languages spoken here ranged from the native tongues of the Lenape as well as those non-native tongues of Dutch and English. The land knew very little other than migration, even the ancestors of those initial Lenape people would have migrated from Russia thousands of years ago. Thanks to its strategic location, New York City quickly became one of the most important port cities in the New World whilst it was under British control. It became the gateway for goods and people into North America and its population rapidly grew. By the mid-eighteenth century, the city housed just under 20,000 people, which made it one of the most populated cities in the Americas. This grew rapidly and, in just fifty years, the population boosted to over 200,000 people, making it *the* most populated city in the Western Hemisphere.

This boom in residents was thanks to migration. During the nineteenth century, various groups arrived in the city. People came from places as far as Italy and even China with the aim of starting a new life in the land of opportunity. New York had built this enigma around itself, an enigma it still holds on to to this very day. Toward the end of the nineteenth century, so many people were arriving in the city that New York decided it needed a whole facility to process everyone. This led to the establishment of Ellis Island. The complex founded on this island existed solely to integrate and process the many people coming into the county. Ellis Island has built up a legend around itself as the starting point for the people entering this new world. Many families in the US today are still able to trace their roots back to Ellis Island. The complex formally opened in 1892. Six years prior to this, in 1886, that Mother of Exiles was finally erected in the Hudson River, beckoning those who had made the arduous journey over land and sea to their new home.

Upon arrival, it would have been in the hallowed halls of Ellis Island, with the Statue of Liberty watching over them, that many Ashkenazi Jews from Eastern Europe found themselves. In most cases, their travels would have consisted of escaping their homes without being caught by the Russian Empire who had ordered their deaths. Trekking across Europe, finding passage to Britain, and then travelling onward to New York City. This wasn't the first arrival of Jews in New York. The earliest evidence we have comes from 1654, when a small group of Jews migrated from Brazil to avoid the Inquisition. Yet, the 1880s saw Jewish migration (Ashkenazi or otherwise) really pick up momentum. During this decade, 200,000 Jewish people arrived in New York and, while some fanned out across the wider USA, a majority stuck around in the city. Key areas they congregated in include the Upper East Side of Manhattan and various parts of Brooklyn. These people must have enjoyed their new lives in New York and sent word back to their old home in Europe since, after the 1880s, Jewish migration from Eastern Europe only increased. From the 1880s until the 1920s, four decades, a resounding three million Jews moved to the USA from Eastern Europe, with a majority finding themselves at home in NYC. This was one third of the Jewish population of the Russian Empire. A staggering amount of people and one of the speediest migrations of a group in history. By 1920, 29 percent of New York was Jewish, the largest single ethnic group of the city.

Migration died down in 1924 when something called the Johnson-Reed Act was introduced with the very intention of lowering migration numbers. Jews did carry on migrating to New York in smaller numbers after this year, however. These smaller migrations happened due to events occurring over in Europe. The largest movement of Jews around the world during the twentieth century happened due to one of the most evil and tragic events to take place in world history: the Holocaust. This was the systematic genocide of the Jews at the hands of the Nazis. Doctors, grocers, and other upstanding citizens were taken away from their lives and split from their families. They were forced to work in concentration camps and, in many cases, met their death, primarily due to the fact they were Jewish. Seemingly no Jews were safe from the hands of the Nazis. Men, women, and children all met this same fate. There is a myriad of reasons why the Holocaust happened in the midst of the Second World War, much of it stemming from those thousands of years of antisemitism that Jews in Europe had faced. The Holocaust came to an end in 1945, but by this point it had already taken the lives of six million Jews. Even to this day, the Jewish population is lower than it was before the Holocaust. This event turned the world upside down for Jews across Europe; those who weren't captured by the Nazis escaped with as much as they could carry. Jews would go on to find refuge all across the globe, from other parts of Europe to the wider world. For so long at this point, NYC had already proven itself to be a safe haven for Jews, so it's understandable why so many traversed the Atlantic to a country which, for so long, had been famed for its freedom. Where these European Jews went, their languages came along too. A large portion of these Jews spoke Yiddish and, by the time of the Holocaust, Yiddish already had a base in New York City, so more of these speakers were only welcomed.

Today, New York City has the largest Jewish population outside of Israel and the religion is a strong part of the city's identity. Iconic things about the city, like one of its signature foods, the bagel, is Jewish in origin. Many even believe that the New York accent was heavily influenced by the Jews who call the city home. The large Jewish population in NYC is reflected in the amount of Yiddish spoken there. A study which examined the spoken languages of the city between 2011 and 2015 revealed that just over 86,000 people who live in New York use Yiddish as their main spoken language at home. That's around 2 percent of the city's entire population. It's not just spoken behind the closed doors of home though, but by whole communities in the city who live in the many Orthodox and Hasidic neighbourhoods dotted around New York. This might make New York the home of the largest population of Yiddish speakers on the planet, but some sources point to Israel as having that title.

Despite how many Yiddish speakers New York has, it is far from the number one language. That honour goes, unsurprisingly, to English. Within the city, these two languages have become intermixed with one another. Words of English sprout up in Yiddish, but Yiddish has also made an impact in English. Not just in NYC but in the wider language. Words like "klutz," "schlock," "chutzpah," "shtick," "tush," and of course "bagel" itself are all of Yiddish origin. Even the word "glitch" is thought to possibly be Yiddish in its roots. These words can be heard by English speakers in the USA but also in the UK, Ireland, Australia, and New Zealand. Yiddish has migrated just as much as the people who initially uttered this language have.

The world the Holocaust happened in can seem like one from the ancient past, but in reality, it was just less than a hundred years ago at the time of this writing. There are still people alive today who would not only remember the Holocaust but be survivors of it. The world marched on after the Holocaust, and—although it sounds like science fiction—less than twenty years after it came to an end, humans and their languages found themselves leaving this planet behind.

ТО БЕСКОНЕЧНОСТЬ
AND BEYOND!

LANGUAGES IN SPACE

When Yuri Gagarin looked down, he saw a sight no human had ever seen with their own eyes. Earth. We had seen drawings of what it potentially looked like and images via satellite, but now we knew for sure the appearance of our blue marble. His orbit of the earth in 1961 made him the first human in outer space and was an integral moment in the Space Race which had captured the world at this point. The mid-twentieth century saw the world locked in the Cold War. This period of tension spotted with occasional fighting pitted the USA and USSR against one another as they both attempted to assert themselves as the world's leading superpower in the aftermath of the Second World War. This was also influenced by their political ideologies of communism and capitalism for the USSR and USA, respectively.

Each side wanted their ideology and influence to spread as much as possible and to be the world's default. This battle grew so intense that just bickering over the planet itself did not suffice. Space became a theatre for the USA and USSR to show off their technological prowess. It was also thought that having claim over parts of space could give them an upper hand strategically. Satellites could detect what was going on in enemy soil, so ruling over space could allow your missiles to fly freely. In some ways, the Space Race was the next evolution of the Age of Colonisation that came centuries before it. Powers wanted to plant their flags and assert their influence in lands that were previously unreachable. This would logically mean languages reaching places that words had never been uttered before.

A huge amount of mythology has seemingly been built up around Gagarin and what he said during his orbit. One thing we know for sure he said is "Let's go!" as his ship launched. It's after this that things get a little murky. The line "I see no god up here" is often attributed to him, but there's no actual evidence he ever said this. Other quotes like "I see Earth! It is so beautiful!" and "The Earth is Blue, how wonderful" are linked with him too. A translated log of his communication back with Earth during his flight shows us none of these quotes appear exactly. He did, however, talk about how blue and wonderful the earth looked from space. He also commented on folds he saw in the terrain and the blue halo which appeared over Earth as he floated around it. It was these humble musings as opposed to one prophetic line which were the first words uttered in space. And the language they were uttered in was none other than Russian.

Russian is the most widely spoken of all the Slavic languages. The tongue that sits on the Balto-Slavic branch of Indo-European hasn't migrated too much outside its own vast borders. Nearby nations like Belarus and Kyrgyzstan have given it official status, but Russian never found its way to being a dominant tongue in the New World nor did the language gain any grounds during the Scramble for Africa. Russia didn't play a large role in the Age of Colonisation for a variety of reasons, but when you already have a nation that dwarfs all other countries on the planet, you probably have enough to worry about without thinking about overseas claims. When Gagarin flew in space, the country we know as Russia today didn't exist. Instead, the aforementioned USSR stood in its place, which contained modern Russia and more land that form other nations today. The Russian languages' farthest migrations, however, weren't across the Atlantic or in the depths of the Southern Hemisphere but instead in the skies. Since Yuri's first flight, Russian has had a key role in the realm of outer space linguistics. Yet, it wouldn't stay as space's only tongue for all that long. Just because the USSR had gotten someone into space first did not mean the race was over, in fact, the feat only made the USA more driven to be the ultimate winners.

Less than one month later in 1961, the USA launched their very own Alan Shepard into the heavens. He is not only the second person ever in space, but the first American and first English speaker. The story goes that, during this flight, Shepard coined the term "A-OK," which has since become deeply linked with space flight. In reality, this was said by someone else after his flight in relation to how it went. Shepard did speak during his travels, communicating on all manner of things to ground control. This meant that English had arrived in space along with Russian and, for some time, these were the only two languages spoken in the void. Across the 1960s, the US and USSR attempted to outdo one another in the space field. A culmination of sorts happened in 1969, as it was in this year that the feet of a human stepped out onto land that wasn't earth for the first time. Neil Armstrong became the first human on the moon, shortly followed by Buzz Aldrin. In a short three-year period between 1969 and 1972, twelve people found themselves walking on the moon, and since then no one has been back. Of these twelve people, a resounding 100 percent of them are American, meaning the only language that has ever been spoken on the moon specifically is English.

Beyond the moon, across wider space, more linguistic diversity emerged. People from other parts of the world found themselves launched into the stratosphere. In 1978, Czechoslovakian political figure and cosmonaut Vladimír Remek became the first person in space not from either the USSR or the USA. This would have made Czech, of all tongues, the third language ever spoken in space. Since Yuri Gagarin was shot into the heavens, forty-eight nations have sent people into space, with their respective languages tagging along for the ride. Some of these space faring nations don't even exist anymore, like the USSR as well as East and West Germany. This means that, besides English, Russian, and Czech, other languages that have been spoken in space include European tongues like French, Italian, German, Swedish, and Ukrainian. Spanish has been uttered up there too, thanks to not only Spain sending people but also nations like Mexico and Cuba. Likewise, thanks to Portuguese and Brazilian space exploration, their shared tongue has been spoken in space as well. Space has also found itself with a variety of Asian languages too. Tongues such as Chinese, Japanese, Korean, Vietnamese, Mongolian, Arabic, and even the tongue of Pashto—thanks to a lone Afghani astronaut—have been spoken in space. This is a huge variety of languages that you don't find mingling all too much with one another on Terra Firma.

This might make space sound like a linguistic paradise, but that really isn't the case. Initially, space travel was fleeting, it consisted of simple trips up and down. While these languages would have been spoken, they weren't exactly thriving as the foundations of communities like we have seen with languages here on Earth. Language became a more permanent fixture in space with the creation of space stations—huge constructions which orbit our earth and allow people to live in space for extended periods. They mainly exist for carrying out experiments otherwise impossible on earth. The USSR's Salyut 1 was first launched into orbit in 1971 and, since then, many have come and gone from our night sky. Today, the most well-known is the International Space Station, or the ISS for short. Launched in 1998, from its name alone, it's easy to see that this is an international affair, meaning it houses people from all around the planet. One of the more remarkable things about the ISS is how it strips away many of the relations countries may have with one another back on earth. Astronauts from both the USA and Russia can be found on board, people from nations that were once bitter rivals in the conquest of space now work up there side by side.

The ISS is run by the space agencies of the USA and Russia—called NASA and Roscosmos, respectively—along with Canada and Japan's—called CSA and JAXA, respectively—and the European Space Agency (ESA), which represents many nations across that continent. This means that many of those aforementioned languages have found somewhat more permanent homes on board the ISS, though still not long term, as the average stay on board is only around six months. It should also be noted, not only spoken languages have found themselves on board the ISS. The humble sign language with its origins in

France, ASL, was used when, in 2010, American chemist and astronaut Tracey Caldwell Dyson sent a video message back home to her Deaf children in ASL.

While the ISS doesn't by law have any kind of official language, English is very much the go-to tongue of the station, as all the tech on board is largely operated in that language. This means everyone going to the ISS for any kind of stay has to have a working knowledge of English. They seemingly don't need to be fluent but have to know enough to operate their home for the next few months. This is not the only tongue which is required for the ISS. To reach this station, traditionally astronauts have to be launched in a vessel called a Soyuz spacecraft. This is a Russian creation and is operated in the Slavic tongue. Suffice to say, if the controls of the vessel that is hurtling you into space are all written in Russian, you are going to want to learn Russian! This means that, in addition to English, all residents of the ISS have to have a working knowledge of the tongue of Mother Russia too. Those onboard the ISS, as well as having acquired all kinds of qualifications to be there in the first place, also have to learn Russian and English if they don't already speak one or the other. British astronaut Tim Peake said that learning Russian was the toughest part of his training.

Space exploration started with Russian and English and it's these two languages which have persisted to become the most widely spoken in space today. The only issue is that these two languages are incredibly different from one another. While everyone on the ISS has to understand each of them to a degree, very few are perfectly fluent in both of them. This means that a space creole of sorts has formed on the ISS, one known as Runglish. As its name implies, Runglish is a combination of English and Russian. In reality, Runglish has been spoken before we ever took to the skies in Russian-speaking communities within the English-speaking world. Yet, the idea has become deeply linked with space and the term itself was adopted by NASA in 2000. This tongue allows those who are more adept in either English or Russian to converse with one another well enough to get things done in their floating home. Runglish can simply exist by using words of both languages in a single sentence or even adding word-forming elements of either tongue into words of the opposing language. It doesn't seemingly have a defined lexicon as people use this tongue when needed.

The ISS is a truly international affair; people from all over the world work side by side with one another as they watch the Earth go by. Though, out of all the languages you will hear on the ISS, something you won't hear is any form of Chinese language. Since they first sent someone to space in 2003, China has become a big player in space. So much so that they have their own space station. The Tiangong space station launched in 2021 and through this and their expanded presence in space, Chinese is the third most spoken language above our heads, even though you won't find it on the ISS.

Having earthly words spoken in space can in some ways seem like the zenith of language migration. It's remarkable that tongues formed over thousands of years, that have moved across the planet via ships, hooves, and our own feet, have now found themselves spoken in the great beyond. This is a remarkable collective achievement of humanity, and one that all started as a one-up-manship contest between the US and USSR in the mid-twentieth century. The Space Race eventually came to an end, as did the wider Cold War between these two nations, in the dying years of the twentieth century. Since then, the world map has stayed more or less the same as it is to this very day. Likewise, the languages of the planet on the whole have stayed put, though not entirely. Languages have carried on moving across the globe, even after the turn of the millennium. For myself personally, one of these migrations happened a lot closer to home.

BOGNOR OR BUST

POLISH IN ENGLAND

A 2012 news story claimed a prison in Poland had plastered posters on the walls telling its inmates to visit Bognor Regis. This coastal town found in the southeast of England is famed for a few things, in addition to its being my home. King George V supposedly declared "Bugger Bognor" when told the sea air there would be good for his ailing health. The image this statement conjures has followed the town since. Once a popular tourist seaside destination in Victorian Britain, Bognor has seen a decline in popularity in the following decades. This has given the town an image of being run down and a little rough around the edges. This was highlighted in a short lived 2004 quiz show dubbed *Bognor or Bust* which featured a trip to the town as a booby prize for the losers. By 2012, however, Bognor Regis had picked up a new image, an image which portrayed it as a town overrun with Polish migrants. This news article reflects the wider sentiment of the time. There was this idea, peddled by people of a certain inclination, that the

Polish were flooding into Britain. Claims varied from accusations that they were taking all the jobs, to the belief that they weren't working and living off the UK's welfare system. It takes a certain kind of person to wilfully believe that a group of people can take all the jobs and not be working at the same time. People also claimed that only the criminally inclined Poles were arriving in the UK, with the intention of causing more chaos and disruption. This ultimately stemmed from the belief that the Poles were going to drastically change Britain and, in the eyes of many, this change would be for the worst.

Obviously, there was little to no evidence to back up the claims of a "Visit Bognor Regis" poster on a Polish prison wall. This sense of Polish panic that swept across small towns like Bognor Regis and wider England stemmed from a small kernel of truth. Not the making-the-country-worse claims—those aren't true. Most Polish migrants who arrived in the UK during this period were seen as hard workers and upstanding citizens. The truth comes from the fact that, during the 2000s, there was a rise in Polish migration to the UK and especially England. This did alter England on a ground level basis, and I remember these changes happening during my own youth in Bognor Regis. Shops that were once empty were brought to life as Polish supermarkets selling all kinds of exotic goods opened for business. In school, new kids started to appear, speaking a language amongst themselves that probably not many British kids had experience with. Eventually, this language would spill on the streets and become commonly heard in my small hometown.

Polish is, unsurprisingly, a product of Poland, the Eastern European nation nestled neatly between Germany and Belarus. This Slavic tongue is believed to have emerged from some kind of Proto-Slavic language in the tenth century AD as Old Polish, the language in its earliest form. It was also around this time that speakers of this new tongue came together and lived in a recognised land known as the Kingdom of Poland, which was established in 1025 under the Piast Dynasty. This dynasty adopted Roman Catholicism as its main religion and this choice brought about one of the biggest changes to the Polish language. A huge influx of Latin words found their way into Polish via Catholicism and its deep link with the tongue of Rome. This bucks the trend of other Slavic languages, as many of their speakers instead follow the distinctly Slavic Eastern Orthodox denomination of Christianity. For example, the Polish word for plumber, *hydraulik*, comes from the Latin *hydraulicus*. In other Slavic languages like Russian, it is instead *vodoprovodchik*. Polish has so much Latin influence that it even uses the Latin alphabet, unlike many other Slavic tongues which use the Cyrillic script.

As Old Polish morphed into Middle Polish and eventually modern Polish, the Latin influence stuck around; Catholicism itself stuck around in the modern nation too. Today, Poland is one of the most religious nations on the planet. The early twenty-first century saw the arrival of many modern Polish speakers in England, but even prior to this, it's not like the UK had been completely devoid of Polish settlement. In the far past, most Poles in the UK would have come over on an individual basis, and in a lot of cases it was for religious reasons. The Protestants of Poland's past found refuge in the also-Protestant UK after Henry VIII's formation of the Church of England (CoE). Polish traders would have been found settling within the nation too. These kinds of migrations are interesting but have minimal impact on the wider country and its languages. The nineteenth century saw a tad more Polish migration to the UK, with various uprisings happening in the nation during this century, forcing many to migrate. The twentieth century too saw Poles enter the UK thanks to the world wars which have come to define this century. The Polish fought alongside the British during the Second World War and the nation formed the Polish Resettlement Act which helped many of those Poles stay in the UK.

This brought the Polish to England in dribs and drabs. What really got the ball moving was an event in 2004. It was this year that saw Poland join the European Union. This grouping today consists of twenty-seven states found across Europe with economic ties to one another. Another defining feature of the EU, as it is more commonly known, is the freedom of movement it offers between member states. Someone from one member nation can not only visit another, but freely live and work there too, more or less as if they had simply moved to another part of their home country. It's a truly marvellous thing and it's unsurprising that many European nations not part of this union wish to join in on the fun. Poland's entrance to the EU in 2004 opened up a whole new world to the people of the land. Suddenly, they were not confined to just their own homeland. They could now call many of the other nations within the Union their home too. From this moment, Polish people have set up shop and found new lives all across the European Union. This admission into the group resulted in many Poles gazing westward to an island nation and fellow EU member…at the time, anyway.

Poles at this time had many possible nations to choose to make a new life in, yet several factors led to the UK being the home for many of them. A key reason was money. In 2004, Poland's economy was not in the best of shapes. Unemployment was at 20 percent and those with jobs were earning a drastically small amount. At this time in England, jobs were plentiful and wages were no less than four times higher than they were in Poland. For those struggling financially in Poland, it made all the sense in the world to migrate across to this island nation bountiful in cash and work. The UK was also much more accommodating for these new EU citizens too. When Poland joined, most other EU nations put transitional restrictions in place, which delayed Poles arriving and working there. The UK, meanwhile, was just one of three nations that forewent this notion and allowed Poles into the country immediately.

Also, Poland had, for some time, been a nation with migration built into it. It was very common for Poles to migrate to Germany in the name of work and back. In the nineteenth century, a vast number of Poles travelled across the Atlantic to start a fresh life in the Land of the Free. Movement is in the blood and bones of many Poles it seems. Another factor which ushered in this surge of movement was the stagnation that the nation had been under for decades prior. For a large portion of the twentieth century, Poland was a Communist country and part of the Eastern Bloc, a coalition of Communist nations. During this period, it was difficult enough to visit other Eastern Bloc nations—seeing nations beyond those was pretty much out of the question. Communist rule in Poland came to an end in 1989. Their 2004 admission into the EU came just fifteen years after. When this happened, life in Communist Poland would have been fresh in many people's memories. It's understandable why they felt so strongly about spreading their wings and finally settling in the wider world after so many years of it being closed off from them.

All this led to a large influx of Poles arriving in the UK, and especially England, across the 2000s. In some cases, whole families would arrive, but in others just one member would come to England. They would leave their family behind, find a job which was high earning relative to Poland's wages, and send money back to their loved ones. It takes a lot for people to pack up their lives and leave their homes and even more to leave their beloved families behind too. This sending of finances back to Poland drew heavy criticism from those against the new

Polish migrants, as money was being removed from the British economy. Other concerns people had over these new residents of England ranged from issue to issue. For one, it included concern over the pressure all these people would put on services like housing and schools. Then there was the worry they might bring unruliness with them too and cause tension with the natives. It was not all doom and gloom, however, as many saw the benefits they brought like new skills and the boost in the economy.

Since 2004, an estimated one million Polish people have arrived in the UK to call the country home, bringing along with them their customs, culture, and language. Polish and English haven't intermixed in the same way we have seen with previous languages. This is mainly down to the fact that the introduction of this immigrant tongue is still relatively new. Languages can take centuries to form and change. As of this writing, this kind of time has not passed for the Polish being spoken in England to change in any meaningful way. While Polish hasn't affected England in a particularly linguistic way, it has in a statistical sense. Polish is now the second most widely spoken language in England, only behind the tongue of English itself. This is *just* England however, the largest of the four nations that make up the UK. Factoring the language of every UK resident, Polish is the fourth most spoken tongue. Sitting behind Welsh, Scots, and English. Welsh and Scots are languages formed in and native to the UK, meaning Polish takes the honour of the most widely spoken, non-native language across the UK. That's nothing short of an incredible feat considering it was a little over twenty years ago (at the time of this writing) that Poles were first allowed to come live in the UK so easily.

As quickly as Polish arrived in England, it could disappear just as promptly. In 2016, the majority of people in the United Kingdom voted to leave the European Union. My little hometown of Bognor Regis, which had become a haven for Polish people, largely voted in favour of leaving. This removed many of the benefits that being in the EU offered. Not only for those native to Britain, but non-natives too, who were living there like the nation's Polish population. This included freedom of movement and the ease to live and work in any other EU nation. Leaving the EU has thrown countless spanners (wrenches in American English) into the lives of Poles living in the UK, resulting in many returning back to their homeland. One source estimates a quarter of Poles living in the UK have since left. Many of those who have remained, meanwhile, still hold on to their Polish roots with pride. Countless more shops and restaurants have sprung up across the nation. There's even Polish heritage days and festivals found all across the country.

This is an incredibly modern language migration, as well as one that is currently in flux. It's also one I had the pleasure of seeing happen with my own eyes. While we can only hypothesize what it felt like to those ancient Celtic speakers in Iberia seeing Latin take over their land or envision how the Māori felt when English suddenly dwarfed their own tongue, here we can truly get a grip of what a language arriving in a new place is like. I can personally remember the anger that English-speaking natives felt when the Polish started to arrive. I remember the jokes, the hesitancy, and, unfortunately, the prejudice. Thankfully, I also remember the people who were on their side and allowed them to integrate into life in England. For those Poles who decide to stick around in the UK, even after the country's decision to leave the EU, I can only hope the two cultures and languages intermix even more so. In the same way that English has intermixed with so many other tongues across the globe. This is perhaps the most interesting thing about how Polish emerged in England as the land's second tongue. It shows us the homeland of English, a language which has immigrated to so many corners of the earth, is just as open to immigrant tongues too.

MADE IN CHINA

MANDARIN ACROSS THE GLOBE?

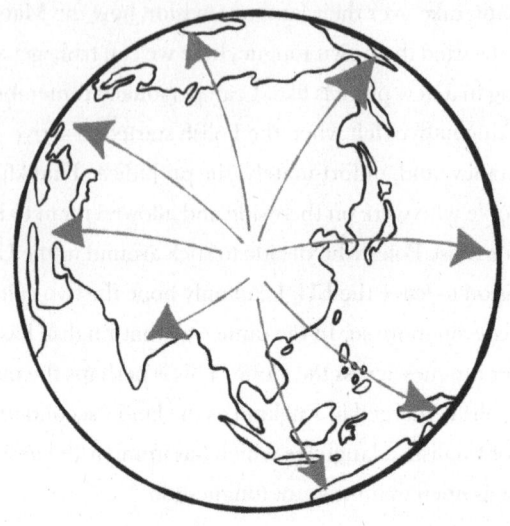

We have now arrived at the point in our immigrant tongues journey where, in our modern world, English is the undisputed lingua franca of Terra Firma. The tongue landed in that position through the dominance of the British Empire in the past, along with all the good and horrendously bad that empire brought. What boosted English significantly, however, was the emergence of the USA becoming the world's only superpower in the aftermath of the Second World War. The thing about lingua francas, however, is that they aren't set in stone. For the majority of people alive today, all we have known is English as top dog. Yet, we know that before our time, other tongues served as bridges between peoples. From Latin across the Roman Empire to Nahuatl for the Aztecs. This shows us that a lingua franca can come and go. Some believe that a tongue formed in the Far East has the potential to migrate all across the globe to become the world's next global language, supplanting even English.

Of the many varieties of the Chinese language the country has produced, Mandarin is the most widely spoken by a long shot. Over a billion people speak Mandarin as their first tongue. For comparison, the previously mentioned Cantonese variety found in Hong Kong and Macau has eighty-five million native speakers, a measly number in comparison. Mandarin easily eclipses the number of native speakers of languages like English, Spanish, or Hindi too. What this all means is that Mandarin is the most widely spoken native language on the planet, but English still takes the upper hand when factoring in people who speak it as a second or third tongue. This language took some time to form into the tongue it is today. China is a supremely ancient part of the world and the earliest evidence we have of some sort of Proto-Sino-Tibetan language morphing into a language we now dub Old Chinese is from the eleventh century BC. That's well over 3,000 years ago. This Old Chinese language would have split into the various Chinese languages we have today over the centuries. The language we now call Mandarin has its earliest records in the twelfth century AD.

It has its origins in the north of the country, a primarily plains-covered land which made traversal far easier in the past, allowing the language to reach a wider audience. It was heavily influenced by the Chinese dialects spoken in the cities in Nanjing and Beijing. This proved to be extremely important, as both these cities have served as the nation's capital. It was the Ming Dynasty who moved the capital from Nanjing to Beijing in 1424. Being the tongue spoken in the capital meant it was the language spoken by the nation's most prestigious people, so it only makes sense why its use became even more widespread. Even the name of Mandarin relates to the noble people who spoke it. It derives from Portuguese explorers in China around this time who noticed the unique way the magistrates of Beijing spoke—they were known as mandarins, so the name was applied to the way they spoke. In China itself, Mandarin is simply known as *Pǔtōnghuà*, which just means common speech. This all led to the modern tongue of Mandarin we have today. Modern Mandarin, however, is not one singular language. It still has a variety of different dialects spoken in China. In a desperate attempt to give China some kind of singular definitive language, something known as Standard Chinese was created and brought into use in the early days of the twentieth century. This is a version of Chinese that can be used across the country, understood, and learnt by the masses. This version of Chinese was formed in the capital, meaning it is heavily influenced by Mandarin. So much so that Standard Chinese is also known as Standard Mandarin or even just Mandarin.

Today, nothing can really compete with the amount of native speakers Mandarin has, yet, unlike English, those native speakers aren't found in large numbers in multiple countries. Mandarin hasn't migrated to the Americas, or Africa, or the South Pacific in the same way English has. The majority of Mandarin migrating has taken place within the vast nation of China itself. This could all be on the cusp of changing. The juggernaut of a language that is Mandarin may finally start spilling out from the borders of China in a big way and become our next global language. People are theorising that Mandarin may supplant English as the world's lingua franca due to the immense rise in power the nation has seen over the last few decades. Over this time period, China has grown in pretty much every way. From their economy to their army, they are teetering on the verge of becoming the world's next superpower alongside the USA.

China is a country growing more powerful and wealthy by the day. A few leading drivers behind this growth are some of the huge companies and businesses born in the nation, from tech giant Tencent to electric car manufacturer Li Auto. China produces a huge swath of modern goods, like computers and other electrical devices. In many ways, China is the home of the building blocks that make up our modern world. Even companies that don't have their origins in China depend on the nation to bring their products into fruition. China has been the world's manufacturing hub for some time now. Products conceptualised by the wider world are more often than not put together and made into reality in China. You probably won't have to look too hard to find something you own with the words "made in China" written on it somewhere. This has all created a situation where many companies and people around the globe are at the behest of China or even want a slice of China's monetary pie for themselves. A terrific way to be in China's good books, do trade/business with them, and acquire some of that lucrative Chinese money, is to speak the lingo.

In the quest to get a leg up when conducting business with China, more and more people are starting to learn Mandarin. In 2015, Facebook founder Mark Zuckerberg gave a twenty-minute speech at a Beijing University in fluent Mandarin. Zuckerberg learnt Chinese primarily to speak with his wife's extended

Chinese family, but it also acts as a show of good faith to the nation, in the hopes that one day China may give its people access to his social media platform. Multi-awarded WWE world champion John Cena is also able to speak the language, surprising everyone at a 2016 WWE press conference in China. Cena has been more outspoken about why he learnt the tongue, saying one of his key intentions was to use the language to help bridge the gap between the WWE and China, allowing the pro wrestling juggernaut to finally make headway (and ultimately cash) in the nation. Zuckerberg and Cena might not have all that much in common with one another. But something they share is the fact they are the poster boys of two products deeply linked with the USA. Their understanding of Mandarin shows China just how committed they are to making those products a success in the land.

It's more than just celebrities and brand ambassadors who are learning Mandarin. In schools, there has been a huge rise in Mandarin lessons. In some cases, kids are being tempted into learning the language over tongues like Spanish and French, mainstays of the education system. The reason behind this surge in Mandarin classes is the idea that knowing the tongue will give kids an advantage once they enter the workforce. The theory is that, by the time they are adults, an understanding of Mandarin will be a much-coveted skill. For decades, kids in countries like India and Nigeria have been urged to learn English to give them an upper hand in the workplace. Now, a similar thing is happening to kids in English-speaking nations like the UK and USA in regard to Mandarin for the exact same reason.

This might make it sound like a one-way system but, in reality, China is just as eager to teach the world Mandarin as many across the globe are eager to learn it. China wants to be seen on the global stage as a true world leader in the same way many of us view the USA. This is done in a variety of ways. The 2008 Olympics held in Beijing was something of a coming-out party for the nation. It was the first time many saw what the nation was like in the modern world and what exactly they could now achieve. China is also attempting to exert more soft power on the globe too. Soft power is how a nation claims influence on the world stage through less aggressive means. Things like movies, TV shows, and other products are prime examples of soft power. The English-speaking world, especially the USA and UK, have had a lockdown on soft power, with things like musical artists, actors, and other media giants from these nations becoming household names across the planet.

While it might seem odd at first, this kind of soft power wields a huge amount of influence, especially in regard to spreading a language. Many people have learnt English primarily through watching English language films and television.

China would love to have this level of soft power and, in more recent years, media of Chinese origin which is spoken in Mandarin is starting to find a wider appeal. Nowhere is this more evident than with the release of the 2024 video game *Black Myth: Wukong*. It is considered to be China's first big budget AAA video game. It is heavily inspired by Chinese mythology and the beloved Chinese novel *Journey to the West*. The entire game can even be played in Mandarin to fully immerse players in the Chinese culture. This game has been a roaring success for exporting the image of China and the tongue of Mandarin to the world stage. A user even posted on the Chinese language subreddit that, after playing the game, they wished to improve their understanding of Mandarin—that is soft power in action. Perhaps one day in the future Mandarin will be the language most linked with entertainment. Then there's TikTok. The Chinese mobile phone app specialising in short form videos became a global sensation in the early days of the 2020s. While the app hosts videos in all kinds of languages, its origins as a Chinese product are known to the masses. TikTok is undoubtedly one of China's most successful exports and has cemented the nation as an entertainment hub as well as just a manufacturing one.

Even away from China's superpower intentions, Mandarin has been able to find a home in other parts of the world. The Chinese diaspora communities found around the planet have allowed Mandarin to migrate in the more traditional way we have come to expect of languages. Those who were born in China but now live in another nation, as well as their descendants, are collectively referred to as the Overseas Chinese. They are single handedly the largest diaspora of people on the planet with sixty million Chinese people living as expats in other countries. That's roughly the population of South Africa. Chinese migration across the globe can really be traced as far back as the days of the Silk Road way over 2,000 years ago. The route that passed through China into Europe traders would use to move their goods such as silk as the title suggests. Larger migration happened from the sixteenth century onward. By this time, European powers had not only integrated themselves more into China itself, but wider Asia as well. This meant China had been opened up to the wider trading routes of the world too.

Europeans arriving in China was not just a one-way system, as many in China took the opportunity to sail to new lands and set up shop there too. Money was a driving factor for this migration—the idea of earning money elsewhere in the world to provide for family back home.

Chinese communities outside of China have popped up all across the globe, with these areas often being referred to simply as Chinatown. Chinatowns tend to be the historic hubs of Chinese migration in cities and many of them share their heritage with pride. Paper lanterns can be found hung across the streets and the shop signs and store fronts are even presented in the symbols of China. The oldest Chinatown in the world is believed to be Binondo, found in the Filipino city of Manila. It supposedly came into being in the late sixteenth century. Since then, many more have sprouted up across the globe, noticeably in two of the planet's most global cities. Across the nineteenth century, Chinatowns sprung up in both London and New York, and have become not only hubs of life for Chinese migrants but tourist attractions unto themselves. New York's Chinatown is seen as the largest concentration of Chinese people outside of Asia. People from all across China settle in these places, meaning they don't all speak just Mandarin. Other Chinese tongues like Cantonese are commonly heard here too. Even the languages of the land they are in could be heard too, like English in New York's Chinatown. The nation of China looks happily upon the Overseas Chinese. They see them in many ways as ambassadors for the country who bring the ideals of the nation to other nooks of the globe.

The Overseas Chinese are proof that Chinese languages, including Mandarin, have made their way outside of the nation and become spoken in other parts of the world. Though, by no means does this make it a global language. The idea of Mandarin becoming the next global lingua franca is still very much hypothetical. There are just as many people who think Mandarin won't become a global language as those who think it will. A huge barrier to the language is the ability to learn it. Mandarin is unique in a multitude of ways. First off, it's tonal, meaning the tone in which you say a word affects what that word means. For example, the Mandarin word meaning "to buy," *mǎi*, is resoundingly similar to their word meaning "to sell," *mài*. Suffice to say, getting these mixed up could lead to some confusion. It's also resoundingly different in its written form too. The symbols it shares with Japanese and Korean reflect whole ideas and things, as opposed to singular sounds like the characters of the Latin alphabet. The character of 人 means "person" for instance. While Japanese and Korean also use these types of symbols, they also have sound-based alphabets to go along with them too. This isn't the case with Mandarin. The language solely uses these logographic symbols in their written form. The only way to understand what a character means is to just know it; you can't sound it out in the same way you can an English language word. On top of this, there are thousands of them, with the average Mandarin speaker knowing around 8,000.

In contrast, English is much easier to get to grips with for many than Mandarin is. English also received this spot as the world's lingua franca via centuries of empire-building and global domination. Planting their tongue, as well as their flag, in parts of the world it hadn't been uttered in prior. We are most likely past the age of empires and colonising of yore, meaning Mandarin's path to global language would be very different to English's. The general consensus is that, if Mandarin ever does become the next global language, then that won't happen for a very long time.

If we imagine Mandarin does get its way and becomes just as prevalent as English, then we could also imagine how much it would change in different parts of the world too. Every country would have its own unique dialect of Mandarin, such as Nigerian Mandarin, Icelandic Mandarin, Bolivian Mandarin, Canadian Mandarin, and even Fijian Mandarin. However, I have no doubt that, if this somehow becomes a reality, then those who speak hypothetical British Mandarin and American Mandarin would probably still be constantly arguing over who speaks the correct version.

PART IV

LOOKING FORWARD

WHERE ARE YOU GOING?

This book started with me being asked the simple question, "Where are you from?" So, why not end it with me asking all of you a similarly deceptively simple question. Where are you going? There's obviously not a single answer to this one. You could be going to work, rattling away on a train or bus. You could be going on holiday, miles above the sky in a plane or crashing through the waves on a ferry. You could even be going to the toilet, doing your business while reading mine. The simple answer to this question is that you really could be going anywhere, and that is also the case for the languages of the world.

From the moment we began talking, tens of thousands of years ago, the words that have come out of our mouths and on to paper have travelled far and wide across the globe. From those early migrations of Bantu tongues to the release of China's first big video game. The history of language migration shows us that languages can quite literally end up in any possible corner of the earth, and even beyond it. Many languages even end up in places that the initial speakers of those tongues had no idea even existed. When English came into being on the island of Britain all those years ago, the initial speakers would have had no idea that the eventual product of their tongues would be the same thing spoken on a landmass full of emus and koalas on the other side of the earth. Yet today I could travel from my home in Britain all the way to Sydney, Australia and the shift in language would be minimal. There'd be the occasional word of Aussie English I may slip up on, but our tongues would be two sides of the same coin.

Though, perhaps the biggest effect all these language migrations have had isn't on the lands they are spoken in directly, but rather in how they have defined us. The way we speak and the languages we use are some of our most defining features. They say so much about who we are as people and what led to us being where and who we are today. They can also shape how we view other people too, and unfortunately in many cases it's not always for the best. The huge influx of immigrant tongues across our planet has led to languages in specific parts of the globe gaining a stigma of some kind. This can be seen in both languages native to a land as well as those tongues that have travelled. Many native tongues now find themselves as minority languages in their home. Languages like Navajo, for example, are now only spoken in small pockets in the land it originates from. It's a tiny droplet in a huge pool of English. This can divide people. English speakers in the USA might view someone who speaks solely Navajo in a different light. They may simply understand that they come from a different culture and carry on with their day, or they may brand them as different or other, which can lead to things like racism and xenophobia. It is a sad fact for any native tongues which now find themselves on the decline.

This idea only gets exacerbated when an immigrant tongue takes a small holding in a different part of the world. Many people who speak Polish in England might have found themselves dealing with all kinds of abuse and accusations of being lazy and violent, with those accusations more or less boiling down solely to the language that comes out of their mouth. This was even seen in the past with the likes of Jewish Hebrew speakers across Europe being ostracised for the tongue they speak. And, of course, we have Afrikaans. A language which, once upon a time in South Africa, was the tongue of power is now seen by many in the nation as the language of their former, racist, oppressors. This division that languages can cause can even be seen within the same language. An English-speaking American might judge another English-speaking American simply down to the fact that one speaks the African American dialect of English while the other uses what is dubbed the standard.

These kinds of divisions very rarely tend to be fifty-fifty splits. The more people who speak the same language in one part of the world, the easier it is to point out those who don't and label them as different. As history has shown us, being different often leads to anger and hatred. We can be hopeful, however. The more people learn about how these languages moved and evolved around the world before coming to define us, the better we can all understand one another. Suddenly, those who seem different to us now, based primarily on the tongues they speak, won't seem all that different anymore. We will all understand that, more or less, all of us speak an immigrant tongue of some kind. Even us here in Britain wouldn't be speaking English if it weren't for the migrations of those Germanic tribes. For now, however, languages come with a huge amount of

baggage at times, and that baggage can come with them and even expand in
their travels.

As for the actual nitty gritty of these language travels, we have seen that,
historically, it involves great physical migrations. It involves boats crossing oceans
or human feet marching thousands of miles. Heavy handed force has been a
focal point too. The languages of the world wouldn't be where they are today,
unfortunately, without that brute force, that insistence that the land you have
arrived on belongs to you, and the devastating destruction of lives this attitude
has wrought in many cases. The final thing language migrations have depended
on for success in the past is time. Languages rarely, if ever, simply arrive in an
area and go from unspoken to undisputed. It can take decades or even centuries
for a tongue to become entrenched enough in a land that it becomes the go-to
language. Often, over the course of this time, it takes on a variety of influences
from the land it has arrived in. This is how language migration has happened
historically and, while the journeys covered in this book have been tales from
the past, language is undoubtedly still on the move. In this day and age, the
movement of a tongue doesn't depend on mass human migration, great ships
surviving storms, or even rockets being blasted into space.

In 1991, British computer scientist Tim Berners-Lee released his invention of the
world wide web to the public. This changed our world forever. The world wide
web, often simply referred to as just the internet, has become a mainstay in the
lives of many, and one of our greatest and most influential tools. You probably
don't need me to explain to you everything that is achievable online. One of its
greatest successes is the open availability of information it has provided. The
majority of the world's knowledge is now available in an instant. At first through
clicks on a glowing monitor, now via finger taps on a device that lives in most
of our pockets. Among all the information online is a plethora of facts about
language, from their histories to how to learn them. Languages that in the far
past would have been inconceivable or at least only accessible in an extremely
niche resource. Now, someone like me living in Britain, can read and hear these
tongues in just a few clicks. Tahitian, a native Polynesian tongue from the island
of Tahiti—which would have been seen as extremely exotic to Britons just a few
centuries ago—now has entire online courses and videos teaching anyone from
anywhere how to speak it from the comfort of their own home. No need to make

the months-long journey to the faraway island like explorers did in years gone by. The internet has made the movement of language from one part of the world to another almost seamless.

The internet is also bringing cultures from other parts of the world to our homes too. With this has come the desire and demand to learn languages that were once rarely taught in traditional classrooms. In the 2010s and 2020s, there has been a huge rise in interest in South Korean media, from films to music to television shows. This has fuelled a boom in people wishing to learn the Korean language, to more easily understand the K-pop bands and shows they now idolise. This isn't to say that Korean will replace English as the lingua franca, nor does it mean that countries in the West will find themselves speaking Korean or become littered with Korean-speaking communities. Though, Toronto is already home to Koreatown. What it does tell us, however, is that the internet connects our planet in a way trade routes and ships could have once only imagined. Online communication has made it far easier for languages to find a new home in a different part of the world. Unlike the brutality which often accompanied language migration in the past, these days (in most cases) not a single drop of blood needs to be spilled.

This surge in Korean language learning across the English-speaking world shows us that languages aren't showing any signs of slowing down. Their movement is going to carry on as it has for thousands of years. Languages once alien in certain places may very well become the norm, or at least more commonplace, in lands where this concept was once unimaginable. Except, now it doesn't take a boat full of colonisers to get the job done. A hit Azerbaijani TV show, a Swahili boy band who becomes a global phenomenon, or a viral video spoken in Maltese, could kick off the next global language learning trend. We can only wonder what language will be next to migrate and find a new home.

ACKNOWLEDGMENTS

The initial concept of this book, a series of disconnected chapters explaining how languages ended up in new places, grew dramatically in scope as my writing continued. It slowly shifted into this wider, somewhat chronological history of the world told through the migrations of languages. While the scope of this book changed, my word limit stayed the same. Writing an entire history of the world while trying to not go over a specific word count means certain things have to fall to the wayside. Some elements I covered in this book were either glanced over, way oversimplified, or not mentioned at all. That's not even going into many of the language migrations I had initially intended to cover. We didn't get to talk about Spanish in the Philippines, Hindi in Fiji, or even South America's German-speaking communities. What this means (hopefully to the joy of my readers and my publisher) is that there's ample room for a sequel.

This book could not have been written without the plethora of research done by countless people who have come before me. I am a mere regurgitator of knowledge. Many books, articles, papers, blog posts, and the occasional forum comment, made the writing of this book possible. A special thank you to sources such as the BBC, World History Encyclopedia, Babbel and their terrific blog posts, and my dear friend Wikipedia. While Wikipedia often comes under scrutiny, I feel it is a bastion of knowledge when used correctly and double checked. Sources available upon request.

Thank you to everyone at Mango Publishing who took a chance on this book and crafted it into the final product it is now. It's resoundingly different to my previous works, so I appreciate the chance you have given it. Thank you to anyone involved with the editing and neatening up of the words on these pages. For turning them from an incoherent mess into something somewhat understandable. Thank you to my ever-expanding group of friends and family who have supported me yet again on another one of these silly projects. Somehow, this whole YouTube and book writing thing is still going—I am just as shocked as all of you.

None of the words you have read in this book were generated by AI, nor was AI used in the research of this book.

ABOUT THE AUTHOR

Patrick Foote is the creator of the YouTube channel *Name Explain*, where he uncovers the origins of names and highlights many other aspects of language. He founded the channel in 2015 whilst working in retail, as a creative outlet and as a means to share his love of all things language. Since then, *Name Explain* has amassed hundreds of thousands of subscribers and millions of views. The channel's success led Patrick to write his first book, *The Origin of Names, Words and Everything in Between*, in 2018. It went on to be a bestseller and was followed by a sequel. Patrick was born in London, spent a large portion of his life in the coastal town of Bognor Regis, and now lives in Plymouth in South West England. When he isn't reading or writing about language, he enjoys walks with the dog, wild swimming, playing video games, and watching pro wrestling.

Mango Publishing, established in 2014, publishes an eclectic list of books by diverse authors—both new and established voices—on topics ranging from business, personal growth, women's empowerment, LGBTQ studies, health, and spirituality to history, popular culture, time management, decluttering, lifestyle, mental wellness, aging, and sustainable living. We were named 2019 *and* 2020's #1 fastest growing independent publisher by *Publishers Weekly*. Our success is driven by our main goal, which is to publish high-quality books that will entertain readers as well as make a positive difference in their lives.

Our readers are our most important resource; we value your input, suggestions, and ideas. We'd love to hear from you—after all, we are publishing books for you!

Please stay in touch with us and follow us at:

Facebook: Mango Publishing
Twitter: @MangoPublishing
Instagram: @MangoPublishing
LinkedIn: Mango Publishing
Pinterest: Mango Publishing
Newsletter: mangopublishinggroup.com/newsletter

Join us on Mango's journey to reinvent publishing, one book at a time.